Understanding the World Language edTPA

Research-Based Policy and Practice

A Volume in
Contemporary Language Education

Series Editor:
Terry Osborn, *University of South Florida Sarasota-Manatee*

Contemporary Language Education
Terry Osborn, Series Editor

Intercultural Competence in Instructed Language Learning:
Bridging Theory and Practice (2016)
by Paula Garrett-Rucks

Identifying and Recruiting Language Teachers: A Research-Based Approach (2013)
by Peter B. Swanson

Demystifying Career Paths After Graduate School:
A Guide for Second Language Professionals in Higher Education (2013)
edited by Ryuko Kubota

Consilio et Animis: Tracing a Path to Social Justice Through the Classics (2012)
by Antoinette M. Ryan

Critical Qualitative Research in Second Language Studies: Agency and Advocacy (2011)
edited by Kathryn A. Davis

World Language Teacher Education:
Transitions and Challenges in the 21st Century (2011)
edited by Jacqueline F. Davis

Language Matters: Reflections on Educational Linguistics (2009)
by Timothy Reagan

Spirituality, Social Justice, and Language Learning (2007)
edited by David I. Smith and Terry Osborn

Identity and Second Language Learning (2006)
edited by Miguel Mantero

Early Language Learning: A Model for Success (2006)
edited by Carol M. Saunders Semonsky and Marcia A. Spielberger

Teaching Writing Genres Across the Curriculum:
Strategies for Middle School Teachers (2006)
edited by Susan Lee Pasquarelli

Teaching Language and Content to Linguistically and Culturally Diverse Students:
Principles, Ideas, and Materials (2006)
edited by Yu Ren Dong

Critical Questions, Critical Perspective:
Language and the Second Language Educator (2005)
edited by Timothy Reagan

Critical Reflection and the Foreign Language Classroom (2005)
by Terry Osborn

Understanding the World Language edTPA

by

Susan A. Hildebrandt
Illinois State University

and

Pete Swanson
Georgia State University

Information Age Publishing, Inc.
Charlotte, North Carolina • www.infoagepub.com

Library of Congress Cataloging-in-Publication Data

CIP data for this book can be found on the Library of Congress website
http://www.loc.gov/index.html

Paperback: 978-1-68123-578-3
Hardcover: 978-1-68123-579-0
E-Book: 978-1-68123-580-6

Printed in the United States of America

CONTENTS

Preface vii

Acknowledgments ix

1. What is edTPA? 1

2. Getting Started With Program and Course Suggestions 15

3. Context for Learning 39

4. Beginning at the End: Assessing Student Learning 49

5. Planning for Teaching and Learning 79

6. Instructing and Engaging Students in Learning 103

7. Activities for the Methods Classroom 127

8. Concluding Thoughts 157

References. 193

Appendixes 207

About the Authors 217

PREFACE

Leslie Schrier
The University of Iowa

In the 1990s, I presented analytics on the changing face of the foreign language teaching population and emphasized that over 75% of current foreign language teachers would be retired by this decade (Schrier, 1993; Schrier & Hammadou, 1994). Predictively, the surge in retirement of the first generation of professional language teachers has created a void of expertise that needs to be replaced. However, the traditional language teaching environment and expectations of teachers are changing, and we are now challenged to ensure inexperienced foreign language teachers are prepared to meet the academic needs of all students. Furthermore, this new generation of language teachers must be ready to teach with the necessary skills needed to support student learning from the first day they enter the classroom, and prior to being licensed to teach, these novice teachers are assessed on these skills. Evaluating teachers is a growing concern in this century, and the glaring void of specific efforts by the overall foreign language profession to address this situation is lamentable.

Fortuitously, Susan A. Hildebrandt and Pete Swanson present in their book *Understanding the World Language edTPA: Research-Based Policy and Practice* a much needed guide for the profession as we are challenged with developing new foreign language teachers to meet the needs of the 21st century classroom. Basing their book on current research related to foreign language teacher assessment (Hildebrandt & Hlas, 2013; Hildebrandt & Swanson, 2014), Hildebrandt and Swanson patiently guide the foreign language teacher educator on how to use the teacher performance assessment known as edTPA.

Understanding the World Language edTPA: Research-Based Policy and Practice
pp. vii–viii
Copyright © 2016 by Information Age Publishing

edTPA is the product of the partnership between Stanford Center for Assessment, Learning and Equity and the American Association for Colleges of Teacher Education. For the first time, edTPA gives teacher preparation programs access to a multiple-measure assessment system aligned to state and national standards—including Common Core State Standards and the Interstate Teacher Assessment and Support Consortium—that can guide the development of curriculum and practice around the common goal of making certain new teachers are able to teach each student effectively and improve student achievement.

Hildebrandt and Swanson's book is the beginning of the professionalism much needed in foreign language education; the authors take charge of edTPA and demonstrate how it can be used effectively for foreign language teacher development. Further, they guide the teacher educator through the consequential portfolio assessment, which is integral to edTPA. Unique to this book, the authors also invite the readers to contribute to an ongoing research agenda needed to help validate this assessment to the foreign language teaching profession.

ACKNOWLEDGMENTS

We are grateful to our institutions' language teacher candidates, and we are especially grateful to "Anna" the teacher candidate who gave us permission to analyze her exemplary edTPA portfolio. We would also like to thank Dr. Leslie Schrier (The University of Iowa) for her contribution to our book. She has been an inspiration for a generation of language teachers, teacher educators, and academics. Also, we greatly appreciate Dr. Robin Huff (Georgia State University) for generously giving of his time and knowledge in proofreading this work. He is a wonderful colleague and genuinely interested in the success of language teacher candidates. We also must thank Dr. Judith Shrum (Virginia Polytechnic Institute and State University, emerita) for her assistance. She has served as the American Council on the Teaching of Foreign Languages/Council for Accreditation of Educator Preparation specialized professional associations coordinator and has been a source of information that guided our thoughts during the writing of the book. Additional thanks go to Elisa Palmer (Illinois State University) for answering our numerous questions about available edTPA resources and implementation practices. We also thank Dr. Terry Osborn (University of South Florida-Sarasota Manatee) for serving as the editor for this book. Over the years Terry has become a mentor and friend, as well as advocate for language teachers on a global scale. He leads by example and truly makes a positive difference in our profession. Finally, we are grateful to the world language teachers and teacher educators who contributed their voices from the field in our final chapter: Ms. Sydney Earley (Lowndes High School of Valdosta, Georgia), Dr. Jennifer Eddy (Queens College of the City University of New York), Mrs. Nancy Ferrill (Illinois State University), Ms. Alicia T. Hiers (Colquitt County High School of Norman Park, Georgia), Dr. Anne Hlas (The Uni-

Understanding the World Language edTPA: Research-Based Policy and Practice
pp. ix–xi
Copyright © 2016 by Information Age Publishing
All rights of reproduction in any form reserved.

versity of Wisconsin-Eau Claire), Dr. Sarah Jourdain (Stony Brook University), and Dr. Victoria Russell (Valdosta State University).

FROM SUE

This year is the 10th anniversary of my dissertation defense, so I am particularly cognizant of the exceptional preparation I received at The University of Iowa. I am especially grateful to Drs. Leslie Schrier and Michael Everson for their support over the last 17 years. They have taught me how to carry out meaningful research and apply the findings to the work of teacher education. Their guidance has been invaluable. The friendships made with bright and energetic classmates are another exceptional feature of my time at The University of Iowa. I am especially glad to have studied, worked, and shared a tiny office in Lindquist Center with Dr. Anne Hlas during our graduate work. Over the last 16 years, I have valued our countless collaborations on professional presentations, writing projects, and joyous hijinks.

My mom, dad, and brother deserve many thanks for their years of caring support. Their work has been different than mine, but they have respected my work in schools as I have respected theirs on the farm. Ten years ago at my graduation party, I reflected to my dad that I had been in school for 30 years, either taking classes or teaching. His response: "I knew you liked school, Susie. I just didn't know you liked it that much!" I am also grateful to Marc, my husband of 16 years, who has followed me across the country and back as I looked for, and ultimately found, a professional home. His sense of humor and objectivity have helped me in more ways than I can name. And, finally, I am so glad to have crossed paths with Pete, whose work ethic, consistency, and humor have made co-authoring this book such a pleasant endeavor.

FROM PETE

Since I became a teacher several decades ago, the notion of teacher effectiveness was ever-present in my mind and practice, thanks to several individuals. I was fortunate when I was a first year Spanish teacher in that the German teacher, Kevin Tonkovich, walked into my classroom one of the first days of class to see how things were going. He had a strong German program and wanted to see me succeed. He remembered his own experiences as a new teacher in a new school, and he was well aware of the challenges that new teachers must overcome. He took me under his wing and helped me navigate my journey as a language teacher. He taught me the value of collaboration, networking, and attending professional development opportunities. I thank him for spending his time and sharing his knowledge and love of language teaching because it has helped shape me as a public school teacher and teacher-educator.

Additionally, I am grateful to Dr. Carol Semonsky because she mentored me as a junior faculty member at Georgia State University. She developed our language teacher education program and was intrinsically interested in preparing highly effective language teachers. She supported my research and has become a wonderful colleague and friend. I thank my wife Karen and my daughter for their support as Sue and I developed the book. Karen offered ideas and Petra enjoyed the many Skype calls with Sue as we worked on the project daily. Finally, I thank Sue for the breakfast invitation at American Council on the Teaching of Foreign Languages in Philadelphia. It has been great to get to know her and work with her on this research. I look forward to many years of collaboration together.

CHAPTER 1

WHAT IS edTPA?

Teacher performance assessments, such as edTPA, evaluate teacher candidate (TC) knowledge, skills, and effectiveness. They can provide valuable information to world language methods instructors, colleges of education and language department faculty, teacher education program directors, and TCs themselves. In this book we seek to support these various audiences as they prepare for edTPA implementation and the accompanying licensure or certification decisions, program evaluations, or accreditation reports.

The ultimate purpose of this book is to help world language TCs understand and perform successfully on the three edTPA tasks. World language teacher education programs can use this book to stimulate TCs' early thinking about developing and measuring K–12 student communicative proficiency development in meaningful cultural contexts with authentic tasks and performance assessments. We also offer world language teacher education coordinators and faculty members suggestions on how to create edTPA implementation plans for their programs. Advice offered is based on the first author's experiences writing early drafts of the world language handbook, along with both authors' efforts to implement edTPA into their teacher education programs and research TC performance on the assessment. Readers of this book will be able to:

- name the three edTPA tasks and the 13 rubrics' foci;
- summarize impacts of edTPA on world language teacher education programs;

Understanding the World Language edTPA: Research-Based Policy and Practice
pp. 1–14
Copyright © 2016 by Information Age Publishing
All rights of reproduction in any form reserved.

- report the pros and cons of edTPA as a TC effectiveness evaluation tool;
- compare and contrast rubric performance levels;
- evaluate gathered evidence of student learning; and
- create an edTPA implementation plan for their own edTPA performance or that of their world language teacher education program.

Throughout this book, the authors will refer readers to books and resources published and sold by the American Council on the Teaching of Foreign Languages (ACTFL). Although we are ACTFL members and ACTFL is the flagship organization of language teachers, advocating daily for language learning, we are not trying to sell their products or any other books mentioned. We are simply providing readers suggestions for additional resources of which they may not be aware. To that end, we do not include in this book edTPA documents created by the Stanford Center for Assessment, Learning and Equity (SCALE), such as the *edTPA World Language Assessment Handbook* (2015a) or *Understanding Rubric Level Progressions* (2015b), but readers should obtain their own up-to-date copies of those documents online or from on-campus edTPA coordinators or others in the college of education.

We seek to join practical suggestions and research-based findings to provide a scholarly, yet approachable, book exploring edTPA through the lenses of world language teaching, learning, and TC development, fleshing out theory and providing examples. As will be seen, we have taken what educational research suggests, aligned those suggestions with one another, and integrated them into a pedagogical model specific to language TC development. The first chapter provides an historical context for and description of edTPA. The second chapter introduces the shared vocabulary of edTPA (e.g., evidence of teaching practice, artifacts, learning segment, commentaries), offering suggestions to get started with edTPA in methods courses and teacher education programs. These suggestions, we hope, will help teacher educators familiarize TCs with the handbook and its vocabulary, expectations, and format, well before its high-stakes completion.

Subsequent chapters guide readers as they examine each of the three edTPA tasks and their accompanying rubrics. Checklists and sample activities to use prior to final field experiences are provided. Structured around the 13 rubrics used to assess an edTPA portfolio, we intend these chapters to help world language teacher educators develop TCs' skills and habits of mind to develop successful edTPA portfolios. For each rubric, we compare and contrast the performance levels and offer suggestions on how to improve TC performance. Additionally, we share research findings, based on our own programs' TCs and their experiences with edTPA, including a case study of one high-scoring portfolio created by a TC in one of our programs. The penultimate chapter includes in-class activities that can be used by methods instructors or student teacher supervisors to develop TCs' abilities, as assessed by each rubric. The last chapter offers final thoughts on edTPA in university-based world language teacher education, including the next steps for our programs and suggested areas of investigation.

While there are certainly areas of improvement for edTPA, we examine the portfolio requirements and point out that much of what edTPA looks for is what world language teacher education programs have already been doing under different auspices. This book is not just about edTPA; it is about making better teachers who are able to develop student learning and communicative proficiency in meaningful cultural contexts. Implementation of edTPA may require TCs and programs to examine more deeply the skills being addressed in their teacher education curriculum. In our programs, as well as many other language teacher preparation programs, there have been less formal work sample portfolio requirements in place. The final field experience, usually a semester-long student teaching assignment, requires students to complete a work sample that includes many, if not most, of the activities required in edTPA. That is, TCs submit lesson plans regularly and reflect upon their impact on student learning. Today, edTPA brings about a more standardized means of evaluating beginning teacher learning and effectiveness than had been used by many of us in the past. Specifically, language teacher preparation programs will be able to be compared across states and even the nation. Previously, this variant of teacher performance assessment relied on teacher educators to evaluate the performance of TCs in their own programs. edTPA provides a means of setting professional criteria for beginning teachers to meet and another evaluation tool by which to compare candidates and teacher education programs, for better or for worse.

HISTORICAL CONTEXT

For the past several decades, teacher education has been both a political and social focus in the United States. As part of President Lyndon B. Johnson's War on Poverty, Congress passed the Elementary and Secondary Education Act of 1965 (ESEA) in 1965 (P.L. 89-10). This groundbreaking federal legislation placed an emphasis on equal access to education while setting high standards for academic performance and demanding accountability from schools and districts within a framework of six titles. Additionally, the ESEA funded primary and secondary school education, with the goal of decreasing the achievement gap. A year later, two amendments were proposed and passed: Title VI–Aid to Handicapped Children and Title VII–Bilingual Education Programs.

Over the first 15 years, the act was reauthorized every 3 years and focused on funding allocation. Following the Jimmy Carter administration (1976–1980), the act was reauthorized every 5 years. Early in President Ronald Reagan's first term (1981–1989), the Education Consolidation and Improvement Act (1981) was proposed to reduce the federal regulations of Title I, reflecting that administration's belief that funding and the provision of resources should be governed by the states and local jurisdictions, rather than by federal government. Additionally, Reagan's Secretary of Education, Terrill Bell, formed Reagan's National Commission on Excellence in Education, working under the latter's suspicion that the United States' educational system was failing to meet the need for a competitive global workforce. The commission's publication, *A Nation at Risk* (National Commission on Excellence in Education, 1983), noted that "the educational foundations of our society are presently being eroded by a rising tide of mediocrity that threatens our very future as a Nation and a people" (Introduction, p. 1). The commission advocated fiercely for improving education within 38 recommendations set in five areas: Content, Standards and Expectations, Time, Teaching, Leadership and Fiscal Support. In the Content category, the commission proposed that high school students take 4 years of English, 3 years of mathematics, 3 years of science, 3 years of social studies, and a half year of computer science. Additionally, the report recommended 2 years of study of foreign languages. In fact, the recommendation read:

> Achieving proficiency in a foreign language ordinarily requires from 4 to 6 years of study and should, therefore, be started in the elementary grades. We believe it is desirable that students achieve such proficiency because study of a foreign language introduces students to non-English-speaking cultures, heightens awareness and comprehension of one's native tongue, and serves the Nation's needs in commerce, diplomacy, defense, and education. (Recommendations, p. 2)

At the turn of the century, the George W. Bush administration reauthorized the ESEA under a new name, No Child Left Behind (NCLB, U.S. Department of Education, 2002). This unfunded mandate called for even more rigorous testing and accountability of K–12 student learning, while including foreign language as part of the core curriculum. The philosophical merits of having *highly qualified*[1] teachers in the classroom were favorable to many, but the top-down requirements placed on schools and teachers were met with criticism. Many state and district officials found that the highly qualified definition placed too much emphasis on teacher candidates' content knowledge (Center on Education Policy, 2007). By focusing solely on having highly qualified teachers, NCLB could narrow K–12 curriculum and prioritize reading, mathematics, and science instruction over nontested content areas, such as foreign languages (Rosenbusch, 2005; Rosenbusch & Jensen, 2004). With increasing financial pressures, schools and districts worked to increase standardized test scores and achieve annual yearly progress. Additionally, this shift in resources and downward demand were found to be a contributing factor to the already alarming shortage of world language teachers (Swanson, 2008, 2012).

Even as the Obama administration began its sunset, ESEA's reauthorization further scrutinized schools and their practitioners. Under Education Secretary Arne Duncan's leadership, Race to the Top required that states measure beginning and veteran teacher effectiveness to receive full federal funding (U.S. Department of Education, 2009). After the 2008 recession, states were eager to gain federal dollars and created legislation focused on preservice teacher preparation and licensing/certification standards, underscoring teacher performance and effectiveness at the state level (e.g., Georgia Professional Standards Commission, 2014; Illinois State Board of Education, 2012). State recipients of the Race to the Top funds were additionally required to use student learning as evidence in teacher evaluation practices (Darling-Hammond, 2012). In many states TCs must now demonstrate "the results of classroom processes, such as impact on student learning" (Goe, Bell, & Little, 2008, p. 4), often through teacher performance assessments.

In December of 2015, the ESEA was reauthorized as the Every Student Succeeds Act (ESSA). NCLB, the new act's predecessor, brought the term *highly qualified teachers* into public conversation and prompted states to introduce massive testing initiatives for both students and teachers. With the new act, however, most of the details of teacher education, qualifications, and certification/licensure procedures is left up to the states (U.S. Department of Education, 2015). This change of approach will be of great interest to teachers and teacher educators as ESSA is fully implemented across the country.

MEASURING TEACHER EFFECTIVENESS

Teacher effectiveness is central to current national, state, and local educational policies, and the ongoing push for accountability recognizes the central role of teachers in student learning. While traditional TC assessments have focused on measuring TC knowledge and skills, along with teacher education program inputs (e.g., courses taken, curriculum), more recent assessments have focused on measuring teacher effectiveness, a notoriously slippery construct (Muijs, 2006).

Federal educational policies often form the framework by which states construct their own K–12 and postsecondary teacher education policies. These federal policies have spawned the current climate of measuring teacher effectiveness. While the Tenth Amendment to the Constitution theoretically allows that all issues not allotted to the federal government go to the states, federal legislature frequently uses funding as the carrot for states to comply with their policies or intentions (Ryan, 2004). Race to the Top provided a fiscal carrot, coaxing some states to include certain teacher assessment practices in their initial teacher certification and licensure process, as well as inservice teacher evaluation. Both federal- and state-level policies have increased requirements to assess TCs' effect on student learning.

The question of what teacher effectiveness is and how to measure remains a challenge (Mujis, 2006). Some states use standardized tests to measure how effective a teacher is, with the results used in complicated algorithms, à la value-added measurements, to determine individual teacher's effect on students' learning. Foreign languages have the mixed blessing of being an untested content area for federal, and frequently state, policy mandates. Despite being one of the content areas named as fundamental to K–12 education by *A Nation at Risk*, foreign languages are usually electives with 2 years recommended for college applications.

Assessment of teacher skills and knowledge starts early, takes place frequently, and depends on the context in which a TC is prepared to teach. TCs knowledge is typically assessed before, during, and after their coursework. The American teacher education system has many masters; the federal government, state governments, universities, and accreditation agencies all set requirements for TC evaluation. Individual teacher preparation programs must follow all of those requirements in order to graduate teachers who can then be licensed or certified in the home state. All of these assessments vary depending on the context in which the TC is prepared—most importantly the state.

Teacher knowledge and skills were codified through standards development and supported by federal funds during the Clinton administration (Smith & Scoll, 1995). In the same way that student standardized assessments are often based on content-specific standards, emerging teachers must now demonstrate their knowledge of teaching and ability to instruct learners of varied backgrounds. Developed in the 1990s, student content standards provided a framework for instruction in K–12 settings (Smith & Scoll, 1995), which later informed various teacher development standards, such as those of the National Board for Professional Teaching Standards, the Interstate Teacher Assessment and Support Consortium, and the National Council on the Accreditation of Teacher Education, which recently became the Council on the Accreditation for Educator Preparation (CAEP). Those frameworks for what teachers should know and be able to do at various stages in their careers, whether as a veteran, novice, or preservice teacher, have informed development of edTPA as a tool of TC assessment.[2]

As a consequence of the standards movement, prior to entering to teacher education programs, TCs in most states must complete and pass a basic skills test, like Praxis I or Educational Testing Service's Basic Skills Test, to assess TC abilities in math, reading, and writing. Some states have mandated basic skills assessments specific to their state, developed by testing companies like Educational Testing Service and Pearson. For example, Illinois licensure and university education program admission require teacher candidates to pass the Test of Academic Proficiency or achieve an acceptable score on the ACT Plus writing or SAT.

Before or during student teaching, TCs also need to show that they possess the necessary knowledge to teach their subject. NCLB's call for highly qualified teachers to prove that they know the subjects they teach necessitated additional TC assessments prior to licensure or certification. Those content knowledge assessments spurred the adoption of tests like Praxis II or other state-specific assessments. World language content tests usually evaluate a TC's familiarity with the geography, cuisine, culture, and holidays of the target language-speaking countries, often through multiple-choice items. Some may require brief speech samples from TCs as part of the content knowledge test, and still others may have a section on pedagogical content knowledge, in which TCs answer questions about content-specific methodologies, pedagogy, or research. Another requirement to deem a teacher highly qualified requires TCs to pass a test of general pedagogical knowledge for the level(s) that they intended to teach (e.g., pre-K through third grade, K–12, middle school, etc.) at around the same time as the content tests above are administered. Before September 2015 in Illinois, for example, TCs seeking licensure had to pass the Assessment of Professional Teaching for teaching a particular grade span, although that requirement has been dropped as edTPA is now required across the state.

Accreditation bodies also influence the means by which TC knowledge and skills are assessed. TCs educated in CAEP-accredited institutions must complete additional assessments outside of those required by federal- and state-level entities. World language teacher education programs seeking CAEP accreditation must create reports in which they demonstrate TC performance on six to eight assessments, including the Oral Proficiency Interview and a content test (if required by the state). Those assessments must address the six ACTFL/CAEP Program Standards

(Foreign Language Teacher Preparation Standards Writing Team, 2013) and have been administered at least twice to form a snapshot of TC performance in that world language teacher preparation program. TCs do not often have a long enough experience with students to impact student learning until student teaching, and teacher education programs have had to rely on assessment of TC knowledge and skills. Brief microteachings with peers give valuable experience to TCs, but they do not allow future teachers to realistically measure student learning.

All of these calls for teacher effectiveness measures have elicited a number of criticisms against the TC assessment proliferation. Cost worries some. An individual studying to become a language teacher in Georgia, for example, can expect to pay at least $800 above and beyond tuition and living expenses to meet the requirements for a beginning teaching license (Hildebrandt & Swanson, 2014). Another criticism is that many of the TC knowledge and skills assessments have multiple-choice formats and do not allow TCs to truly show what they know and are able to do. They can contain discrete, multiple-choice items, eliciting the criticism that they are decontextualized and simplistic (Darling-Hammond & Snyder, 2000).

Performance assessments, on the other hand, allow TCs to provide a more robust sample of what they know and are able to do in the classroom. Performance assessments can be used to assess TC language production abilities (i.e., speaking and writing), along with their teaching competencies. They allow TCs to be evaluated in a more realistic context and can provide a means for them and their teacher education programs to gauge improvement over time.

Language proficiency assessments are currently used in many programs to demonstrate TC ability to speak or write the language they wish to teach. The Oral Proficiency Interview and the Writing Proficiency Test assess world language TCs' second language oral and writing proficiency, respectively. The Oral Proficiency Interview is a required assessment for ACTFL/CAEP accreditation, with 80% or more of TCs in the program required to pass with Advanced-Low proficiency (Foreign Language Teacher Preparation Standards Writing Team, 2013). Performance assessments of second language proficiency can also be part of state licensure and certification. In Wisconsin, for example, world language TCs must demonstrate intermediate-high proficiency on both the Oral Proficiency Interview and the Writing Proficiency Test as a prerequisite to licensure.

Portfolio assessments, which have been used for decades, have also been a means by which TCs can demonstrate that they are ready to teach and can make an impact on student learning, either as part of postsecondary teacher preparation programs or licensure/certification. One tool used by university preparation programs is the *Teacher Work Sample*, developed by Renaissance Partnership for Improving Teacher Quality (2002). This portfolio assessment asks TCs to create an assessment plan, provide evidence of instructional decision making, use student learning to adjust their teaching, interpret student data, and communicate with others about students' progress.

Some states have created legislation that mandates teacher performance assessments prior to teacher licensure or certification. In July 2008, the California legislature mandated the Performance Assessment for California Teachers as part of preliminary teaching credential requirements in that state. That teaching performance assessment was designed to measure the candidate's knowledge, skills and ability to teach and assess K–12 students (Sato, 2014). Modeled on National Board certification processes for veteran teachers, Performance Assessment for California Teachers influenced later edTPA development (Sato, 2014.)

While local assessments of teacher skills can be useful, a nationally standardized test of teacher abilities can bring about positive changes to the teaching profession (Peck, Singer-Gabella, Sloan, & Lin, 2014). By having independent assessors evaluate TC performance according to professionally agreed upon criteria, Darling-Hammond (2010) argued, teaching can reach a higher level of professionalization, such as that enjoyed by doctors, architects, and accountants. That standardization can also bring about a shared vocabulary for teacher development (Peck et al., 2014), as well as a more "common and concrete language of practice" (p. 22), thereby "achieving deeper levels of communication, collaboration, and coherence, both within and across programs of teacher education" (p. 23).

edTPA DEVELOPMENT

Based on the aforementioned Performance Assessment for California Teachers from California, edTPA is a nationally available performance assessment of novice educators' readiness to teach. Developed by SCALE, in collaboration with the American Association of Colleges for Teacher Education and administered by Pearson, edTPA seeks to evaluate beginning teacher effectiveness by assessing Planning for Instruction and Assessment, Instructing and Engaging Students in Learning, and Assessing Student Learning in 27 different content areas (SCALE, 2013a). Among their objectives, edTPA's developers sought to create a national common performance assessment that can be administered across institutions and reliably scored by experts in teaching (Sato, 2014).

Typically, edTPA is carried out during the TCs' final field experience, usually student teaching. Its three main components attempt to measure teacher candidates' abilities to plan, instruct, and assess student learning and proficiency development. Described in the *edTPA World Language Assessment Handbook* (SCALE, 2015a), edTPA can be conceptualized as a cycle of effective teaching: planning (intended teaching), instruction (enacted teaching), and assessment (impact of teaching on student learning). Unlike elementary education with 18 rubrics and other content areas with 15 rubrics, world language teacher effectiveness is measured with 13 Likert-scale rubrics. Early in the world language handbook development, it was decided that academic language was already an inherent part of language teaching. Therefore, the need to assess TCs' ability to develop students' academic language did not exist since it was so central to the very work of language teaching.

As mentioned above, teacher education programs must also meet requirements of accreditation agencies, such as CAEP, that allow programs to continue preparing TCs. The case is no different with the ACTFL/CAEP standards (Foreign Language Teacher Preparation Standards Writing Team, 2013) that outline six standards that programs must report on in order to carry out their work at CAEP institutions. edTPA is aligned most closely with three of the six ACTFL/CAEP standards for the preparation of new language teachers:

- Standard 3: Language Acquisition Theories and Knowledge of Students and Their Needs
- Standard 4: Integration of Standards in Planning, Classroom Practice, and Use of Instructional Resources
- Standard 5: Assessment of Languages and Cultures–Impact on Student Learning

The other three standards, Standard 1 (Language Proficiency: Interpersonal, Interpretive, and Presentational), Standard 2 (Cultures, Linguistics, Literatures, and Concepts from Other Disciplines), and Standard 6 (Professional Development, Advocacy, and Ethics) are important, of course, but Standards 3, 4, and 5 center on the teaching and learning of the second language. For example, as part of edTPA's *Task 1 Planning for Instruction and Assessment*, TCs must "demonstrate an understanding of key principles of language acquisition and create linguistically and culturally rich learning environments" (Foreign Language Teacher Preparation Standards Writing Team, 2013, p. 13). Regarding Standard 4, TC's must "use the *Standards for Foreign Language Learning in the 21st Century* and their state standards to make instructional decisions (p. 19). Finally, Standard 5 requires that TCs "reflect on results of assessments, adjust instruction, and communicate results to stakeholders" (p. 24).

ACTFL initiated a review team of language teacher educators to align edTPA to the CAEP standards for world language teacher education, and the two of us serving on that team to create a crosswalk for the standards and edTPA rubrics. The committee members individually indicated how much evidence each of the 13 edTPA rubrics could provide for assessing the CAEP standards. It was determined that edTPA did not show evidence to meet the first or second standard, but evidence is present in the assessment to meet parts of Standards 3, 4, 5, and 6. Stronger evidence was found for the third, fourth, and fifth standards than for the sixth. The final crosswalk in Excel can be found on the ACTFL webpage (ACTFL, n.d.-a).

Thirteen 5-point rubrics describe emerging language educator proficiency on a continuum. Each rubric describes five levels of candidate knowledge and skills:

- Level 1: the knowledge and skills of a struggling candidate who is not ready to teach;
- Level 2: knowledge and skills of a candidate who is possibly ready to teach;
- Level 3: knowledge and skills of a candidate who is ready to teach;
- Level 4: solid foundation of knowledge and skills for beginning teacher;
- Level 5: advanced skills and abilities of a candidate very well-qualified and ready to teach (SCALE, 2013a, p. 12).

Beginning teachers are not expected to be in the advanced range of the rubrics, and a score of 3 across all 13 rubrics would elicit a solid passing edTPA score in most states at present.

Passing scores in many states have yet to be determined, but during its national standard-setting meeting, the American Association of Colleges for Teacher Education recommended that areas with 15 rubrics have passing scores of 42 (Pearson Education, 2016a). The American Association of Colleges for Teacher Education further adjusted the score of 42 to consider a full standard error of measurement lower, thus helping state policy makers determine an initial cut score ranging from 37 to 42 total points for content area assessments with 15 rubrics. In order to determine cut scores for content areas with more or fewer than 15 rubrics, an adjusted professional standard must be used (Pearson Education, 2016a). Such proportional adjustments are used (1) to ensure that the score for each rubric contributes equally to the total score across all academic disciplines and content areas and (2) to reduce decisions influenced by measurement error (e.g., false negatives). According to Pearson Education (2016a), this [professional performance standard (PPS)] was calculated upwards for credential areas with more than 15 rubrics (where a higher total score is possible) and downwards for credential areas with fewer than 15 rubrics (where a lower total score is possible). These calculations in PPSs are proportional to the number of rubrics and maintain the same average rubric score. (para. 2)

Content areas with fewer or more than 15 rubrics, like world language, use proportional adjustments to establish passing scores in order to ensure that each rubric score contributes equally to a TC's total score (Pearson Education, 2016a). For example, the edTPA handbook for elementary education has 18 five-point rubrics that can have a range of total scores from 18 to 90, constituting a cut score ranging from 44 to 50 total points with the professional performance standard adjustment. The *edTPA World Language Assessment Handbook* contains 13 five-point rubrics with a range of total scores from 13 to 65 points. Using the same adjustment, recommended passing scores for world language TCs ranging from 32 to 36 total points are suggested (Pearson Education, 2016a).

States are able to determine the levels to which teacher candidates must perform on edTPA and most teacher assessments. In short, state boards of education or legislatures determine the acceptable cut scores for the various teacher assessments put into place (Goldhaber, 2007). Some states informed stakeholders years in advance that edTPA would be used for licensure decisions. In Illinois, for example, 2012 legislation required that TCs seeking licensure complete a teacher performance assessment and that approved teacher preparation programs begin in 2013 (Illinois General Assembly, 2012). Before fall of 2015, when scores became consequential, colleges of education and individual teacher education programs were able to familiarize themselves with edTPA expectations and process. Cut scores in Illinois increase incrementally year by year (Pearson Education, 2016b).

In the case of California, based on the standard setting activities described in the *Recommended Passing Score Standard for the Use of the edTPA in California* (California Commission on Teacher Credentialing, 2014) report, a cut score of 34 points was recommended. That score is slightly lower than New York's passing score of 35 (New York State Board of Regents, 2013) and higher than Washington state's passing score of 30 (Pearson Education, 2016c), as shown in Figure 1.1.

While other states like Hawaii and Oregon, for example, have yet to set passing scores some states, like Georgia, required that teacher education programs implement edTPA as an evidence-based assessment of teacher effectiveness beginning in fall 2015 (Georgia Professional Standards Commission, 2014). In early July 2015, a cut score of 29 for world lan-

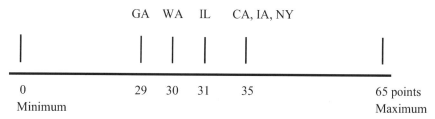

GA   WA   IL   CA, IA, NY

0   29   30   31   35   65 points
Minimum   Maximum

Figure 1.1.   edTPA range of known pass scores by state.

guage and classical language was set in Georgia for fall 2015 enactment (Georgia Professional Standards Commission, 2015). In 2017, the required score in Georgia will increase to 32 for world language TCs (Georgia Professional Standards Commission, 2015). Other states have yet to announce their cut scores, despite the fact that edTPA will be consequential in the not too distant future.

States are encouraged to set their own passing scores based on each state's standard-setting panel that takes into account state-specific data, pilot test results, and state policy considerations (Pearson Education, 2016a). As it stands at the moment of this writing, some states have cut edTPA cut scores and also have chosen to raise scores as time passes to soften the blow of initial implementation, allowing teacher preparation programs the time to get their TCs used to edTPA requirements. For example, New York State Board of Regents (2013) was one of the first states to set the cut score for the world language edTPA at a score of 35 total points, which requires TCs to score an average of 2.73 points on each of the 13 rubrics. The state of Washington set the minimal passing score at 30 points (Pearson Education, 2016c), which requires individuals to score an average of 2.31 points on each of the 13 rubrics.

However, other states are in the process of developing policies regarding the use of edTPA. At present, edTPA is in various stages of implementation in 683 Educator Preparation Programs in 38 states and the District of Columbia participating in edTPA and is being used to inform initial licensure and certification decisions in 13 states (American Association for Colleges of Teacher Education, 2016). For example, Hawaii is going to require a performance-based assessment such as edTPA for teaching candidates beginning in 2017, while Illinois began requiring a performance-based assessment of teaching for program completion in September 2015. Nevertheless, most teacher preparation programs in Illinois have pilot tested and phased in edTPA over the past several years (Alliance for Excellent Education, 2014).

CONCLUDING THOUGHTS

The genesis of this book can be traced back to a breakfast conversation at ACTFL 2012 in Philadelphia. During that meeting, we decided to pool our knowledge and resources and begin to study edTPA in our programs for several reasons. To begin, the first author worked with SCALE early in process of developing the content-specific *edTPA World Language Assessment Handbook* and had a head start on most of us. Second, we coordinate two of the largest world language teacher education programs in the country. Thus, when we combine our data for research purposes, our sample size is relatively large. We can see the impact of our curricular changes on a broader and deeper scale. Additionally, our almost daily conversations have facilitated our two programs' transformation to accommodate edTPA. Third, we have more than 45 years of combined experience in teacher preparation and P–16 language teaching. Finally, we were both P–12 Spanish teachers. We earned degrees in Spanish and curriculum and instruction, maintained teaching certificates in several states, and had a lot of shared experiences that help us relate well to our TCs. In fact, we believe our experiences as classroom teachers have helped our TCs be successful because they know we have done much of what is being asked of them now.

Our scholarship informs the content of this book, as well. As recipients of ACTFL's second round of the Research Priority grants in 2013, we began to analyze edTPA data from our own programs in order to lay a path for other world language teacher education programs to follow. In this project, our scholarship informs our program development, while our program development informs our scholarship. Simultaneously, our scholarly and programmatic experiences with edTPA inform our teaching and vice versa.

NOTES

1. To be considered highly qualified in the United States under No Child Left Behind, teachers must have: a bachelor's degree, full state certification or licensure, and proof that they know each subject they teach (U.S. Department of Education, 2004).
2. While in-service teachers' knowledge and practices are also assessed for purposes like National Board certification, licensure advancement, and on-the-job assessment, exploration of many of those practices, however, falls outside the parameters of this book. We recommend that those interested in the issue of in-service teacher assessment consult Shinkfield and Stufflebeam (1995) and Stronge (2005).

CHAPTER 2

GETTING STARTED WITH PROGRAM AND COURSE SUGGESTIONS

At first sight, edTPA can be daunting to not only teacher candidates (TCs), but also to teacher education programs. The stakes are high. Without scoring at or above their state's edTPA cut score, TCs may be prohibited from earning a teaching license or being recommended for certification. If they are unsuccessful at passing edTPA, they may also need to complete their university degree late or choose another major altogether. The current cost of $300 to have one edTPA dossier scored, in addition to other expensive requirements of teacher education and licensure or certification, can also be problematic for TCs.

Teacher education programs can be taken to task by federal and state departments of education. The U.S. Department of Education's most recent efforts to modify teacher education suggest using TC effectiveness assessments in determining which teacher education programs to support financially. Among other objectives, the U.S. Department of Education seeks to help distinguish between "high- and low-performing teacher preparation programs" (U.S. Department of Education, 2014, p. 1) by measuring new teacher placement and retention rates and *customer satisfaction* (p. 2), through surveying graduates and their principals about new teacher effectiveness. State legislatures may also use edTPA or other TC assessment data to allocate resources to their various universities within the state.

Understanding the World Language edTPA: Research-Based Policy and Practice
pp. 15–37
Copyright © 2016 by Information Age Publishing

We hope that this book will alleviate some of the anxiety related to edTPA as readers come to understand more clearly what it is, what it measures, and what they can do to implement it. In this chapter, we focus on three areas. First, we provide some general advice, based on what we have done thus far to help our own TCs succeed on edTPA. This advice speaks to both the programmatic and the classroom levels, before and during the student teaching semester. Second, we discuss some resources prepared by SCALE, as well as information from the state level. Then, we offer advice regarding the roles that various people can play in colleges of education and language departments as edTPA is implemented. We briefly touch on technology integration as it is related to creating and submitting the portfolio. Afterward, we share some ideas that we have been using in our methods courses, as well as some advice from the field placement perspective and helping stakeholders in K–12 clinical settings understand their role in TCs' edTPA success.

We have to admit that edTPA was a shock to our systems as teacher educators when it first was unveiled. We experienced various degrees of anxiety about the changes that would need to take place to implement it. Those anxieties were not only about the final field experience (i.e., student teaching or internship), but also about the necessary curricular changes to set the stage for TC success on the new, standardized assessment. For us, the first semester was trial and error, combined with many conversations with college leaders about how to phase edTPA into our programs. The next semester was still challenging, but it helped us realize the changes we needed to address. One purpose of this book is to help others in our positions avoid trial and error as they implement edTPA into their own programs.

The ideas we advance are intended to help teacher educators not only include edTPA in their programs but also to help them make any programmatic changes that may need to occur. It is important to remember that not every state has adopted edTPA yet and teacher education programs are at various stages of implementation. Although listed under particular categories, these suggestions are not meant to be exclusive to the category in which they are placed. That is, suggestions may be implemented at other times or in other contexts at the discretion of the user. We share ideas that we have implemented as we revised our unique teacher education program contexts and requirements, and we understand the need to consider context in all educational endeavors.

Readers cannot and should not prepare for edTPA implementation alone. Teamwork within and across settings is paramount. Without agreement and support from all levels, success may be tenuous. However, by working together and communicating roles and expectations, edTPA can be implemented with less anxiety and chaos to programs. Collective plan-

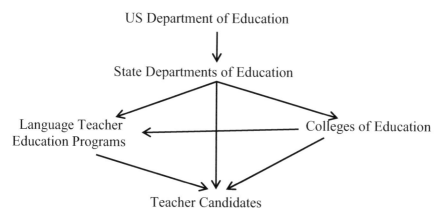

Figure 2.2.   The interplay among educational stakeholders.

ning and delegating responsibility becomes necessary as more voices come to the mix.

There is a complicated interplay among the federal and state departments of education, colleges of education, language teacher education programs, and TCs, as shown in Figure 2.1. From there, the state places pressures on colleges of education, language teacher preparation programs, and TCs themselves. In addition to the state pressures, language programs are influenced by colleges of education, and colleges of education in turn influence TCs. CAEP further influences each educational stakeholder in Figure 2.1, save for the federal department of education. Such influence is dependent upon individual states', institutions', and programs' adherence to CAEP standards. As can be seen, the federal government's educational policy generally flows one way to the states and their departments of education.

Backwards design (Wiggins & McTighe, 2005) can be a useful tool as programs and their TCs begin putting edTPA portfolios into practice. Beginning with the end in mind, programs can plan for edTPA implementation within their departments, colleges, and universities. The end that programs will most likely have in mind will be for all TCs leaving the program to earn a passing score on edTPA. To get to that point, TCs must be notified of impending requirements, timelines for submission to external review, and expenses as early as possible. It is important to update catalog descriptions, program advisement resources, and websites/blogs in order to alert TCs of the upcoming edTPA during their schedule planning as early as freshman year. Holding regular advising meetings with TCs to discuss program completion requirements can assist TCs in graduating from teacher education programs in a timely manner. Making expectations as clear as possible as early as possible to both TCs and faculty working with TCs will help keep everyone aware of the programmatic changes that need to take place or that are in the process of occurring.

As we first began learning more about edTPA, we started talking with our TCs at all levels of the programs—those who were new to the program as well as those about ready to complete the program. As new information came to us via program coordinator meetings and meetings with SCALE, we passed information via email and face-to-face meetings to our TCs so they knew what we knew. In effect, we opened a conversation about how our programs were going to be affected and how we were going to address curricular changes. We involved TCs in the conversations so they could have voice. We suggest that program coordinators schedule informational meetings with all faculty members involved in the preparation of teachers (e.g., methods instructors, language professors) to familiarize them with the purposes and challenges of edTPA, along with plans of edTPA implementation.

Shared professional knowledge and use of evidence are central to advancing teaching as a profession. We advocate introducing TCs to the shared edTPA vocabulary, such as *evidence of teaching practice, artifacts, learning segment*, and *commentaries*, early in their preparation. We noticed early in the pilot phase of the implementation that our TCs could generally do the required work; however, they were confused by the terminology from time to time. Additionally, candidates in our edTPA pilot tests did not have exemplars showing what a successful edTPA portfolio looked like. Using previous candidates' portfolios for instructional purposes, with permission, of course, teacher educators can demonstrate to current TCs the various components of a successful portfolio and its writer's successes and challenges.

Promoting a culture of evidence- and research-based decisions can help teacher education programs acclimate to the exigencies of edTPA. TCs and their educational programs must develop habits of mind to make teaching decisions based on solid evidence, instead of opinions and feelings. Part of communicating effectively for edTPA requires TCs to write in a more technical way than they may be used to. While leading up to completing their actual edTPA portfolio, TCs should become used to writing in a clear manner about the instructional decisions that they make. The semester that they complete the consequential edTPA portfolio should not be the first time they justify their instructional decisions with evidence and previous research. Assignments in methods classes can guide TCs to use second language acquisition research and evidence of student learning to describe their teaching decision-making process on the later consequential edTPA portfolio

As readers are most likely aware, teacher education requirements change quickly. The same is true of the edTPA handbooks and commentary templates, so be sure that you and your students are working from the most recent handbook and Word templates. The most recent handbooks and templates should be available to readers through your local edTPA coordinator or state department of education. The handbooks are also available online through a resource library discussed below, but faculty must gain permission from the edTPA coordinator or teacher education office.

Recent graduates can also be helpful as programs implement edTPA. For example, those graduates who previously performed well on edTPA can be invited as guests to talk to methods classes and student teachers about time management, useful resources, and other topics of interest to TCs. Individual graduates can be asked to serve as mentors to current TCs, listening to ideas and giving feedback on their various edTPA portfolio components. While faculty members, methods instructors, and student teacher supervisors can guide TCs in their portfolio construction, advice from someone who has experienced edTPA firsthand can be invaluable. Finally, recent graduates can be asked to contribute financially and aid financially strapped TCs who must complete the $300 process of edTPA portfolio submission.

SUPPORTING TEACHER CANDIDATES

Support, other than financial, can also be offered to TCs according to SCALE, the developer of edTPA. Although TCs must work independently on their official final edTPA submission, there are a number of ways that instructors, supervisors, cooperating teachers, and others can provide aide to TCs as they work on and submit their portfolio. In this book, we offer a number of means of supporting candidates as part of a language teacher education program and during the methods class. We also offer questions that TCs should consider as they create their responses to the three tasks.

The *edTPA Guidelines for Acceptable Candidate Support* (SCALE, 2014) highlights the acceptable practices for the edTPA handbook and rubrics to be used formatively throughout teacher education programs. For example, SCALE suggests that TCs become familiar with the rubrics throughout a variety of courses and that instructors provide feedback on assignments intended to develop TCs' skills measured by the edTPA portfolio. They list 11 "acceptable forms of support for candidates within the edTPA process" (p. 2), ranging from making arrangements for technical assistance to discussing samples of previous TCs' edTPA materials.

Despite much conversation across the country about the line between acceptable and unacceptable support, this document includes "Asking probing questions about candidates' draft edTPA responses or video recordings, without providing edits of the candidate's writing or providing candidates with specific answers to edTPA prompts" (p. 2) as permissible TC support. After the initial 11 acceptable forms of support describing permitted assistance, the same document provides the following "Unacceptable forms of candidate support" (SCALE, 2014, p. 2):

- editing a candidate's official materials prior to submission;
- offering critique of candidate responses that provides specific, alternative responses, prior to submission for official scoring;
- telling candidates which video clips to select for submission; and
- uploading candidate edTPA responses (written responses or video-tape [sic] entries) on public access social media websites.

As can be seen, SCALE permits ample means for teacher educators to support TCs as they work on the final edTPA portfolio. They also provide a number of resources for other stakeholders.

RESOURCES FROM SCALE

SCALE offers a multitude of other resources of which program coordinators may not be aware. In addition to the *edTPA World Language Assessment Handbook* (SCALE, 2015a). SCALE provides the *Understanding Rubric Level Progressions* (SCALE, 2015b) guide, which helps faculty and TCs know the difference between a weak and a strong performance on each of the edTPA rubrics. Another document vital for helping TCs understand edTPA requirements and what they need to do in a chronological manner is *Making Good Choices: A Support Guide for edTPA Candidates* (SCALE, 2015c). These resources will undoubtedly be updated in the future, so we urge readers to stay tuned. Another useful resource was created at Illinois State University and is called *Commentary Thinking Organizers and Helpful Hints (World Language Version)* (Palmer, 2015a). Each of the content areas assessed by edTPA has its own, specific thinking organizer document. All of these resources can be found in the online edTPA Resource Library, although readers should use the URL listed in the references to access the thinking organizer is only available using its URL, not via the library's search tool.

While we could continue to list and discuss the various publications provided by SCALE, we recommend readers take time to get to know the edTPA Resource Library, which contains a substantial amount of useful information and can be located by searching in a web browser. Some documents on that site are available to the public, while others are password protected. If interested, readers should contact their local edTPA coordinator for logon credentials or create an account on the library website. Further, we recommend that readers subscribe to American Association of Colleges for Teacher Education's edTPA community newsletter and make a point of reading the growing body of edTPA research. We encourage the reader to stay tuned to the edTPA Resource Library and other websites to be able to take advantage of new resources as they are released.

INFORMATION FROM THE STATE LEVEL

We recommend that readers become aware of their individual state's requirements regarding edTPA. Details, such as when edTPA becomes consequential in their particular setting, pass scores, and retake processes, will assist language teacher preparation programs with implementing future curricular changes. By working collaboratively and sharing valuable existing resources, faculty members involved in edTPA can initiate the transition. In our research, many states, colleges of education, and SCALE frequently offer a variety of resources to assist in edTPA preparation.

To begin, state departments of education, as is the case in Illinois, may have resources such as permission forms in various languages to explain the video recording requirements. For example, the Illinois State Board of Education (2013) provides a support letter to districts from the State Superintendent of Education that explains edTPA and its use during the student teaching semester. Also provided by that Board (Illinois State Board of Education, n. d.) are release forms for K–12 student participation in English, French, Japanese, Polish, and Spanish. Finally, examples from early edTPA adopters are shared on the Illinois State Board of Education website to let teacher preparation programs build off of others' previous successes.

Also of use for clinical placements may be the state department of education website about edTPA and its implementation. Showing school district teachers and administrators that edTPA is state mandated and not a department- or institution-chosen assessment may alleviate fears related to video recording learners in their schools and district. That assurance may comfort administrators enough to allow student teachers into the district once edTPA is fully implemented.

COLLEGES OF EDUCATION

As teacher educators, we acknowledge that world language teachers are prepared in different environments (e.g., colleges of education, collaboration among colleges). To that end, we contextualize our comments using our specific programs as examples. At Illinois State University, the preparation of world language TCs takes place in the College of Arts and Sciences. At Georgia State University, these individuals are prepared via a collaborative endeavor that includes the College of Education and Human Development and the College of Arts and Sciences. Thus, in this section we discuss the role of colleges of education.

Many times our students think about or even declare their major in Spanish Education, for example, and we do not know about it until they arrive in one of our foundations or pedagogy classes. While it would be helpful if the program coordinators were notified so that advisement could begin early, it is not always the case. From the moments TCs begin taking general coursework, they can begin to learn about world language education. We have found that general education faculty appreciate being given context-specific information about teaching world languages, such as the *World-Readiness Standards for Learning Languages* (National Standards Collaborative Board, 2015), the *ACTFL Proficiency Guidelines*, and even the National Council of State Supervisors for Languages-American Council on the Teaching of Foreign Languages *Can-Do Statements*. Those resources can assist them in creating content-specific assignments that incorporate edTPA language and constructs. Such information aids the TCs as they prepare for assignments in their general and language-specific teacher education courses.

To that end, TCs in general education courses can be introduced to information that will be helpful as they progress through the program. Faculty members in colleges of education as well as those preparing teachers outside of a formal academic setting (e.g., Teach for America, Georgia Metropolitan Regional Educational Service Agency) should have necessary introductory information to help world language TCs contextualize their learning, beginning at program admission. One major difference for education faculty to understand about world language edTPA is that it does not have an academic language component. That is, it does not contain a section regarding the "set of words, grammar, and organizational strategies used to describe complex ideas, higher order thinking processes, and abstract concepts" (Zwiers, 2004/2005, p. 20). World language TCs can focus on other critical, world language-specific edTPA construct, such as the three modes of communication and the three Ps of the cultures standard, while other content area TCs explore how to more effectively integrate academic vocabulary into their instruction.

Universities and colleges of education can also support programs and candidates to prepare for edTPA use in their contexts. World language teacher education program directors would be wise to get to know their campus edTPA coordinator and others responsible for assessment in their colleges of education and across campus. To help directors avoid beginning from scratch, these people may be to able to identify local programs that have been successful in preparing their candidates for edTPA. Those individuals may be able to put directors in contact with others at the state or national levels with further edTPA experience. On-campus personnel may also have in place steps for remediating candidates who have not been able to pass edTPA on the first try, should that be necessary.

Some universities, like both of ours, may offer teacher education programs edTPA vouchers purchased with university funds for pilot tests. In that way, a number of TC portfolios can be sent for external review as programs get ready for implementation. While helping TCs and programs know more about the evaluation process, the submissions provided real data that informed our programs as we continued to develop policies and practices to implement edTPA. Additionally, the data allowed us to compare locally scored portfolios to those externally reviewed and to ascertain how reliably we had evaluated our own students' work.

Illinois State University has been a leader in developing materials to support TCs of all content areas as they compile their edTPA portfolios. As an example, Figure 2.2 shows the resources available to that institution's world language teacher candidates to maximize their success. Earlier assignments in the semester can also prompt the TCs to read the various parts of the edTPA handbook before they begin writing. In that way, candidates can gain insight as to what will be expected of them once they begin compiling the portfolio. In particular, the *LiveText* interface allows an electronic clearinghouse for helpful documents. At the end of the LiveText page that TCs use to upload their instructional task, a number of documents appear, such as helpful suggestions for video recording, guardian consent forms, the handbook, the commentary template, a commentary review sheet, thinking organizer, and a completion checklist. In addition to the previously completed assignment to read each task in advance, these organizational tools can guide TCs to complete and submit all of the necessary parts of a rather complicated assessment.

Illinois State University also offers a one-credit, online summer course called "Preparing for the edTPA" (Illinois State University, 2016), which was offered for the first time during the summer of 2016. Its purpose is "to allow students to explore, practice, and review the essential components of the edTPA" (p. 1) and is targeted to TCs who anticipate student teaching in the upcoming academic year. TCs enrolled in the class will create and review instructional materials, while addressing critical concepts addressed by the assessment, such as backwards design, objective writing, and student feedback. edTPA TC supports will also be featured in the course.

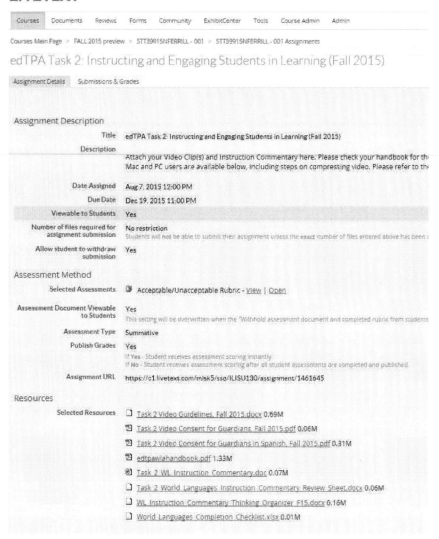

Figure 2.2.   LiveText interface for instructional task, including additional resources useful for submission.

While edTPA can be viewed as another financial impediment to becoming a certified teacher, we are working with our TCs early to begin planning for all of the costs associated with preservice teacher education. During meetings it has become evident that edTPA, alongside other assessments, can deter individuals from pursuing a career as a language teacher. However, we believe that by alerting TCs early on about the financial commitments, they can begin to plan financially, eliminating potential surprises as they are about to enter their final field placement. Program sheets showing the required coursework, deadlines for certain requirements (such as officially applying to the teacher education program), and state examinations are listed on the sheets alongside URLs. TCs are advised early of the costs associated with becoming a certified teacher so that they can plan. Additionally, as a matter of trying to help students plan financially, we are working with the Office of Financial Aid to investigate if financial aid can be used to pay for edTPA.

TECHNOLOGY INTEGRATION

Technology plays a serious role in edTPA implementation. TCs need to provide no more than two unedited video clips of themselves teaching in the classroom that last a maximum combined length of 15 minutes total. SCALE provides information about file sizes and supported file formats that need to be checked prior to recording any video files. *Education Week* (2014) and Ithaca College (n.d.) have additional tips about recording for edTPA. Because working with video for high-stakes assessments can be stressful, we advise faculty members to include video recording in methods courses in order to not only help with TC preparation pedagogically, but also various aspects of video recording. For example, cell phones have relatively good video capabilities, but we have found that their microphones have difficulty recording voices in classrooms because of the distance between the camera and the subjects. Also, cell phones tend to lack the ability in some cases to be put on a tripod for ease of recording. We have also found that flip cameras and other video cameras have improved lenses and microphones and the ability to be placed on tripods. It is important to remember that the external evaluators must be able both hear and see the teacher and students during the videos. Finally, recording videos in landscape, as opposed to portrait, gives the viewer a richer picture of the classroom and is highly recommended. We will more fully explore video recording particulars in Chapter 6.

To that end, while today's youth certainly appears to love shooting amateur video with cellular phones and many are avid videographers, we recommend that other video recording tools be investigated for edTPA purposes. Some of our TCs have used tablets and iPads for filming. Others use flip cameras and specialized video cameras. The technology director at Georgia State University purchased 10 new video cameras and tripods for our TCs to use during coursework and field placements. While we feel fortunate to have such technology available, the purchase most likely would not have taken place were it not for a meeting we had with the language lab director to discuss edTPA and how technology plays a role in TC success. The funds to purchase the equipment came from an internal university technology grant. As we have mentioned earlier, it is important to include every stakeholder in the conversation about edTPA.

ROLES FOR FACULTY IN LANGUAGE DEPARTMENTS

In addition to what needs to happen within traditional colleges of education, world language faculty members have a role to play in the preparation of language teachers, too (see Figure 2.3). Department organizational structure and individual personnel's duties will greatly inform the decisions made at the departmental level, and each university's or college's language teacher education program is unique. For example, TCs from some institutions may graduate from colleges of education with degrees in curriculum and instruction or perhaps in teaching and learning. Others whose degree programs are set in language departments may graduate with a degree in a particular language with a concentration in world language teacher education. Other possibilities exist as well. In our experience, some language departments have only one faculty member specializing in K–12 world language education. It is that person who is responsible for teaching the methods classes, supervising student teachers, and even directing the program. Other departments have multiple faculty or instructors who work with TCs in methods classes and field placement settings. Some departments have one advisor for all of their majors and minors, while others have all faculty advise individual students, both teaching and nonteaching students. World language programs can vary dramatically, even when they are in the same state (Hildebrandt, Hlas, & Conroy, 2013).

Regardless of departmental structure, language programs have a serious role to play in educating future teachers. We highly recommend a department-level edTPA implementation plan because it can guide programs and TCs as they prepare for consequential use of edTPA in the future. Program directors should clearly communicate expectations and inform faculty of necessary changes. Such communication is vital in securing buy-in from others in the department who may have less responsibility in the teacher preparation process. Helping others to understand edTPA's impact on the program, along with the importance and high stakes nature of the assessment, will help coordinators delegate responsibilities within the language department.

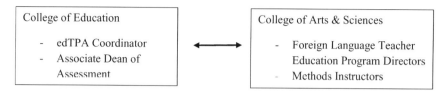

Figure 2.3.   An example of productive interaction for edTPA implementation.

Some members of the department will be, by job description, the most involved in the edTPA process. For example, student teacher supervisors work directly with TCs in the field; foundations of second language learning and methods instructors introduce TCs to the details of how to teach languages. Clearly, the world language teacher education program director is at the head of this group. We recommend that the director maintain constant communication via emails and scheduled face-to-face meetings in order to keep others aware of the ongoing efforts and to advocate for resources as the edTPA changes become permanent.

There are, however, a number of other individuals in a language department who can make the transition to full edTPA implementation easier. To begin, department chairs can play an important role by reallocating financial and time resources to those more directly involved in implementing edTPA. Taking the time to discuss the changes during faculty meetings can be helpful so that faculty specializing in other areas of the language department, such as literature and civilization, understand the changing landscape of teacher education and how to support the teacher education program. Additionally, the chair along with the program director can help bring higher level administrators into the conversations (e.g., associate deans, deans). It is critical that everyone understand the high stakes nature of edTPA, not just the TCs and associated faculty members. For example, at Georgia State University, during a faculty meeting the changes to the state content language exam were presented, and the presentation included the need for more francophone coursework in the curriculum. The world language teacher education faculty discussed the new exam content as well as the key points from the edTPA. The conversation helped the French faculty members understand the new requirements for our future teachers. Existing courses were modified and new courses were discussed, a process that excited faculty members.

Other language faculty and staff in the department can also join the transition team to edTPA implementation. Curricular committees certainly play an important role as necessary curricular changes are made to make room for edTPA in curriculum or coursework. Setting deadlines as new courses are developed is critical to timely implementation. Advisors, with their knowledge of departmental context, are in-house experts responsible for guiding TCs though course selections. These advisors can become powerful advocates as departments prepare TCs for edTPA success. Also, sharing information about edTPA with out-of-the-department advisors who work with freshman can benefit TCs early in their university studies. These advisors and others who encounter freshmen can alert TCs of the financial planning necessary for a myriad of teacher preparation costs such as edTPA, state content exams, et cetera, that come into play in the final year of the program. Well-trained advisors can raise TCs' attention to the courses in which they will develop the skills necessary to succeed on edTPA and in the program in general. They can also help curricular committees and program directors communicate efficiently with TCs as changes take place.

edTPA OPPORTUNITIES IN METHODS CLASSES

We set out to establish a road map for other instructors to follow, highlighting central language teaching concepts through meaningful methods activities, with the objective of engaging TCs in edTPA before it becomes high stakes. In this section we will advance our ideas for integrating edTPA throughout the entire teacher preparation program starting when we first have TCs in a world language teacher education foundations or pedagogy class (see Figure 2.4). Once TCs reach their language pedagogy classes, new opportunities to influence their performance come into being. Traditionally, methods classes are the place where future teachers combine what they have learned in their language classes and what they have learned in their general college of education pedagogy classes. The content-specific methods class is a critical time for TCs to establish the vocabulary and habits of mind to succeed on edTPA and in their future careers.

Essential edTPA vocabulary (e.g., evidence of teaching practice, artifacts, learning segment, commentaries) should be introduced in those general pedagogy, but they must also be reinforced during the second language-specific prestudent teaching coursework. Developing TCs' understanding of that shared vocabulary early will set the stage for a shared professional vocabulary across content areas. By using the shared vocabulary of edTPA throughout teacher preparation coursework, TCs become familiar with the underlying assumptions of the assessment. And incorporating content-specific edTPA vocabulary into methods courses is critical to TCs' success. Vocabulary, like meaningful cultural context, modes of communication, proficiency development, et cetera, should

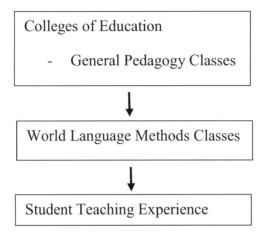

Figure 2.4.   Sequence of candidate edTPA familiarization.

become second nature well before submitting the official edTPA portfolio during student teaching. As one of the first assignments in the methods class, instructors can have TCs read the edTPA handbook glossary.

A practice edTPA, prior to the student teaching semester, can increase TC familiarity with the tasks. If left until the last semester of their teacher education programs, edTPA can be unwieldy for TCs and may demand a steep learning curve at an already stressful time. Microteaching assignments can play an important part in preparing TCs for the exigencies of edTPA, while encouraging meaningful reflection on teaching in action and reflection on action (Schön, 1983). The real-life setting can allow TCs to integrate the edTPA planning and instruction components into their work with real students. A whole-class service learning project, such as the one described in Hildebrandt (2014), can provide an authentic setting to let TCs put into practice the pedagogical skills central to edTPA. A mini-edTPA portfolio in the world language methods classes or an early field experience can provide a trial run with low stakes, familiarizing TCs with the format of the assessment and its evidence-based exigencies. When scoring the informal, mini-edTPA during methods classes, instructors may wish to avoid the numbers used to officially score the portfolio, using instead a three-column approach with scores of 1 and 2 being below target, 3 at target, and 4 and 5 above target. Otherwise, using the same rubric content can help TCs get familiar with the more formal expectations later on.

Other tools can be used to help TCs prepare for submitting effective edTPA portfolios. For example, providing lesson plan templates for TCs to use in methods class and student teaching can set TCs up for success, with consistent lesson plan templates across purposes and classes eliminating some of the guesswork associated with beginning lesson planners. The authors recommend at this time *The Keys to Planning for Learning* (Clementi & Terrill, 2013) for an outstanding thematic unit planning template and the accompanying lesson plan template for use in methods classes and student teaching settings. These helpful templates can be found on the ACTFL website (ACTFL, n.d.-b).

Letting TCs peek behind the curtain of methods instruction can provide TCs the modeling that they may not otherwise have. Explaining clearly the decisions made by the instructor as the course develops also enhances TC buy-in. For example, if on a reading quiz an item is disputed, the methods instructor can show TCs an item analysis carried out by the instructor and discuss how that analysis informed her decision to mark it wrong or accept alternative answers. Explaining the considerations made, in a reading quiz for example, can make explicit to TCs what seasoned teaching veterans take for granted.

Backwards design can inform practice in the methods class. By modeling the various lesson planning and assessment practices required of TCs in their edTPA portfolio composition, methods instructors can provide powerful *apprenticeship of observation* (Lortie, 1975) for TC. A critical aspect of successful edTPA portfolios and language instruction involves TCs connecting state and national standards to learning objectives, which are then connected to the assessment tools used to determine whether the desired learning took place. Using ACTFL/CAEP standards (Foreign Language Teacher Preparation Standards Writing Team, 2013) to establish in-class objectives for each lesson during the methods class and tying those objectives to the assessments/activities carried out during class can provide powerful modeling and make more explicit the connections that we hope TCs internalize. Addressing the targeted standards at the beginning of each class and how they are operationalized for assessment provides TCs an insight into their own learning, as well as a model for their future language instruction.

STAKEHOLDERS IN K–12 CLINICAL SETTINGS

We strongly recommend that everyone associated with preparing language teachers and even those outside of higher education (e.g., mentor teachers, district world language coordinators, principals) have a working knowledge of edTPA and its requirements. First, student teacher supervisors are critical to TC success once edTPA counts in a given state. Their efforts in preparing TCs cannot be overestimated, as it is during their shared time that TCs generally submit the portfolio to be evaluated by

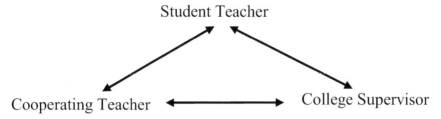

Figure 2.5.   Triadic reciprocity of edTPA information in clinical settings.

external reviewers. Further, the score earned on edTPA may determine the TC's ability to earn a teaching license or certificate. Figure 2.5 makes the critical roles of relationship and communication among the student teacher, cooperating teacher, and college supervisor visual.

SCALE has assembled a variety of handouts that can support stakeholders in the K–12 settings and are accessible on the edTPA Resource Library. For example, a two-page document entitled *edTPA Support and Assessment Program* (SCALE, 2013b), which outlines highlights of edTPA, including that it was developed "*by* the Profession *for* the Profession" (p. 1, italics in original). It further provides information about edTPA's foci on student learning and program renewal, as well as the content specificity of the assessment. Further information about stakeholder support can be found on the websites of SCALE and the American Association for Colleges of Teacher Education. Further information about technology resources, common expectations, and reciprocity across states can be found this document.

A second two-page document entitled *Using edTPA* (SCALE, n.d.-a) gives background information on the assessment's architecture and purposes. It further outlines the five critical dimensions of teaching, including planning instruction and assessment, instructing and engaging students in learning, assessing student learning, analysis of teaching effectiveness, and academic language development. The document also outlines information about how portfolios are assessed and who does that assessing. It closes with the 22 licensure areas (now 27) that edTPA addressed at the time. That number of content areas has increased to 27 since the publication of this document.

Although now rather dated, an edTPA fact sheet (SCALE, n.d.-b) gives background information on edTPA and its foci on evaluating teaching performance and student learning via authentic performance assessment. It explains how edTPA works, that it is based on professional expectations, and the status of edTPA use throughout the country. It goes on to outline how edTPA is "helping to meet education's top priority," which is to "provide an effective teacher in every classroom" (p. 2), The document closes with an explanation of how edTPA supports change in teacher preparation, along with a list of the 33 states and District of Columbia that were participating in edTPA at the time of the document's publication. It is of note that 38 states and the District of Columbia are participating in edTPA at the time of this writing (American Association for Colleges of Teacher Education, 2016).

A fourth document available from the edTPA Resource Library to support stakeholders is entitled "Making Culturally Relevant Pedagogy Relevant to Aspiring Teachers" (Lynn, 2014), in which the author explores the disconnect "between what is taught, how it is taught and who is being taught" (p. 1). He makes a case that teachers need to be better prepared to "effectively serve African American males and other critically underserved populations" (p. 1). He further expresses his confidence in edTPA's ability to help teacher candidates move beyond deficit thinking and toward understanding "where student potential lies and demonstrate that they can leverage it" (p. 2).

edTPA Myths and Facts (SCALE, n.d.-c) provides stakeholders seven pages of responses to myths about a number of issues related to edTPA and its implementation, including scoring practices, Pearson's role, handbook and rubric quality, and retakes. It also briefly addresses acceptable candidate assistance by faculty, instructional approaches espoused by edTPA, culturally relevant pedagogy, and the representativeness of instruction recorded for Task 2. It closes with myths and facts about edTPA's ability to inform program decisions, "teaching to the test" concerns, the $300 price tag, and edTPA's psychometric characteristics. The document encounters each myth with a relatively short response, but points readers to electronic resources available to support the facts presented.

The final resources among the stakeholder handouts available from the American Association for Colleges of Teacher Education's Resource Library are for supervising teachers and P–12 administrators and leaders. The first is a four-page document entitled *Teachers Who Support Teacher Candidates* (SCALE, n.d.-d), which highlights the planning, instruction, assessment feedback loop related to student learning featured in the introductory pages of content area handbooks (e.g., SCALE, 2015a, p. 6). It also explains the critical role that cooperating teachers play in TCs' edTPA success and the process that TCs go through to document their teaching practice. In a section called "What you can expect," the need for a cooperating teacher to share learning context information early and to support additional TC reflection practices precedes an explanation of some necessary video recording considerations. The document goes on to outline acceptable candidate supports, such as discussing edTPA and "asking probing questions about candidates' draft edTPA responses or video recordings" (p. 3), and unacceptable supports, such as editing TC materials before submission and instructing TCs on what video recordings to submit. The last page outlines edTPA scorer qualifications and invites cooperating teachers to become scorers.

The last document, a two-page handout entitled *edTPA Guidance for P–12 Administrators and Leaders* (SCALE, n.d.-e), "provides ... guidance for using edTPA evidence to support new teachers during induction, implement teacher evaluation and discuss best teaching practices" (p. 1). While highlighting the centrality of student learning, this document outlines instructional leaders', cooperating teachers', and TCs' roles in the edTPA process. Like the document for cooperating teachers, this handout provides examples of acceptable TC support that can be provided during the clinical experience. The second page features the same visual representation of the planning, instruction, assessment approach to student learning as shown in each content area's handbook. General information about edTPA rubrics and their alignment with professional standards, like InTASC and CAEP standards, are featured. The handout closes with an exploration of "formative use of edTPA results for professional development" (p. 2), which describes the role of stakeholders in supporting TC development and edTPA portfolio completion, and information about security and confidentiality required.

It is also a good idea for teacher preparation faculty to become trained to score portfolios. In order to prepare for consequential use of edTPA, we have found that there is merit in locally scoring all edTPA portfolios even though they may be sent for external review. Each semester we take time to compare the local scores to the external scores on each rubric in order to learn more about edTPA scoring. Such data analysis has revealed to us several interesting findings. For example, one of our TCs was scored locally on one of the instruction rubrics as a 2, but the external reviewer awarded a score of 4. We scored the TC performance lower for several reasons, but a primary reason was that the TC taught in both languages (French and English) instead of remaining in French the majority of the time. We pointed out the discrepancy to various ACTFL members and quickly learned that teaching in the target language is not a primary concern for the world language edTPA at the moment. Grounded in both theoretical and conceptual frameworks as well as best practices, we have, along with several others, advanced the issue at the national level in order to affect change.

There are several immediate advantages to internally evaluating TC performance even after they have turned in their portfolios. First, by knowing what the external reviewers are trained to look for, it helps teacher preparation faculty know how to structure programs and curricula. Second, it improves interrater reliability by calibrating local scoring to external scoring. Third, having data to discuss helps improve our own TCs' sense of efficacy so that they feel empowered as they create dynamic portfolios. Finally, individual program data can be compared and then discussed with other program coordinators in order to determine ways to improve programs on a larger scale. For example, we combined our data and reported the findings in *Foreign Language Annals* (Hildebrandt & Swanson, 2014). As we were analyzing the data, questions and conversations naturally emerged about why some candidates were doing better than others on certain rubrics. We talked frequently about the structure of our programs in terms of curricula and coursework, for example. Quickly we learned that even though our two programs shared many similar classes and ways of bringing TCs to higher levels of learning, some of the ideas being implemented at Illinois State University worked better than those at Georgia State University and vice versa. We instituted the changes we felt we needed and are still looking at the data. Finally, the examination of data can be combined at a more state, regional, and even national level. Such collaboration can be very helpful to improve programs, regardless of location. Findings can be reported at various conferences and via webinars to help at a broader level.

While such work by faculty in clinical settings is crucial to TC success on edTPA, cooperating teachers and principals in the field play an important role, too. They need to become aware of edTPA requirements, at least in very general terms. During the first week of a student teaching placement, cooperating teachers should be informed of the edTPA submission timeline that TCs must follow. That timeline, as will be discussed below, should include time for the TC to focus on writing the portfolio and perhaps a temporary diminished level of classroom responsibility. While it is ideal to maximize TCs' time in the classroom, the high stakes nature of edTPA should allow at least a few hours' time reassignment.

Principals have the power to accept or deny teacher candidates in their schools. Many times these individuals do not know about new national teacher preparation trends. We have found that by scheduling time with them and helping them understand more about the exigencies of edTPA, they are more willing to work with our programs. Additionally, there is value in meeting with individual teachers. In the past, both of us have met with cooperating teachers in K–12 schools to discuss edTPA requirements, as well as the new licensing issues (e.g., new assessments for preservice teachers). It is important to remember that many teachers not only teach as they were taught (Burke, 2014), but they were also certified to teach under a completely different set of rules and requirements. These individuals work more closely with TCs on a day-to-day basis during student teaching than the college/university supervisor does. It is critical that these teachers know edTPA requirements, the timelines for portfolio submission, the rigor and the time TCs must dedicate in order to complete edTPA, and the many details associated with edTPA (e.g., parental permission forms, quality unedited film clips). By having an open line of communication, mentor teachers can help TCs as they progress toward becoming a certified member of our profession.

University student teacher supervisors and cooperating mentor teachers help TCs put into practice what they studied in coursework prior to the culminating clinical experience. With effective preparation, TCs can successfully navigate their responsibilities to their new school and students while creating edTPA artifacts and commentaries. Communicating with school districts and TCs about edTPA requirements should begin before the student teaching semester.

A timeline for edTPA portfolio submission can be critical to TC success. Beginning at the end with submission dates and working backward are the first steps. It takes approximately one month after portfolio submission to receive a TC's official scores. Therefore, for a semester-long student teaching experience, we recommend having TCs submit their portfolios for scoring approximately halfway through the semester (see Figure 2.6).

We recommend that critical that TCs begin their student teaching experience when the K–12 school year begins because colleges and universities' academic calendars tend to begin after K–12 schools are already in session. By beginning when schools K–12 classes start, TCs can have several additional weeks to begin developing the portfolio. In the case of Georgia State University, in the fall semester K–12 schools typically commence in late July or early August, whereas classes at the university begin the third week of August. Such an approach gives TCs more necessary time to develop, submit, and possibly resubmit tasks that received scores below the passing cut scores before the K–12 semester concludes. Additionally, the approach allows TCs who did not initially pass edTPA to work with the same K–12 students, which is an edTPA requirement.

The timeline shown in Figure 2.6 suggests that TCs choose their target class and begin developing their portfolios early. We recommend that program directors consult Pearson Education website (2016d) for portfo-

Figure 2.6. Timeline for portfolio submission.

lio submission deadlines. In the spirit of beginning with the end, TCs should determine the evidence that will be acceptable to show that students met or did not meet lesson objectives. edTPA completion does not have to take place in a linear fashion. In fact, successful TCs would be wise to look first to the assessments that students complete.

Proper timing for submitting materials is essential for TCs' edTPA success. Spreading each task deadline across the first weeks of the semester will help TCs pace themselves more effectively than if left to their own self-established deadlines. In a similar manner, the order in which tasks are addressed does not necessarily have to be done in a linear fashion by TCs. That is, as TCs are working on the planning task, they should keep in mind the exigencies of the assessment task. Additionally, video recording a number of class periods with a variety of activities will provide the TC plenty of evidence to analyze, should an unforeseen technological mishap take place. Thus, we recommend backwards design when creating edTPA artifacts and evidence. Further, creating multiple assessments for use in the edTPA portfolio is advised, should resubmission be necessary later. Those additional assessments may help avoid the need for a second portfolio or student teaching placement.

The timeline established should leave time at the end of the semester for remediation, if necessary. Despite the best plans, TCs may earn scores that are not sufficient for licensure or certification in their home state. Therefore, building time in at the end of the semester for TCs to rewrite portions of the portfolio can prove wise. In our experiences, however, retakes have not been common (Hildebrandt & Swanson, 2014). With stakeholders from across campus and a given state, programs can collaborate on formulating retake procedures for those TCs who are not successful the first time they attempt edTPA.

CONCLUDING THOUGHTS

In this chapter we have provided a number of ideas for world language program directors and others involved in edTPA implementation to maximize TC success early. Our own programs have served as models for others to follow, but each context will determine the ultimate steps to follow as edTPA is used. We have listed some resources from SCALE and other external organizations to help the reader along the various tasks that can be carried out at the state, college, and department levels. We shared changes that we have implemented in methods classes to get TCs used to the assessment. Finally, we explored what can be done in K–12 settings to help TCs as they work on their edTPA portfolios. We strongly advocate sharing ideas among programs, universities, and states, as edTPA continues to influence teacher education across the country. The next chapter will explore the Content for Learning, which sets the stage for the rest of the edTPA portfolio.

CHAPTER 3

CONTEXT FOR LEARNING

In the first two chapters, we have introduced edTPA and the history of measuring teacher effectiveness in the American pre-K through Grade 12 educational context. We have also shared the purposes for writing this book and the steps that we have taken in our world language teacher education programs to help teacher candidates (TCs) be successful on edTPA. In this chapter, we explore edTPA's Context for Learning. Specifically, we provide suggestions for selecting a school and a particular class, critical decisions in edTPA preparation. We also discuss in detail heritage language learners, English Language Learners, and students with identified learning plans via individualized education programs (IEPs) and 504 plans. We address how TCs should approach diverse classrooms in a positive manner instead of from a deficit perspective.

Once an edTPA portfolio is complete, it is sent for external review by at least two trained scorers. The Context for Learning document allows the TC to give scorers context as to where and who the TC is teaching. It also enables external reviewers, who know nothing of the TC or the setting in which he/she teaches, to situate the TC's edTPA portfolio within the larger picture. While a student teacher supervisor knows many of these details by observation and presence at the school setting, the standardized nature of edTPA submission requires TCs to document what may otherwise seem obvious. As is the case with many aspects of teaching, context is everything. Who the learners are and where the teaching takes place determine much of what is or what should be done in the classroom.

The Context for Learning and each of the three edTPA tasks that follow have a Word document template for TCs to use while writing. Those templates, along with the entire handbook, should be made available to TCs

Understanding the World Language edTPA: Research-Based Policy and Practice
pp. 39–48
Copyright © 2016 by Information Age Publishing

as early as possible so that decisions made throughout can become familiar with them and effectively explain the decisions they make throughout the learning segment. Handbooks and the accompanying Word templates should be available from on-campus edTPA coordinators or other sources. Once candidates have the templates, they will see that they can alter the document by typing between the two brackets (e.g., []) after each of the prompts. As the TC types, the brackets move to allow more space.

Via edTPA's Context for Learning document, TCs provide three levels of detail for scorers to gain a better understanding of the teaching environment. First, TCs describe the school setting in terms of level and setting. The first section also allows TCs to explain any extenuating circumstances that may influence how material is taught, such as the school or district's unique expectations for students or teachers. Then, details about the course, its level, schedule, instructional materials and resources, and grouping or tracking are shared. Finally, information about the students themselves is provided (e.g., grade levels, gender, and differences that might affect instruction). Such differences may include home language, cognitive abilities, IEPs or 504 plans, or reading abilities. The last section of the Context for Learning allows TCs to document the number of students with each of the indicated differences, along with necessary supports, modifications, or accommodations.

SCHOOLS

Selecting a school or a school district for some TCs can be challenging for a variety of reasons. To begin, TCs may not know many inservice language teachers or where they are employed, and they most likely do not have firsthand information about which language teachers demonstrate the best practices in language teaching (e.g., teaching in the target language at least 90% of the time, assessing and building student proficiency in the target language) on a daily basis. Furthermore, we have found that some TCs want to take a path of least resistance and just randomly select a school and hope that the language teacher can serve as a quality mentor. From such a lack of knowledge about schools and the teachers who work in those schools, problems can and do arise.

We strongly urge TCs to work closely with teacher education faculty and the field placement faculty member(s). The faculty member(s) can recommend districts and schools with vibrant language teaching programs and reputations for excellence in language learning and teaching. They may even be able to recommend specific teachers who would be excellent mentors. At Georgia State University, we have the TCs investigate schools and districts via the Georgia Department of Education website (http://www.gadoe.org/Pages/Home.aspx). TCs can learn more about schools and districts by reading the school's Report Card and NCLB/ Annual Yearly Progress pages. They can also learn about the school population via the school's published demographics statistics, usually found on school's individual web pages.

Each teacher preparation program has a different way to assign TCs to districts and schools for student teaching. Some university placement offices ask language program faculty to recommend individual teachers who may be interested in serving as cooperating teachers. Others do not consult language departments at all when making placements. We have found that state language teacher conferences can be an ideal context to solicit teachers to mentor TCs. Teachers who regularly attend conferences tend to be up to date on current methods and pedagogy, and may be more willing to allow TCs to demonstrate the target teaching practices required by the language teacher education program.

Once potential schools are identified, we recommend that TCs select a school near where they live in order to decrease commute time. In rural and suburban contexts, commute times may be relatively short. However, in urban areas, commutes of 10–12 miles can take up to an hour at peak times. These individuals will be spending a lot of time at schools and having a short commute can be helpful. Additionally, we have found that successful TCs choose to meet with the mentor teacher in the school well before the student teaching placement begins. By becoming familiar with the teacher and the school, the TC comes to understand early the mentor teacher's expectations as well as those of the administration. Conversations about edTPA and its requirements can take place so that mentor teachers understand how different teacher education is now, as opposed to when they completed licensure or certification requirements. For example, during the initial student teaching interview, TCs could offer cooperating teachers a handout that explains edTPA and ways that veteran teachers can support student teachers during the edTPA process. The educational landscape has changed in many states since the introduction of edTPA and in-service teachers serving as cooperating teachers may have little knowledge of or experience with the assessment.

Information requested about the school on the Context for Learning document includes indicating what type of school in which the edTPA portfolio was composed: elementary, middle, high school, or other, which must then be described. The TC also indicates whether the school is located in an urban, suburban or rural setting.

SELECTING A FOCAL CLASS

The information requested about the focal class in the Context for Learning document is intended to provide a richer portrayal of the class and instruction provided. TCs are able to briefly explain their setting in order to provide edTPA scorers the information necessary to evaluate the TC's classroom performance. Helping TCs think through and highlight what they may take for granted is a necessary part of this portion of edTPA. For example, a course that meets every day for 48 minutes is going to differ in critical ways from another that is on a block schedule of 90 minutes every other day. If a textbook is not used in the class, instruction is obviously going to be different than one in which the textbook is the primary source of input for students. Ability grouping or tracking will directly affect the interactions among students in the classroom, informing instructional decisions made by the TC.

Choosing the best class to feature in edTPA is a critical decision, with the demands of edTPA informing the choice. Given the timeline restrictions, it is wise for the TC to choose the class and content with which he or she is most familiar and a schedule of instruction (e.g., 45-minute class, block) that he or she is most comfortable teaching. Generally, the class that the TC has taught the longest is a wise choice because the TC knows the students and course content the best. An additional consideration, however, is the amount of opportunities available for the TC to show differentiation of instruction, to help learners of various backgrounds and abilities learn. As the TC must show student learning evidence from three learners of varying backgrounds, there must be sufficient student diversity to show a variety of instructional approaches and decisions. In the September 2015 handbook, which is the most recent as of this book's writing, requires that at least one student whose work is examined have a specific learning need. Therefore, in order to meet the requirements of edTPA, TCs much choose a class with some diversity of learners.

The case study portfolio used throughout this book was generated for a Spanish II honor's class, and Anna indicates that there were no students with IEPs, 504 plans, or specific learning needs in the class. Under the auspices of the 2013 handbook (Stanford Center for Assessment, Learning, and Equity, SCALE, 2013c), she was able to earn high scores on the rubrics without having that diversity of learners. We caution that, given the most recent edition of the handbook, TCs would be wise to choose a focal class that has at least one student with some specific learning need so that they can give specific examples of differentiation in their learning segment.

STUDENTS

Every child in every classroom of every school in every district is unique in a myriad of ways. Some differences are visible while others are less so. Each student brings his or her own unique perspective to the class and to learning. The edTPA Context for Learning document provides TCs the opportunity to provide details on students' profiles and their needs, which ultimately should inform the way that the lessons are constructed and carried out.

By the time they are placed for student teaching, TCs should know the difference between an IEP and a 504 plan. In short, an IEP is a plan or program to ensure that a student who has a disability identified under the law and is attending an elementary or secondary school receives specialized instruction and related services. A 504 plan differs in that it ensures that students with an identified disability as defined by law who are attending an elementary or secondary school receive accommodations that will ensure their academic success and access to the learning environment. Under the law not all students who have disabilities require specialized instruction. We recommend that TCs understand more about IEPs and 504 plans and the students who are identified in accordance with the two. Additionally, federal legislation is revised, reauthorized, or reconfigured routinely and so readers are urged to remain aware of existing changes to mandates influencing all aspects of education, with special attention to special education.

One of the most important ways for a TC to get information about students' needs is from IEPs and 504 accommodation plans, legal documents that detail a student's disability and his/her needs. Initial legislation that would culminate in the Individuals with Disabilities Education Act (2004) was passed in 1975, when up to 80% of students with disabilities were not able to go to public schools (Yell, Katsiyannis, & Bradley, 2011). Over the years the act has been revised. In general terms, an IEP lists modifications and accommodations for the learner and has been put together by a team of stakeholders, including teachers, counselors, and parents. Gorman (2013) describes a modification as a practice that "substantially changes the general education curriculum" (p. 6), while an accommodation "provides opportunities for an adjustment in the presentation of the material or assessment but does not change the content in any way" (p. 6). Section 504 of the Rehabilitation Act of 1973 "provides protection against discrimination for individuals with disabilities" (Gorman, 2013, p. 6), either mental or physical, whose life activities are limited. A 504 plan generally includes only accommodations for the learner, most often a secondary school student (Gorman, 2013).

As part of their new school familiarization process, TCs who are in their final clinical experience should ask to see the IEPs and 504 plans of the students in their classes. As they are legal documents that set the parameters for student assistance, the IEP or 504 plan provides invaluable information about what teacher must do to best teach the individual.

Cooperating teachers should be able to direct TCs to where IEPs and 504 plans are housed and how to gain access to those documents.

According to Kelleher (2010), the term *heritage language learner* can be used to describe someone studying a language "who has proficiency in or a cultural connection to that language" (p. 1). Interestingly, and perhaps less well known, there are different types of heritage language learners. Those differences may be of import for preservice teachers as they begin edTPA. There is not one profile of heritage language learners because the term describes a heterogeneous population (Wang & García, 2002). For example, Kelleher (2010) noted that for members of indigenous communities, such as Navajo, any member of the community studying the language might be considered a heritage language learner. In K–12 schools with English as the primary language of instruction, other languages like Spanish may be offered as foreign or world languages. Nevertheless, some of the students in those classes could have a connection to the second language through their families and have some level of proficiency in the target language. These students, too, are heritage language learners.

In short, heritage language learners do not constitute any one group, as defined by specific linguistic or even racial background. Valdés (1999, 2001) suggested that heritage language learners raised in homes in which English is not the first language speak or understand the heritage language to varying degrees, with most at least somewhat bilingual in English and the heritage language. She has found that heritage language students can be categorized into one of four major groups: new arrivals/migrant students, foreign-born students who arrived at a young age but have been in U.S. schools for a number of years, ethnic-American students who were born in the United States to immigrant parents or ancestors, and indigenous American students who would like to strengthen or reestablish their ties to their heritage language and culture (Wang & García, 2002). While the students' linguistic and educational needs can vary widely no matter which group they identify as, these individuals and the American society would benefit from developing heritage language learners' first languages alongside English

Additionally, and equally important, world language teachers need to acknowledge and use what Moll, Amanti, Neff, and Gonzalez (1992) refer to as students' funds of knowledge—"the historically accumulated and culturally developed bodies of knowledge and skills essential for household or individual functioning and well-being" (p. 133). Equipped with such information, language teachers can start to understand that the students' lived experiences contain rich cultural and cognitive resources, and that such resources can be leveraged in the classroom in order to provide meaningful, culturally responsive activities that build upon students' prior knowledge. Furthermore, as Wang and García (2002) noted, teachers must attend to heritage language learners' sociolinguistic issues. For example, students may need to learn how to speak to teachers in certain situations (Hymes, 1974).

In sum, language teachers not only need to know that heritage language learners are part of their classroom, they also must learn to engage them in culturally responsive teaching. Gay (2000) suggested that the process of building culturally responsive communities of learning is important for teachers. Instead of approaching teaching from a deficit perspective, one that views students based upon "our perceptions of their weaknesses rather than their strengths" (Gorski, 2010, p. 2), teachers should gain knowledge of the cultures of the various ethnic and cultural groups of the community, how those cultures may affect learning behaviors, and how classroom interactions and instruction can be changed to embrace these differences (Gay, 2000, p. 114). A deficit perspective deteriorates expectations for students and weakens educators' abilities to recognize giftedness in its various forms (Ford & Grantham, 2003). The most devastating brand of this sort of deficit thinking emerges when teachers mistake difference—particularly difference from themselves—for deficit. We recommend that readers become familiar with the topic and consult Gay's (2000, 2010) and Nieto's (2010, 2013) work as a point of departure to understand more about engaging diverse populations in the classroom. We also recommend that readers consult Osborn's (2006) and Glynn, Wesley, and Wassell's (2014) work on social justice. These leaders in the field provide readers with a wealth of information and ideas about a variety of culturally relevant topics.

ENGLISH LANGUAGE LEARNERS

In addition to heritage language learners, English language learners (ELLs)—students who do not have English as their native language—provide a specific set of challenges for teachers across the content areas. Over the past 3 decades, the foreign-born population of the United States has nearly tripled (Camarota, 2011) and is expected to continue to grow each year in the foreseeable future. Based on current projections, the foreign-born population in the United States of 9.6 million in 1970 will increase to 65.2 million by 2033. ELLs now comprise 10.5% of the nation's K–12 enrollment, up from 5% in 1990. Demographically, ELLs are found in higher concentrations in cities as opposed to rural settings. For example, the National Center for Education Statistics (2014) reported that in 2011–12, ELL students in cities constituted an average of 14.2% of total public school enrollment, 9% in suburban areas, and 3.9% in rural areas of the country.

Teachers will need strategies and skills in order to work with an even more heterogeneous student population. Much like the heritage language learner population, there is not a single profile of an ELL. Some ELL students come from homes in which English is not spoken. Others come from homes where only English is spoken, while others have been exposed to or use multiple languages at home. Some are new to the United States while others have lived in the country for years (National Council of Teachers of English, 2008).

Depending on students' level of English language proficiency, they may characteristically these individuals may be timid or have a low sense of efficacy in their academic abilities, be overly reliant on visual stimuli, and even become resistant to interacting in small group activities. Therefore, there are specific strategies that can be employed to help ELLs learn in the language classroom. Blackburn (2015) suggests (1) using visuals, (2) monitoring teacher language use, and (3) layering meaning.

First, visuals are helpful for just about any learner. However, ELLs can benefit from *word walls*, an ongoing activity in which important vocabulary is placed on the wall or bulletin board. In some cases, having a piece of paper folded in half with the word written on the outside and a picture or graphic of the word on the inside can make huge differences for ELLs. Second, teacher communication matters. Blackburn notes that, whenever possible, teachers should simplify instructions and streamline questions in order not to interfere with a student's native language. Moreover, consciously avoiding the use of idioms, unless idioms are part of the learning objectives for the unit, can help clarify meaning for ELLs. For those individuals who are struggling with English, Blackburn recommends that teachers pose questions that require ELLs to complete a thought, rather than generate a new idea. By starting with a partially constructed response, ELLs can build confidence and a strong base for future learning. Finally, Blackburn advocates that teachers layer meaning. For example, many times ELLs struggle with academic language found in textbooks. Teachers can find an article or a selection from a different source on the same topic that is easier to read. ELLs can be asked to read and understand the easier text first, gathering original material, vocabulary, and background knowledge before attending to the material in the textbook.

Some ELL students could also be categorized as heritage language learners and may have differing academic needs. Thus, it is important to keep in mind that these students may have differing academic needs. Teachers must be aware of their students' similarities and differences as they approach planning and instruction. Differentiation can be vital. While some instructors may feel they are differentiating instruction for all learners, it is good practice to remember that differentiation involves presenting the same task to all learners but in different ways and at different levels of understanding so that all students can learn in their own ways.

CASE STUDY

Throughout the following three chapters, we will use an exemplary portfolio submitted by Anna, one of our TCs who scored exceptionally well. While we do not explicitly share her commentaries or artifacts, we do reexamine her portfolio from a number of angles, using it as an externally scored model. She has graciously allowed us to use her edTPA artifacts, for which we thank her. Anna was a student in one of our programs, taking our classes during the fall of 2013 and student teaching during the spring of 2014. In her world language pedagogy courses, she performed very well and paid close attention to detail. She was a successful student teacher and graduated from the program in May 2014. Her edTPA rubric scores ranged from the median score and higher on all 13 rubrics. Scores with .5 (e.g., 2.5, 3.5) generally indicate that the TC's performance fell between two levels or that the two scorers were one level apart in their scores on the particular rubric. The scores she earned placed her above the score of 3 on each of the 13 rubrics that we tell our TCs to aim for in order to score at least 39. At the time of this writing, that score is well above the cut scores set in all 13 states using edTPA scores for licensure and certification decisions.

Our purpose in using this example is not to provide a template for TCs to blindly follow. Instead, we use this former student's lesson plans and assessments to provide an example of edTPA-approved language teaching practices, as determined by official scoring. This and other models can provide powerful ways for TCs to encounter teaching practices that they may not have experienced firsthand as language learners.

Anna was placed in a suburban high school Spanish class. She described her classroom setting as *average* without any special features. She noted that none of her students were recent immigrants to the United States. One hundred percent of the students were native English speakers and they were learning Spanish as a world language. She also mentioned that her mentor teacher did not have any specific lesson plan template for her to use so she used the lesson plan Clementi and Terrill (2013) lesson plan template available for not cost on the ACTFL website. For her focal class, she chose a Spanish II Honors class that students attended the entire academic year for approximately 45 minutes Monday through Friday. She mentioned briefly that the high school offers two world language tracks: regular and honors. The honors classes are taught at a faster pace, she explained to the reviewers. In addition to the textbook listed by name, she wrote that she also used the Flash Cultura Video Program, the textbook's workbook and online component.

She described her students as 10th graders with only 12 students in the class, six females and six males. None of her students were working under the provisions of a 504 plan or an IEP. When Anna developed her edTPA portfolio and submitted it for review under the September 2013 handbook (SCALE, 2013c), edTPA required that TCs include at least one student with a special learning need as part of the three focus students. However, the handbook did not state the nature of the learning need. So her one focal student was gifted along with the rest of the students. Nevertheless, as of the September 2015 handbook, one of the three focus students must have a specific learning need (SCALE, 2015a). In total, she used approximately two and a third pages for her Context for Learning. The maximum allowed is three pages.

CONCLUDING THOUGHTS

In this chapter we have provided a number of ideas as TCs begin working on the edTPA Context for Learning. We explored edTPA's Context for Learning. We provided suggestions for selecting a school/district and a particular class within the school. Due to edTPA requirements along with best practices, we provided information about heritage language learners, English Language Learners, and students with identified learning plans via IEPs and 504 plans. Importantly, we discuss how TCs should approach diverse classrooms in a positive manner instead of from a deficit perspective. TCs should become knowledgeable about IEPs and 504 plans and what accommodations are needed before their placement officially begins.

In the following three chapters, we discuss each of the three tasks of edTPA: Planning for Instruction and Assessment, Instruction and Engaging Students in Learning, and Assessing Student Learning. In each of the chapters, we provide readers strategies, ideas, and activities. In the spirit of backward design, we begin with Assessment.

CHAPTER 4

BEGINNING AT THE END

Assessing Student Learning

Despite the order of tasks presented in the September 2015 *edTPA World Language Assessment Handbook* (i.e., planning, instruction, assessment), we approach the tasks and the chapters of this book based on our teacher education programs, teacher candidates' (TCs) needs, and philosophies of language teacher education. As discussed earlier in Chapter 2, we dissuade our own TCs from creating the portfolio in a linear matter, warning that progressing from Task 1 to Task 2 to Task 3 may not be the most effective way to approach edTPA and teaching in general. Therefore, we also begin with Task 3, Assessing Student Learning, which *backwards design* (Wiggins & McTighe, 2005) tells us is connected intimately with planning. In the following chapters, we address the other two tasks in their turn, Planning for Instruction in Chapter 5 and Instructing and Engaging Students in Learning in Chapter 6, offering background information along with research-based and practical suggestions to help TCs encounter the tasks and accompanying rubrics.

Throughout this chapter and the next two chapters, we will address various components of effective language teaching, as relevant to the task of each chapter. Afterwards, we explore the chapter's focus task through a case study, highlighting critical vocabulary and questions for each of the 13 world language edTPA rubrics, followed by possible resources to help TCs develop additional background on the topic of those rubrics. We

Understanding the World Language edTPA: Research-Based Policy and Practice
pp. 49–78

close each chapter with our own TCs' edTPA performance and concluding thoughts.

Thus far, we have offered general suggestions to help world language TCs be successful on the edTPA portfolio. We have examined the programmatic and course-level steps that can be taken to develop systems aiding TCs before and during their portfolio preparation. We have outlined the logistics of how we implemented edTPA into our existing language teacher education programs and steps that we take to aid TCs as they create their portfolios. Now, we increase the level of specificity by examining key concepts in language education and assessment with models, activities, examples, and results from our own teaching and research. We also explore rubric by rubric the September 2015 *edTPA World Language Assessment Handbook* (Stanford Center for Assessment, Learning, and Equity, SCALE, 2015a) to help stock directors' and teacher educators' instructional toolkits and to develop TCs' habits of mind necessary to show their best work on edTPA.

Notice that the title of the third edTPA task is *Assessing Student Learning* rather than *Testing Student Learning*. The difference between testing and assessing may seem subtle, but it is anything but subtle. Testing is a subcomponent of assessment, which has a much larger place in the classroom. Brown and Abeywickrama (2010) illustrated this interrelationship by showing a small *tests* circle within a larger *measurement* circle, within a larger *assessment* circle, within a still larger *teaching* circle (p. 6). That is, all that is taught is not assessed; in the same way, all that is assessed is not tested. Testing suggests summative evaluation, which places a score on student work at the end of instruction, while assessment suggests ongoing development and feedback with the purpose of improving later student learning. Clapham (2000) explores other differences between assessment and testing, including the heavier focus on validity and reliability for the latter.

In this chapter, we will first explore backwards design (Wiggins & McTighe, 2005) and writing effective and measurable instructional objectives to be used in all three edTPA tasks. We then outline how TCs might apply the *Proficiency Guidelines* to their work, along with how Integrated Performance Assessments could help develop their students' proficiency in the target language. We further situate effective assessment practices within a sociocultural approach to language teaching and assessment, while providing information about useful feedback practices to use while assessing student work.

BACKWARDS DESIGN AND OBJECTIVES

For a successful edTPA portfolio and a future teaching career, TCs must internalize how to backwards design their lessons, developing measureable learning objectives and assessments based on those objectives before engaging in instruction. Wiggins and McTighe (2005) advocate beginning with the end in mind, via backwards design, with teachers determining what learners should be able to do as a result of instruction, followed by determining the acceptable evidence to demonstrate that learning took place. Then, instruction can be designed to help students meet the indicated objectives, as readers will see in Chapter 5. The purposeful design of instruction will aid TCs on edTPA and in their future teaching sites where they may be evaluated by peers and administrators who embrace backwards design. For that reason, we adhere to backwards design by strongly suggesting that TCs formulate learning objectives first, then determine acceptable evidence through assessments, and finally determine instructional activities to carry out. We further encourage our TCs to scaffold (Vygotsky, 1978) instruction, leading up to standards-based performance assessments that are similar to formative tasks already encountered (Donato, 1994) in order to guide learners toward increasing independence. With effective feedback after performance assessment, learners can gain information to improve their performance on upcoming instructional activities and assessments. The design of instruction will be the focus of the next chapter.

Authentic, real world skills should be the center of attention for student instruction and assessment across the curriculum, not just for the purposes of edTPA. Beginning with the end in mind and determining authentic tasks and situations to help students develop their communicative proficiency is the first step. Performance assessments, in which students use language actively and mirror real situations with real people, offer TCs opportunities to gain information about what their students can do in a real world setting. Authenticity in instruction and assessment supports the ultimate purpose of language, to communicate with real people in culturally authentic situations. Establishing a real-world task, which students practice first, and then assessing student progress toward stated objectives can aid in developing students' proficiency (Bachman & Palmer, 2010). Also, such procedures can give purpose to the task for learners, whose motivation is central to their language learning success. When TCs determine the real life tasks for students to perform, their instruction more closely aligns with the expectations of the language teaching profession in general. Finally, designing multiple assessments for edTPA use may be advantageous to TCs, should they not pass the assessment task on the first submission. By having additional assessments administered, TCs can draw on those additional resources if they need to resubmit a task. That extra assessment could mean the difference between resubmitting one task at a cost of $100 and needing to resubmit the entire portfolio at a cost of $300. Further, those additional assessments may help

TCs avoid extending the student teaching placement or needing to find a different placement altogether.

An invaluable tool for writing measurable learning objectives, the first step of backwards design lesson planning, is Bloom's taxonomy. Originally developed in the 1950s (Bloom, Engelhart, Furst, Hill, & Krathwohl, 1956), Bloom's taxonomy contained six major categories in the cognitive domain: knowledge, comprehension, application, analysis, synthesis, and evaluation. Originally ordered from simple to complex and from concrete to abstract, the taxonomy was frequently used to classify curricular objectives and classify test items' psychometric breadth and depth (Krathwohl, 2002). The taxonomy was revised in the early 21st century to change the taxonomy level names from nouns to verbs, rename the final category *create* instead of *synthesis*, and reverse the order of *evaluate* and *create* (Anderson & Krathwohl, 2002).

Each level describes ways that learners encounter content and demonstrate what they know and understand about that content, in an increasingly complex and sophisticated manner. The six levels are described below:

- Remember: "retrieving relevant knowledge from long-term memory";
- Understand: "determining the meaning of instructional messages, including oral, written, and graphic communication";
- Apply: "carrying out or using a procedure in a given situation";
- Analyze: "breaking material into its constituent parts and detecting how the parts relate to one another and to an overall structure or purpose";
- Evaluate: "making judgments based on criteria and standards";
- Create: "putting elements together to form a novel, coherent whole or make an original product" (Krathwohl, 2002, p. 215).

A number of websites unpack each of the six levels, listing appropriate active verbs to use in formulating student learning objectives. Additionally, Shrum and Glisan (2015) have included a selection of those verbs in an appendix to their lesson planning chapter.

The types of knowledge addressed during instruction is at the heart of another substantial change to Bloom's taxonomy. Previously, three types of knowledge were addressed, but the revised taxonomy added *metacognitive knowledge*, which is "knowledge of cognition in general as well as awareness and knowledge of one's own cognition" (Krathwohl, 2002, p. 214), as the most sophisticated type of knowledge. *Factual knowledge* is the most rudimentary of the four and includes "the basic elements students must know to be acquainted with a discipline or solve problems in it" (p. 214), while *conceptual knowledge* includes "the interrelationships among the basic elements within a larger structure that enable them to function together" (p. 214). *Procedural knowledge* is defined as "how to do something; methods of inquiry, and criteria for using skills, algorithms, techniques, and methods" (p. 214).

The levels of the taxonomy and types of knowledge are powerful on their own, but even more illustrative when combined into a matrix, as seen in Krathwohl (2002, p. 216) (see Table 4.1). By forming a table with the six taxonomic levels across the horizontal axis and the four types of knowledge on the vertical, TCs create a visual of how their objectives and assessments align with Bloom's taxonomy and knowledge types. By using such a table, TCs can not only plot their objectives formulated with action verbs, they can also easily see at a glance the expectations they have for learners. Airasian and Miranda (2002) pointed out that the "power of assessments... resides in their close connection to objectives and instruction" (p. 249). The matrix, described above and seen in Table 4.1, can be used to help TCs align their objectives, instruction, and assessments in a visual way, drawing their attention to patterns in their own planning and their students' learning. First, TCs place the declared learning objectives in the appropriate cells of the matrix. Then, they list the assessments of student learning that they anticipate using in the proper cells, aligning with the stated objectives. Finally, TCs place the instructional activities they anticipate carrying out for each of the cells' objectives and assessments. In this way, TCs can literally see if their stated objectives align with their assessments and instructional activities. We will expand on this table in Chapter 7, showing how TCs can align their assessments and activities to the types and levels of knowledge to establish a well-reasoned progression in their assessment and instruction.

Constructing student learning objectives with active, measurable actions via verbs allows assessment to be more meaningfully and con-

Table 4.1.   Bloom's Revised Taxonomy Matrix

Knowledge Dimension	Remember	Understand	Apply	Analyze	Evaluate	Create
Factual						
Conceptual						
Procedural						
Metacognitive						

Source: Krathwohl (2002, p. 217).

cretely connected to instruction and planning (Airasian & Miranda, 2002; Swanson & Early, 2008). Learning objectives should be written in terms of observable second language performance. We urge TCs to write their objectives using the ABCD approach (i.e., audience, behavior, conditions, and degree). First, the audience must be clearly defined; that is, who is the recipient of the instruction? Next, what is the observable behavior or what task are the learners to accomplish? We recommend writing the objectives in terms of action verbs and objects as described earlier. Afterward, it is important to determine the conditions (e.g., independently, for 2 minutes, using note cards) under which the behavior is to occur. And finally, the criteria for acceptable performance or even mastery of the task must be determined and articulated to students (Swanson, Early, & Baumann, 2011). These steps can be taken with the *Proficiency Guidelines* in mind to determine level-appropriate tasks for language learners to carry out.

PROFICIENCY GUIDELINES

The ACTFL Proficiency Guidelines (American Council on the Teaching of Foreign Languages, 2012) describe what language learners are able to do while speaking, writing, listening, and reading in real-world situations, in spontaneous and unrehearsed contexts. For each of the four skills, the guidelines are broken into five primary levels of proficiency: distinguished, superior, advanced, intermediate, and novice. The advanced, intermediate, and novice levels are further divided into high, mid, and low sublevels. The proficiency guidelines serve as a framework to describe learners' abilities to use the target language, regardless of when, where, and/or how the language was acquired. Many programs and teachers use the guidelines as an instrument to measure learner ability in the target language, both formatively and summatively.

Language students should be able to increase their proficiency as they study the language, which makes the assessment of language proficiency a vital part of program effectiveness. By using the guidelines, teachers can provide learners with relevant feedback on their developing language abilities. Class grades are not a valuable tool to measure proficiency because of the various other influences on a student's final grade (e.g., extra credit, attendance). The measurement of target language proficiency places emphasis only on what students are actually able to do with the language. To that end, teacher-created assessments must be realistic for the level of proficiency that students are able to reach. Writing learning objectives as real world tasks with established proficiency levels can aid in both assessment and instruction. Students can use their developing *interlanguage* (Selinker, 1972) to perform those real world tasks in a formative way on a day-to-day basis, building up the skills necessary to succeed on the later more formal assessment of their skills, ideally a performance assessment such as the Integrated Performance Assessment.

The Communication goal of the *World-Readiness Standards* places emphasis on the use of the target language for communication in real life situations. Additionally, the goal focuses on *what students can do with language* instead of *what they know about language*. Therefore, TCs' lesson plans should be based on the standards and emphasize students' abilities to build communicative proficiency in the target language. To effectively develop student proficiency, most assessments should be performance based and not the traditional pencil and paper format (e.g., filling in the blank, multiple choice questions). Rubrics that specifically outline expectations for performance at the various levels of success should be carefully designed and used in order to measure and develop student proficiency. Subsequent feedback to students should emphasize how they can improve their communicative abilities, based on the targeted learning objectives.

INTEGRATED PERFORMANCE ASSESSMENTS

At its core, language instruction in the communicative classroom is dedicated to the ideals and the practices of developing proficiency (Swanson, Early, & Baumann, 2011). If students are to become proficient in a given target language, they must become literate in the three modes of communication: the interpretive, the interpersonal, and the presentational (National Standards Collaborative Board, 2015). Rather than focusing on the four skills (reading, writing, listening, and speaking) in isolation, language learners attend to three parts of a single goal, communication. Using the three modes as a framework, language learners develop and demonstrate proficiency through thematic integrated performance assessments or IPAs. A core aspect of the IPA is its emphasis on a cyclical approach to assessment. That is, it combines continuous modeling, practice, performance, and feedback, essentially a *feedback loop* throughout the assessment process (Glisan, Adair-Hauck, Koda, Sandrock, & Swender, 2003). The IPA can be used to evaluate student target language ability as a cluster assessment featuring three tasks, with each task focusing on one of the three modes (Adair-Hauck, Glisan, Koda, Swender, & Sandrock, 2006). It is a multitask assessment that is conceptualized within a single thematic context, regardless of proficiency level (i.e., novice, intermediate, or advanced).

As shown in Figure 4.1, students first listen to, read, and/or watch an authentic text in the target language (e.g., magazine article, news report,

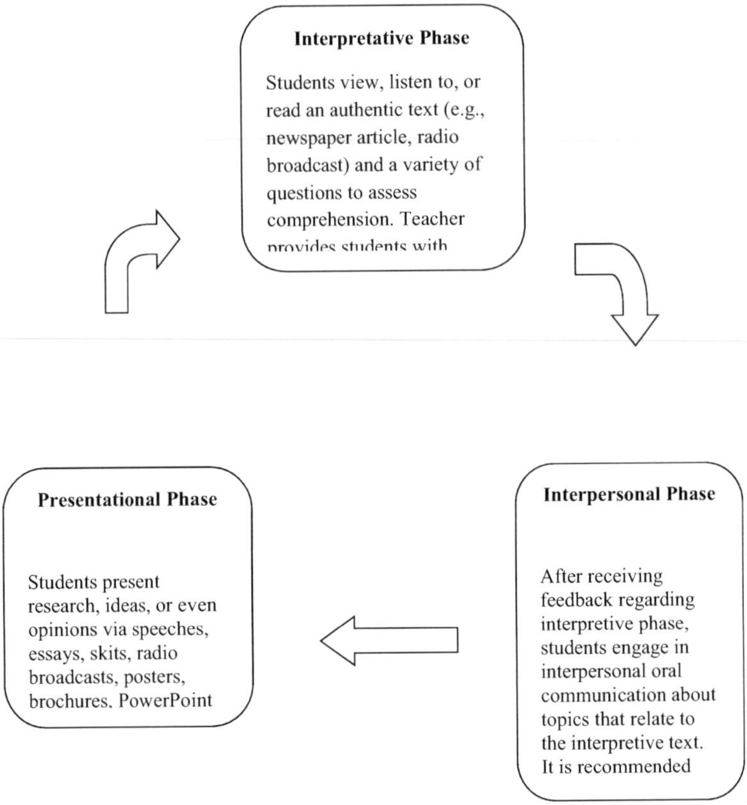

> **Interpretative Phase**
>
> Students view, listen to, or read an authentic text (e.g., newspaper article, radio broadcast) and a variety of questions to assess comprehension. Teacher provides students with

> **Presentational Phase**
>
> Students present research, ideas, or even opinions via speeches, essays, skits, radio broadcasts, posters, brochures. PowerPoint

> **Interpersonal Phase**
>
> After receiving feedback regarding interpretive phase, students engage in interpersonal oral communication about topics that relate to the interpretive text. It is recommended

Source: Adair-Hauck et al. (2006).

Figure 4.1. Integrated performance assessment.

commercial), which serves as a model. Then they answer informational and interpretive comprehension questions. Teachers guide learning by providing students initial feedback on their performance on this interpretive task.

Then, once the learners have received feedback from the interpretative phase, they engage in interpersonal oral communication about a specific topic related to the interpretive text. Afterwards, students perform in the target language by sharing their ideas, findings, research, and even opinions in the form of broadcasts, brochures, dramas, essays, skits, and even speeches, ideally using the input from the interpretive task as a model.

Faculty at one of the National Language Resource Centers, the Center for Advanced Research on Language Acquisition (CARLA, 2013a), advanced a seven-step process for creating IPAs and provided examples of assessment units for instructors of various education levels. First, the creators note that it is important to review the standards as planning takes place. Afterward, the teacher must choose a theme, typically a unit from a textbook. After a theme is identified, the teacher then articulates the goals and learning objectives. In our world language teacher education programs, TCs are taught to write goal statements in terms of observable student performance in the target language. For example, if the theme is clothing, students will describe their choices in clothing and fashion, compare going shopping in the United States to going shopping in a target-language speaking country, and perhaps list ways in which culture impacts one's choice of clothing.

In the fourth step, the instructor develops the three performance assessment tasks and the assessment for each. Beginning with the interpretive mode, learners are given opportunities to listen to, read, and/or watch authentic materials such as podcasts, news reports, speeches, or even video journals. Afterward, they demonstrate understanding on two levels: literal and interpretive. On the literal level, learners demonstrate understanding the surface meaning of the text. On the interpretive level, learners go further and demonstrate that they are capable of providing a more complete interpretation of the message. Ursula Lentz, a member of CARLA's assessment team, notes that it is wise "to give students the opportunity to share what else they notice in an authentic text: it encourages students to be explorers, to be curious, to ask questions" (CARLA, 2013b, para. 4). Students are then given an assessment, typically in the form of multiple choice and true/false questions, in order to give students feedback on their performance.

Following the interpretive portion of the assessment, CARLA (2013a) recommends that instructors move to the presentational task. Here, learners develop an oral or written presentation. Preparation is paramount. Students are encouraged to prepare drafts of any written text and carry out multiple rehearsals of an oral presentation. Instructor feedback is necessary in order for students to have a well-developed final product. In this task, students could research a celebrity's fashion choices and then create a video presentation that contains both photos and short video clips of that person.

Next, instructors and students move to the final phase of the assessment, the Interpersonal task. According to CARLA (2013c), it is helpful for students to complete the presentational task before the interpersonal task because they will gain multiple opportunities to practice new vocabulary and grammatical structures so that the new material becomes part of their permanent memory. This task has two characteristics that influence the way the performance task is set up. First, it is unrehearsed and negotiated. It is unrehearsed because the learners have to engage in a conversation or discussion without any previous plan or script. They cannot read or memorize their conversation or discussion. Second, the interaction is negotiated because the students listen and respond to each other.

Once the assessments are developed, rubrics and objective test items are created. As mentioned earlier, objective measures such as multiple choice and true/false questions are typically used to assess student learning in the interpretative part of the IPA. Unlike the interpretive assessment, assessment measures in the presentational and interpersonal domains take place in the form of rubrics. Care must be taken to identify the criteria and develop quality rubrics that have well-defined performance level descriptions.

The fifth step according to CARLA is to consider what tools (i.e., functions, grammatical structures) the students will need in order to complete the IPA. Next, identifying and teaching the key vocabulary successfully take place, in order to support learners' acquisition. The final step in creating IPAs involves designing a standards-based assessment unit. Planning, as well as carrying out lessons, is critical as students build proficiency in the target language. CARLA (2013d) suggests that finding appropriate resources, especially in the interpretative mode, "is perhaps the greatest challenge in designing a standards-based performance assessment unit" (para. 1).

While CARLA advocates moving from the interpersonal task to the presentational and then to the interpersonal task, others advocate starting with the interpersonal task and then having the interpersonal task take place before the presentational task (Adair-Hauck, Glisan, & Troyan, 2013). Regardless of the approach, one must remember the characteristics of each mode of communication. That is, in the interpersonal mode, teachers should begin with the gist and then move to deeper levels of details. In the interpersonal mode, an unscripted, spontaneous message is key. In the presentational mode, delivery the message is paramount. The presentation is rehearsed and polished in order to maintain the audience's attention (Sandrock, 2008). We encourage TCs to give rubrics to the students in advance to alert them of the required interpersonal and presentational tasks, as well as the criteria for exemplary performances and products. IPAs can be created for learners at all levels of proficiency and a multitude of examples can be found online.

SOCIOCULTURAL APPROACH TO ASSESSMENT

After objectives are developed, determining the acceptable evidence for students to show that learning took place is the next step (Wiggins & McTighe, 2005). That evidence is manifested by both formative and summative assessments that take place in the language classroom. In our experience, performance assessments with opportunities to use instructor feedback for future improvement tend to be scored highly on officially scored edTPA portfolios. Feedback on an assessment offers a TC a meaningful opportunity to establish a zone of proximal development, which is "the distance between the actual developmental level as determined by independent problem solving and the level of potential development as determined through problem solving under adult guidance, or in collaboration with more capable peers" (Vygotsky, 1978, p. 86). While recognized as an integral lens for instruction (González, Moll, & Amanti, 2005), the learners' zone of proximal development can be taken advantage of as students complete an assessment and TCs offer feedback to better student language output. As the more knowledgeable person in the relationship, the TC can guide students' knowledge development. Such support and encouragement from a teacher can further fuel students' performance and develop their proficiency, while students negotiate meaning with the teacher and classmates during instruction (Donato, 1994).

When TCs understand students' *interlanguage* (Selinker, 1972) development, they can set learning objectives, design assessments based on those objectives, and build necessary supports for language learners to advance from one proficiency level to another. Establishing the criteria by which performance will be evaluated and communicating those criteria to students allows learners to anticipate the assessment and understand how the assessment aligns with established objectives and the previous practices leading up to assessment. Central to succeeding on edTPA is the need for TCs to understand student errors, anticipate their occurrence, and design assessments that allow learners to carry out purposeful language output.

When TCs create an edTPA portfolio, they evaluate student performance based on established objectives. Developing assessments that parallel previously encountered scaffolded activities leading up to the assessment gives the learner an opportunity to try out the skills informally before the assessment. In that way, they can develop increasingly independent communication, while developing linguistic functions and greater accuracy of linguistic form.

FEEDBACK

Grading and feedback serve two quite different purposes in the classroom. Grading serves to assign a value or score to student work, whereas feedback is intended to give students information about what a student did well and what that student can improve upon in the future. In this chapter, we focus on feedback on student work, while in Chapter 6 we shed light on the process of giving students feedback in the moment of instruction. Both assessment and instructional moments offer student chances to develop their communicative proficiency. Ultimately, the purpose of feedback is to aid in student uptake—the learners' observable immediate response to the corrective feedback in his/her language production (Lyster & Ranta, 1997)—and continued learning. While uptake cannot guarantee language acquisition, it is an indication that the learner has noticed the feedback (Lightbown & Spada, 2013), and that noticing may, in turn, facilitate the acquisition process (Ellis, Basturkmen, & Loewen, 2002; Loewen, 2005).

Second language acquisition researchers have identified various forms of corrective feedback. Debates about which feedback strategies are most effective may ignore the fact that individual students respond differently to the various feedback strategies. Ellis (2009) reminds teachers that they should not be afraid to correct students' errors because whether corrective feedback comes in the form of a clarification request, a repetition, a recast, an elicitation, a metalinguistic strategy, or even a direct correction strategy, research shows that a combination of various forms can be helpful as students acquire the target language (Mackey, 1999; Muranoi, 2000; Nassaji & Fotos, 2011).

A clarification takes place when the teacher indicates that he/she has not understood what the student said. A repetition is when an instructor repeats what the student said and highlights the error(s). Recasts, a popular form of feedback, take place when a teacher repeats what the student has said but corrects or changes the statement in some way. An elicitation takes place when the teacher repeats a portion of what the learner says but not the part that contains the error. Using intonation, the instructor signals the student to complete the thought. Metalinguistic feedback is a subtler form of feedback requesting the learner to think about what he or she said. The teacher poses questions or provides clues related to the student's formation of the utterance without providing the correct form. Finally, explicit feedback is when the teacher indicates to the student that an error has been made by identifying the error(s) and providing the correction(s).

In general, teachers are advised to focus attention on a few error types rather than try to address all the errors learners make (Harmer, 1983; Ur, 1996). Ellis (2009) recommends that language teachers adhere to several guidelines when using corrective feedback. First, focused corrective feedback appears more effective than unfocused feedback. Thus, teachers should identify specific linguistic targets for correction in different lessons. Second, teachers must be able to use a variety of both oral and written corrective feedback strategies and be able to adapt these strategies to the learners. Moreover, timing of the feedback is important to consider. While oral feedback can be both immediate and delayed, written feedback is typically delayed. Ellis suggests that teachers need to experiment with the timing of their feedback to see what is best for their learners. Next, teachers should create space following the feedback for learners to uptake the correction(s). Teachers do not need to follow a prescribed set of procedures for feedback. Instead, instructors must be aware of the learners' affective and cognitive needs and provide feedback that helps learners improve their second language abilities. Finally, teachers must monitor the extent to which corrective feedback fosters learner anxiety and then modify feedback strategies so that anxiety facilitates learning, rather than debilitating it.

Feedback can help bring students to higher levels of learning, when accompanied by backwards design, well-written learning objectives, quality assessments, and *The Proficiency Guidelines*. edTPA focuses on assessing the practices of novice educators and has become a high-stakes assessment for many preservice educators throughout the United States. In the following section, we begin our discussion of Task 3.

TASK 3: ASSESSING STUDENT LEARNING

When it comes to preparing the edTPA dossier, feedback to learners is critical. A quick perusal of the rubrics shows that edTPA reviewers are looking for language teachers to develop students' communicative proficiency in the target language within meaningful cultural contexts (SCALE, 2015a). The development of proficiency includes the 5 Cs (communication, cultures, connections, comparisons, and communities) and three modes of communication (interpretive, interpersonal, and presentational). TCs are required to assess student progress informally and formally. Specifically, TCs must select one assessment from the learning segment in order to evaluate students' developing knowledge and skills in the target language. The chosen assessment provide opportunities for students to demonstrate communicative proficiency through both interpersonal and presentational modes of communication. In order to do so, TCs must collect samples of student work and analyze them in order to "identify quantitative and qualitative patterns of learning within and across learners in the class" (SCALE, 2015a, p. 27).

Additionally, TCs must select three student work samples that are representative of the identified patterns of learning. That is, "the TC makes make clear what individuals or groups generally understood and what students were still struggling to understand" (p. 27). TCs should include at least one focus student who is classified as having a specific learning need (e.g., IEP, 504 plan, English language learner) for feedback. TC feedback must be documented for each of the three focus students in at least one of three accepted ways: (1) written directly on the student work submitted, (2) as an audio clip, or (3) as a video clip. If via video or audio, care must be taken to ensure that evaluators can hear/see the feedback as it is given. Otherwise, a transcript of the inaudible comments must accompany the submission. Finally, TCs must respond to the commentary prompts listed in the handbook and submit the selected assessment to the Assessment Commentary (SCALE, 2015a).

As a central part of edTPA, TCs must compose an assessment commentary. While the handbook notes that the commentary should not exceed 10 single-spaced pages including the prompts (at the time of this writing), we urge TCs not to focus on the page limit, but rather to focus on the content. First, TCs must include the assessment used to evaluate students' performance (maximum 5 additional pages), which does not count in the 10-page limit. Per the guidelines, TCs must analyze student communicative proficiency in the target language by discussing the specific learning objectives. They must provide a graphic or narrative that summarizes student learning for the entire class, and we suggest that they provide both. Finally, TCs must use the evidence found in the three work samples and the whole class summary to analyze the patterns of learning, which focuses on students' communicative proficiency through the interpersonal and presentational modes of communication (SCALE, 2015a).

Next, TCs refer to specific evidence of submitted feedback to support their explanations in the assessment commentary. The evidence can be presented by showing written feedback on work samples, audio files, or video clips from Task 2 (discussed in detail in Chapter 5). TCs explain how the feedback they provided to the three focus students addresses their individual needs, as well as how the TC will support each focus student "to understand and use this feedback to guide improvement of communicative proficiency" (SCALE, 2015a, p. 29), either within the learning segment or during later instruction. Finally, TCs describe how the data from assessments inform their next instructional steps for the three focus students and the whole class. They must explain how these next steps are aligned with the analysis of student learning, using ideas based on second language acquisition research and/or theory.

CASE STUDY

Anna's focus assessment was a group presentation in which three to four students presented a poster created about a specific Spanish city. Students were required to show a map and pictures of the city on the poster and then present it to the class together. Each member of the group needed to give an individual presentation about one site in the city for 2 minutes. Each student also submitted a written script as part of the assignment. Instructions for the assignment were provided, along with the rubric, on a handout with four questions to address in the individual presentations. (Unless otherwise indicated, all materials used in class were written in Spanish. In our descriptions, we will do so in English to aid readers.) The instruction sheet included three additional questions about their thoughts on their peers' presentations to answer in writing afterwards.

Anna's feedback to her students was handwritten directly on the rubric shared with them via the assignment instructions. A 4 × 5 table provided a description for each of the criteria (*description*, *time*, *poster creativity*, *ability to comprehend*, and *discussion*) at three levels (*so-so*, *good*, and *fabulous*), along with quantitative feedback in the form of numerical scores for each criteria. Placed underneath the rubric was a space for written teacher comments outlining areas on which the student performed well, entitled *How great!*, and that the student needed to improve on, entitled *How can I improve?*

As required by edTPA, Anna submitted the feedback provided to three focus students. On each student's work sample, Anna made grammar corrections (e.g., adding accent marks, changing verb conjugations, crossing out unnecessary words). On each rubric, she circled the description in the column that indicated the level of quality achieved (e.g., so-so, good). To the left of the description column with the number of possible points, Anna wrote the number of points earned by the student for the given criteria. At the left bottom corner, she noted the total number of points earned over the number of points possible. She also tabulated the number of words and the number of grammatical errors. Under the rubric, she wrote several sentences in Spanish about things that each student did well on in the column titled *How great!* and another several suggestions for improvement in the column titled *How can I improve?*

Learning Segment Objectives

As we noted earlier in this chapter, in order for TCs to build successful edTPA portfolios and careers as language teachers, they are wise to integrate backwards design into their lessons, instruction, and assessments. They must develop measureable learning objectives and assessments based on those objectives before engaging in instruction. Our profession advocates using the target language for purposes that are as authentic to the learner as possible, and having students actively use the target language to engage in communicative situations with real people is paramount. By beginning with the end in mind (Wiggins & McTighe, 2005), TCs can determine authentic tasks and situations to help their students develop communicative proficiency across the modes. The use of performance assessments underlies effective language teaching and can help a TC meet the requirements of an edTPA portfolio.

While Anna did not use an IPA structured assessment, her assessment and feedback were well-aligned with the lesson's objectives and edTPA expectations in general. Her assessments were performance-based and her feedback contained both positive and constructive feedback to learners, in both quantitative and qualitative terms. In her commentary, Anna demonstrated proficient writing skills and drew from second lanuage acquisition research and theory.

As shown below, Anna wrote active and measureable objectives for each of the 3 days' objectives were active and measureable, while asking learners to demonstrate various types of knowledge (Airasian & Miranda, 2002) during the lesson at varying levels of Bloom's revised taxonomy (Krathwohl, 2002) across the learning segment. As matter of discussion, we view her objectives using the framework of the three modes of communication. Her first two objectives on the first day can be categorized into the interpretive mode. Objective 3 is an interpersonal activity while the final two objectives for the day are presentational and interpretive activities, respectively.

Day 1 Lesson Plan Objectives

1. Identify the practices, products and perspectives of Spanish city life by listening to a cultural PowerPoint presentation (Objective 1).
2. Identify distinct cultural practices and products of Granada, Barcelona, Madrid, and Málaga by listening to a cultural PowerPoint presentation (Objective 2).
3. Compare and contrast the differences and similarities between American and Spanish city culture by engaging in class discussion (Objective 3).
4. Apply their knowledge of Spanish city culture into a group presentation project that examines several places within a specific Spanish city (Objective 4).
5. Demonstrate their vocabulary knowledge of cities by rewriting a dictated paragraph (Objective 5).

During her second day of instruction, Anna's learning objectives (below) moved from Day 1's more simplistic tasks of identifying practices, products and perspectives to more complex tasks in the higher levels of Bloom's taxonomy. By analyzing Anna's second day's objectives and activity descriptions from her lesson plans, her first three objectives focus on the presentational mode as students are preparing for the group presentation. Objective 4 is an interpretive task (i.e., listening) while the final objective again applies to the presentational mode.

Day 2 Lesson Plan Objectives

1. Describe famous places within a Spanish city in a group presentation using their research notes (Objective 1).
2. Explain the cultural significance of famous places within the Spanish cities of Madrid, Málaga, and Barcelona (Objective 2).
3. Describe the geographic location of Madrid, Málaga, and Barcelona and the relative location of famous places within those three cities using an authentic street map (Objective 3).
4. Identify distinct cultural practices and products of Barcelona, Madrid and Málaga by listening to the cultural presentations of their peers (Objective 4).
5. Apply their knowledge of Spanish city culture by writing a postcard that summarizes places they would like to visit from Madrid, Málaga, or Barcelona (Objective 5).

The third day's four learning objectives continued to push students to higher levels of learning. With respect to her third and final day of planning for instruction, her objectives focused on the interpersonal (Objective 2, Objective 3) and presentational modes (Objective 1, Objective 4).

Day 3 Lesson Plan Objectives

1. Describe cultural practices and products of Madrid, Málaga, and Barcelona in an informal group presentation (Objective 1).
2. Ask for directions to various places within Madrid, Málaga, and Barcelona (Objective 2).
3. Give directions to various places within Madrid, Málaga, and Barcelona using the informal command verb forms (Objective 3).
4. Reflect on their learning by writing a postcard that highlights what they learned about their favorite Spanish city (Objective 4).

Learning Segment Assessments

Not all of Anna's summative assessments require students to analyze, evaluate, and create language. Again, student learning starts by giving new information at lower levels of Bloom's taxonomy and once students master the tools of language (e.g., vocabulary, grammar), they can then begin to build and articulate more personalized discourse.

Anna used three different types of assessments, as shown below.

1.   Assessment A: Group presentations to describe places in Spain
2.   Assessment B: Individual explanations using maps to locate points of interest geographically
3.   Assessment C: A discussion following group presentations

Anna chose to assess four of the stated objectives through students' group presentations and a follow-up conversation that took place after the presentations. As is seen, she was careful to specify how the objectives matched the assessments. By using such a diverse set of assessments, it is clear that Anna demonstrated that her goal was to show that Anna's instruction focused on communication and cultural understanding.

The Assessment Commentary

In this section, we describe Anna's assessment commentary. In the first part of her commentary, Analyzing Student Communicative Proficiency in the Target Language, Anna, a young woman and traditional student in her early 20s, identified the specific learning objectives and standards measured by her assessments (as shown in Table 4.2) for her Spanish 2 Honors class.

After describing each of her objectives and the assessments, Anna provided the mandatory graphic to summarize the whole class performance. The table included the objectives and the percentage of students who either received complete or partial credit for each of the objectives. With regard to the objectives, up to half of her class only received partial credit for an objective.

Next, Anna wrote about using evidence found in the three student work samples and the whole class summary in order to analyze the patterns of learning for the entire class, as well as the groups or individual learners. She keenly focused her analysis on her students' communicative proficiency in Spanish through both the interpersonal and presentational modes of communication. She discussed the criteria she used to evaluate student proficiency development, using the presentational mode in a

**Table 4.2. Learning Objectives
and Assessments for Learning Segment**

Objectives	Assessments	Mode of Communication
Students will be able to describe famous places within a Spanish city in a group presentation using their research notes (Objective 1)	The quality of performance shown via students' group presentations	Presentational
Students will be able to explain the cultural significance of famous places within the Spanish cities of Madrid, Malaga, and Barcelona (Objective 2)	The quality of students' description of their selected place within a Spanish city during their group presentations	Presentational
Students will be able to describe the geographic location of Madrid, Malaga, and Barcelona and the relative location of famous places within those three cities using an authentic street map (Objective 3)	Students' ability to use the Spanish city map to explain the geographic location of each member's place of research	Presentational
Students will be able to identify distinct cultural practices and products of Barcelona, Madrid, and Malaga by listening to the cultural presentations by their peers (Objective 4)	Students' ability to discuss what they learned from their peer's presentations in a follow-up discussion	Interpersonal

meaningful cultural context (i.e., her students had to take on the role of a travel guide, giving advice to their peers on famous places to visit in Spain). She explained clearly that her students were expected to give a brief explanation of what the place was and what purpose it served in the Spanish city. Then, she wrote about how their performance was assessed. Afterward, she discussed how the evidence of their comprehensibility was gathered via a written submission of their presentation.

Next, she presented her data regarding the entire class's performance. She referred to a table created to show how some of the students received complete credit while others did not. She did the same when discussing the three students from the work sample. She continued her commentary discussing the rest of the objectives and how the students performed. Near the end of her commentary, Anna discussed what she felt was one of the greatest learning challenges that her class faced while having their language proficiency assessed. She wrote about her greatest areas of concern as related to errors the students were making (grammatical, lexical and syntactical). She wrote about how the assessment was scored and what determined if the students had passed the objective or not. She explained the grading criteria for each objective and helped the reviewers understand how she assessed the students. Each time she discussed the results from the entire class, she also wrote about the performance of the three focus students. As she continued with her commentary, she keenly wove in the phrase "evidence of the development of students' language proficiency." Finally, she discussed how she conducted a follow-up class discussion that accompanied the students' presentations. She wrote about how the students performed in developing their abilities in the interpersonal mode. From a quantitative aspect, she composed 1164 words in the first section, Analyzing Student Communicative Proficiency in the Target Language.

In the second part of her commentary, Feedback to Guide Further Learning, Anna explained that she gave written feedback on a form that included the original rubric. She specifically noted that she had given the rubric to the students when the project was assigned. She also noted that the rubric included an area where the grade was shown along with a qualitative explanation of each grade. She explained to the reviewers that she felt it was important that her class better understand why they received a given grade for the assignment. Additionally, she mentioned that she gives feedback on the rubric, telling students what they did well and the area(s) in which they can improve their proficiency. Then, she went on to talk about the students' presentations. She noted that evidence of her feedback was present on all three of the student work samples on which she noted grammatical and syntactical errors.

In order to explain how her feedback impacted the three focus students, she discussed each student in a separate paragraph. She wrote to the students about how to improve their language functions, while only briefly touching on the language form errors. For example, she mentioned how well one student had done in giving an interesting and engaging introduction and how well she could understand the student's description of the cultural details with regard to Barcelona. She also noted a few areas of improvement, asking the student to more fully explain the cultural practices of Spaniards living in Barcelona. She also mentioned that she compared the results from the three students' work samples to those of the entire class. She gave a few examples and noted that one of the focus students had achieved the highest score on the assessment. She specifically noted that one of the focus students caused the greatest concern as one of the lowest achieving students in the class.

The next edTPA prompt for this task asks TCs to indicate how they will support students to apply the feedback and improve communicative proficiency in the target language, either within the learning segment or at a later time. Anna wrote that before she returned her written feedback to the class, she would ask her students to share with their partners what they thought their strengths and weaknesses were with regard to the project. She noted the importance of learner self-reflection as a learning tool so that students could discuss how they could improve their proficiency. Following the self-reflective conversations between students, Anna returned her written feedback to the class so the students could read her comments about their interpretive and presentational communication skills development. She stated that she asked students to correct and resubmit their work, using her comments as a guide for revision. She noted that the revision would be included in her students' portfolio assessment developed over the course of the academic year. Finally, she noted that she would require her students to determine five linguistic goals and incorporate a plan for achieving those goals in future presentational assignments; specifically, she asked them to set a goal related to the next unit on employment. She mentioned that she would meet individually with her three focus students to discuss their plans for increasing their linguistic accuracy. In her commentary, she discussed each student's areas for improvement and how she would approach working with each student. Her write-up for this section totaled 1,317 words.

In the third section, Using Assessment to Inform Instruction Section A, Anna noted that although her students performed "fairly well" using language functions to describe, explain, and define the cultural practices of famous places within Spanish cities, they still required continued support as they learn to describe, explain, and define new contexts. She explained in detail that her next unit focused on employment and what her plans were to develop further students' use of linguistic functions. She discussed how her students struggled with the language functions of describing and explaining, so she planned to continue helping students improve those skills, along with their understanding of cultural practices. She mentioned that her students struggled with the cultural misconception that tourists visiting Madrid, Malaga, and Barcelona accurately portray the cultural practices of the Spaniards living in these cities. She discussed briefly a plan to help correct such misconceptions in her next unit of study on employment. She also explored her students' difficulties using language forms and mentioned a rather detailed plan to help students become more aware of their language form errors.

Over the course of the next three paragraphs, Anna discussed each of the three focus students and her plans to help them individually. She wrote about how she planned to use the feedback she had provided each student and to help those students overcome their specific areas for improvement and build their proficiency in the target language. She explained how she took a personalized approach with her individual student conferences. With each student, she discussed what the student did well and in what areas the student needs assistance. In the final paragraph she explained how she would revise the unit if she were to teach it to a different class of students. In her Context for Learning statement, she selected a Spanish 2 Honors class, and in her commentary she explained to reviewers how she would modify the assignment for a different group of students and what she would do if there were ELLs and heritage language learners in the class. The word count for this section was 1,310 words.

In Section B, Anna explained her next steps and how they are supported by second language acquisition/teaching research and/or theory. In her next 660 words, Anna wrote about providing even more comprehensible input as theorized by Krashen (1981) in his Monitor Hypothesis. While she did not explain to the reviewers the tenets of Krashen's ideas, she wrote about how she would provide students with more comprehensible input before expecting output from the students. She speculated that if she were to model a presentation about Spanish cities in Spanish, before assigning the task to her students, they would better understand the assignment. She described how the presentation would look (i.e., using pictures and vocabulary) and that she would add a few linguistic elements that are just beyond the students' linguistic abilities, a clear reference to Vygotsky's zone of proximal development. She also mentioned that her students would be better equipped to "develop their language proficiency in presentational and interpersonal communication using the meaningful cultural context" if she were to model the assignment first.

Next, she discussed how a proposed language form workshop would work based on Long's (1996) Interaction Hypothesis. She wrote that the workshop would help students focus on their linguistic errors (e.g., lexical, grammatical) by having them peer-edit each other's presentations before presenting them. Students would be able to converse about each other's work and continue to build proficiency as they work with each other. Finally, she stated that, because all of her students were continuing to improve their language proficiency at various rates and stages of development, she planned to continue to use group and partner work in her future instruction. Specifically, she is planning to pair her more advanced students with more novice learners on future assignments. She referenced Vygotsky's sociocultural theory of human mental processing that claims that learners gain proficiency when they socially interact with more advanced speakers in the target language. She concluded how these changes in practice would impact her next unit on the topic of employment.

UNPACKING RUBRICS 10–13

By now readers will know that we recommend that world language methods instructors and program directors familiarize TCs with edTPA portfolio requirements and accompanying rubrics early and frequently throughout their teacher education program. As a component of that familiarization process, we suggest that TCs are guided by their more knowledgeable mentors, instructors, and supervisors through the rubrics explicitly, working with them well before their student teaching semester begins. As described earlier, TCs at Illinois State University encounter the rubrics during their world language methods class as they complete a mini-edTPA while working with real students at a local community center.

We realize that not all teacher education programs are able to provide such an experience, so we offer the following activities for teacher educators and their TCs to be used as part of a methods class, student teaching orientation, or other group exercise to address the rubrics' criteria, each in their turn. Having TCs read the various parts of the edTPA handbook as explicit assignments, task by task, and as a group carrying out the activities described below, we hope, will assist teacher educators and TCs in internalizing edTPA constructs.

Deconstructing each rubric and analyzing the various concepts contained within can form a foundation on which to build an effective edTPA portfolio. Carrying out the three steps described below for each of the 13 rubrics, with the guidance of a more knowing mentor, can prepare TCs to explain their planning, instructional, and assessment decisions in a more robust way.

1. *Vocabulary:* Analyze the rubric and pick out the important vocabulary. Define each of the words or phrases. List additional vocabulary that may be useful while writing the commentary for the assessment, planning, or instructional edTPA task.

2. *Guiding questions:* Examine the guiding questions at the top of the rubric. Those questions give clues as to what to address in the commentary. What are those clues? List them and discuss what evidence should be presented to address that question in the commentary.

3. *Characteristics of a score of 3 on the rubric:* What needs to be shown in the commentary and accompanying artifacts to earn at least a score of 3?

As a further means to address each rubric, we encourage teacher educators to examine carefully each rubric and ascertain what challenges can be seen foreseen for TCs as they address these key concepts. That reflection can aid in better constructing opportunities for TCs to engage actively with critical content before they complete the high stakes portfolio.

Below, we have unpacked the rubrics and identified key vocabulary that we thought pertinent for TCs to know and be able to explain. These lists may complement lists assembled by TCs and their instructors or serve as prompts for in-class discussions, activities, or assessments. They may also be part of a homework assignment or included as part of a portfolio self-assessment. Also included for each rubric is a checklist of questions for TCs to pose to themselves while self-evaluating their portfolio.

Also in this portion of this and the following two chapters, we will unpack each of the rubrics and provide evidence of Anna's performance that we, as trained scorers, believe supported the score that she earned. While we are not comfortable disclosing the details of Anna's scores on the 13 edTPA rubrics, we describe aspects of her performance, commentary, and artifacts that make her portfolio exemplary. We discuss Anna's performance in terms of the performance level descriptor at the middle score of 3 on each of the 13 edTPA rubrics. As program directors, we set the goal for our own TCs to earn a score of at least a 3 on each rubric, which results in a total score of at least 39, which, in turn, is well above states' cut scores for a passing performance on edTPA at this time.

Finally, we list existing resources that may be helpful for teacher educators and their TCs to dig deeper into the constructs being measured by the rubrics. Those resources are not necessarily intended to be cited within portfolios; rather, they are resources that readers can consult to gain more background on the concepts being measured in the rubrics. The authors listed have summarized the existing research well and we, in no way, wish to duplicate already existing resources or disclose too specific of information that could be directly applied to a TC's portfolio.

We caution readers to keep in mind that the activities below are based on the 2015 September edition of the *edTPA World Language Assessment Handbook* (SCALE, 2015a) and changes may occur to instructions, rubrics, and commentaries in subsequent editions. SCALE makes available a list of changes to the handbooks with each new edition. In the 2015 list, "Minor subject-specific changes for clarity" (2015d, p. 16) were made to Task 1 instructions; while those changes were minor, future changes may be more substantial.

With respect to Rubric 10, Analysis of Student Communicative Proficiency in the Target Language, central vocabulary includes: performance assessment, quantitative and qualitative data, discrete point, evaluation criteria, student learning, patterns of learning, data analysis, data, results and findings, graphics, formative and summative, informal and formal.

We have developed the following checklist to help TCs and faculty as edTPA portfolios are created.

- Does at least one of the focus students have a specific learning need?
- Does the TC include what students did right in the analysis?
- Does the analysis of student performance go further than what's right and what's wrong?
- Are differences in whole-class learning included?
- Are differences in focus students' learning included?
- Is the assessment used for analysis a performance assessment?

The checklist can be used as a guide when conceptualizing and writing the commentary. Also, it can be used as a review tool before the portfolio is uploaded for review. Anna's analysis contained in the assessment commentary is not superficial. She consistently focused on what students did correctly and incorrectly, as well the differences in the learning of the whole class. She discussed the whole class and then turned to a discussion about her three focal students. Furthermore, her criteria, learning objectives, and analysis are well-aligned with each other. Her analysis is supported by citing specific examples in the student work samples to bring patterns of learning to the evaluators' attention. The write-up was clear and straightforward for the reviewers to understand her analysis.

Turning to Rubric 11, Providing Feedback to Guide Student Development of Communicative Proficiency in the Target Language, we focus our TCs' attention on the following vocabulary found in the edTPA handbook: feedback, student needs, student strengths, language function, language form, feedback type, feedback strategies, positive feedback, meaningful feedback, quantitative feedback, qualitative feedback, and student errors that merit feedback. In parallel fashion, the following checklist helps our TCs as they develop their portfolios to provide evidence of quality feedback to students:

- Is feedback related to learning objectives?
- Are students' strengths included in the analysis?
- Is feedback focused on language form only?
- Is feedback focused on meaning?
- Is feedback specific to one learner and his or her performance?

With respect to Anna's commentary, her feedback to students is directly related to the developmentally appropriate learning objectives she set forth. Her feedback is straightforward, specific, and accurate. Additionally, her feedback addressed not only her students' needs but also their strengths. Her feedback to the three focus students was similar to her feedback to the whole class. All of her feedback was related to communicative proficiency in the target language.

Next, regarding Student Use of Feedback, Rubric 12, we suggest that our TCs focus their attention on the following ideas: summative vs formative assessment, feedback, language form, language function, student application of feedback, sandwich feedback technique, constructive criticism. As TCs work on their portfolios, we also remind them to keep the following questions in mind:

- Is the assessment formative in nature?
- Can the feedback supplied be used by students to improve future performance?
- Does feedback mention what the student did right?
- Does feedback include only what the student did wrong?
- Is feedback focused on student growth?
- Is feedback useful to students?
- Is feedback focused on language form exclusively?
- Is feedback only negative?

In her commentary, Anna's description was specific instead of vague. She clearly described how her students understood and used the feedback in order to improve their proficiency. To that end, she carefully discussed each student's work in a positive manner. She provided plans to help the three focus students overcome their specific areas for improvement and build their proficiency in the target language—essentially demonstrating how she was going about building student language proficiency.

For the final rubric, Using Assessment to Inform Instruction, we ask our TCs to focus on the following vocabulary found in the edTPA handbook: student learning needs, outcomes, learning objectives, three modes of communication, second language acquisition research, pacing, supports, accommodations, standards, and effective and ineffective assessments and feedback. Much like the other rubrics discussed thus far, we have developed a checklist for Rubric 13. We ask:

- Do next steps focus on reteaching?
- Do next steps focus on pacing?
- Do next steps focus on classroom management?

- Are next steps connected theoretically to second lanuage acquisition research?
- Are next steps related to the stated learning objectives?
- Are next steps related to stated standards?
- Are next steps focused on improving student proficiency development?
- Are next steps grounded in the assessed student work?
- Are next steps grounded in what was taught during the learning segment?

As methods instructors and program directors, we feel it is important for our TCs to think and plan beyond the current unit of instruction. Keeping the goal of earning at least a score of 3 on each rubric, Anna's next steps detailed in the commentary were relevant to the learning objectives, rather detailed, and clearly discussed how to improve students' interpretive and presentational communication. She discussed how theory guided her ideas, citing Krashen's (1981) Monitor Hypothesis, Long's (1996) Interaction Hypothesis, and she even hinted at Vygotsky's (1978) zone of proximal development. She noted the need to use more modeling in the next unit.

RESOURCES

A variety of resources are already available for faculty and TCs to gain more information about the four rubrics concerning assessing student learning. In Table 4.3, we list a number of texts that summarize previous research on the constructs being assessed in each of the rubrics. To learn more, readers are advised to consult those texts listed and others. TCs may choose to include these or other resources in their commentaries to support their assessment, planning or instructional decisions. Full citations can be found in the references list at the end of the book.

OUR RESEARCH

In our experience thus far, assessment has been the most challenging of the three edTPA tasks for world language TCs. In a previous study, our TCs ($N = 21$) had the lowest mean for assessing student learning ($M = 3.04$, $SD = 0.96$) across the three edTPA tasks (Hildebrandt & Swanson, 2014). As seen in Table 4, their mean scores were only slightly above 3 on a 5-point scale, with a 3 indicating "candidate who is ready to teach"

Table 4.3.   Resources for TCs to Learn More About Assessing Student Learning

Rubric	*Suggested Resources*
Rubric 10: Analysis of Student Communicative Proficiency in the Target Language	Brown & Abeywickrama (2010); Sandrock (2010); Chapter 11 of Shrum & Glisan (2015); Blaz (2000)
Rubric 11: Providing Feedback to Guide Student Development of Communicative Proficiency in the Target Language	Chapter 11 of Shrum & Glisan (2015); Sandrock (2010); Lee & VanPatten (2003)
Rubric 12: Student Use of Feedback	Lightbown & Spada (2013)
Rubric 13: Using Assessment to Inform Instruction	Lightbown & Spada (2013)

(SCALE, 2013a, p. 12). Many TCs design instruction as part of their education classes and their content-specific methods class(es). Some, then, have the opportunity to teach some lessons to peers or students at their practicum sites, gaining practical experiences in instruction. What TCs generally lack prior to their student teaching experience, however, is using student performance data to inform their own teaching. When teaching isolated, short-term lessons, TCs rarely have opportunities to give feedback on the work of students whom they will teach over a substantial period of time.

Thorough preparation in assessment and evaluation has been historically suggested as a necessity in teacher preparation (Schulz, 2000), but our TCs are not required to take a stand-alone language assessment class. While adding a course of that nature may offer TCs more opportunity to become familiar and practiced in assessing student learning, adding additional credits to existing programs can be very challenging as time to graduation and employment may be extended. Further, university curriculum committees and state accreditation boards may question the need to add credits to an already dense language teacher education program.

Most world language teacher education programs require at least one world language methods class that addresses assessment, although there are universities that do not offer those world language-specific pedagogy courses (Hildebrandt, Hlas, & Conroy, 2013). By their nature, methods classes generally focus on planning and instruction, but rare is a program that requires TCs to take a class with a strong emphasis on language assessment. Each of our programs has a strong assessment component within the methods classes, featuring recent publications (Sandrock, 2010; Shrum & Glisan, 2015) as assigned readings.

**Table 4.4.   Descriptive Statistics
of Each Performance Level of Assessment Rubrics**

	M	SD	1	2	3	4	5
Rubric 10: Analysis of Student Communicative Proficiency in the Target Language	3.38	0.80	0	4	5	12	0
Rubric 11: Providing Feedback to Guide Student Development of Communicative Proficiency in the Target Language	3.19	1.07	2	4	3	12	0
Rubric 12: Student Use of Feedback	2.71	1.05	2	8	6	4	1
Rubric 13: Using Assessment to Inform Instruction	2.90	0.62	1	2	16	2	0

On Rubric 10: Analysis of Student Communicative Proficiency, over half (57%) of the TCs scored 4 on the rubric, meaning that their performance indicated a "solid foundation of knowledge and skills for a beginning teacher" (SCALE, 2013a, p. 12) and that they could analyze student data and identify patterns in student learning. TCs in the study scored higher on Rubric 10 than on the other three assessment rubrics ($M = 3.38$, $SD = 0.80$). Rubric 11: Providing Feedback also had a mean of over 3 ($M = 3.19$, $SD = 1.07$), while Rubric 12: Student Use of Feedback most challenged participants' ($M = 2.71$, $SD = 1.05$), not only in the assessment task but across all three tasks. About a third of TCs scored 1 or 2 on Rubric 12, showing "the knowledge and skills of a struggling candidate who is not ready to teach" and one "who is possibly ready to teach" (SCALE, 2013a, p. 12) respectively. Rubric 13: Using Assessment to Inform Instruction had a mean score below the suggested 3 ($M = 2.90$, $SD = 0.62$), although over three quarters (76%) of the participants showed performance at a level 3 on rubric 13. Less than 10%, or two candidates, scored a 4 on Rubric 13 by providing targeted support to improve learners' communicative proficiency in the interpretive mode and at least one of the other communicative modes (SCALE, 2015a). A comparison with the national dataset from SCALE (2015e) showed that our TCs had higher means on three of the four assessment rubrics than the national average on the four assessment rubrics.

CONCLUDING THOUGHTS

This chapter has addressed second language acquisition theory, language assessment practices, and edTPA rubrics, providing a framework for future discussions on planning for student learning and carrying out instruction. We examined the third task artefacts and commentary created by our former TC Anna, who scored exceptionally well on her portfolio. We also highlighted the central vocabulary and offered a checklist for each of the rubrics, to be used for peer- or self-assessment prior to final submission. A list of additional resources will lead readers to other resources summarizing research on each rubric's topic. Finally, we shared our own early research about our own TCs' edTPA performance, disclosing that assessment is the most difficult of the three tasks. In the next chapter, we address planning instruction after a sound set of objectives and accompanying assessments have been created.

CHAPTER 5

PLANNING FOR TEACHING AND LEARNING

In this chapter, we will explore the first edTPA task, Planning for Instruction and Assessment by employing backwards design (Wiggins & McTighe, 2005). We approached this book in the same way, by addressing the assessment task in the previous chapter and only now are by turning to planning. As explained in Chapter 4, we recommend to our own programs' TCs that they first develop their edTPA learning segments' objectives and assessments. Designing lessons and activities to plan for students' communicative proficiency development is the next step in constructing effective edTPA portfolios.

We begin this chapter by revisiting the earlier discussion on writing performance objectives. Then, we discuss the planning process necessary for creating meaningful cultural contexts in which lessons can take place. Afterward, we briefly review the refreshed national standards, the *World-readiness Standards for Learning Languages* (National Standards Collaborative Board, 2015), and the three modes of communication. We also briefly discuss technology considerations as TCs begin developing their portfolios. Then, we present the core practices for teaching languages, also known as high-leverage teaching practices, and discuss how Anna approached this edTPA task by elaborating on what reviewers are trained to look for when examining and scoring a portfolio. Finally, we advance a few resources that may be helpful and offer findings from our own edTPA research. The chapter concludes with some final thoughts on preparing Task 1.

Understanding the World Language edTPA: Research-Based Policy and Practice
pp. 79–102
Copyright © 2016 by Information Age Publishing

REVISITING OBJECTIVES

The first step in planning is determining the objectives that the students should be able to meet as a result of instruction. As the reader will recall from the previous chapter, we supplied an ample discussion of how to write effective and measurable objectives using Bloom's taxonomy and the principles of backwards design to create effective assessments of students' developing communicative proficiency.

The objectives for learning, formulated prior to planning and instruction, are at the heart of teaching, particularly for edTPA expectations. The centrality of objectives cannot be overstated, and TCs are wise to tie all assessments and activities leading up to those assessments to performance objectives, which are observable second language behaviors. As described in the previous chapter, Bloom's taxonomy and the active verbs that accompany them provide TCs a useful framework to conceptualize outcomes-based learning. That is, objectives help TCs document expectations for learners and measure the quality of learner performances. These objectives and their accompanying assessments help teachers operationalize what it is that learners should know and be able to do, most often through performance assessments.

Planning scaffolded activities that parallel the intended assessments' format and content is this chapter's focus. We seek to describe the steps necessary to familiarize learners with the communicative events for which they will be responsible in later assessments. Developing activities that parallel assessments and scaffold up to them helps learners be able to prepare for performance-based assessments. For example, having students work in groups on an activity and later carry out the activity alone as the assessment is a sound means of gradually leading the learners to independence, while providing them with opportunities to build their communicative proficiency. The group activity and individual assessment may, for example, have the same objectives, but involve different pairings or a different scenario or communicative setting.

Having cultural objectives for students to work toward are a worthy addition to any language classroom. Stating those measurable and active cultural objectives can help students develop their own interculturality (Clementi & Terrill, 2013), as well as give context to their developing communicative proficiency. Providing a meaningful cultural context in which language learning takes place is critical for world language edTPA success.

PLANNING MEANINGFUL CULTURAL CONTEXTS

The centrality of *meaningful cultural context(s)* in the world language edTPA necessitates TC attention to cultures across all three tasks, with three of the four planning rubrics using the phrase in their guiding questions. Cultural contexts are central in language teaching and learning, but until recently the focus has been almost exclusively on the target language-speakers' cultures. Constructing an edTPA portfolio necessitates that TCs guide students in examining target language cultures, along with the cultures to which students belong. Knowledge of learners goes beyond merely knowing their academic achievements and challenges; knowing one's learners requires TCs to know students' personal, familial, and community backgrounds, along with the academic. Knowing what is of interest to students is one way to tailor instruction to the group of learners in front of the TC, not only for the planning task of edTPA but for general success in relating to students and advancing their learning.

A variety of lenses by which to view culture informs world language culture teaching and learning in the U.S. educational context. For example, culture can be broken into *big C Culture* and *little c culture* (Hu, 2002), which focus on the more well-known aspects of the culture, like works of art and theatre, and the more daily and widely ingrained aspects of daily life, like social hierarchies and dating practices, respectively. The world language teaching community has used the national standards as a framework for cultural teaching and learning for the last 2 decades, with the world-readiness standards as the most recent iteration of the professional consensus. With this attention being paid to cultural contexts in edTPA, the three Ps of the Cultures standard become even more critical. Perspectives, defined as "the traditional ideas, attitudes, and values … of a culture" (National Standards Collaborative Board, 2015, p. 80), hold a primary position in the Cultures standard, connecting the products and practices of the target language speaking cultures. That insight gained into the deep culture is the heart of cultural instruction and brings a more profound examination of people's ways of living, well beyond the more tangible surface culture of flags, fashion, and music.

It is not only the target language cultures that are of import for edTPA and for making learning relevant for the most students possible. *Culturally relevant pedagogy* (Ladson-Billings, 1995), along with the more recent *culturally sustaining pedagogy* (Paris, 2012), argue that students bring their own experiences and cultures to the learning experience and that teachers must respect and build on those experiences and cultures, fashioning lessons so students develop the critical thinking skills necessary to succeed in adulthood. Paris' (2012) culturally sustaining pedagogy "seeks to sustain—linguistic, literate, and cultural pluralism as part of the democratic project of schooling" (p. 93), moving away from the previously practiced *deficit approaches* (p. 93) to teaching, in which ways that learners "lack" are of central concern. For example, a child's family's low socioeconomic status may be used as an explanation for her lack of achievement, while her curiosity and tenacity may be overlooked in evaluations.

TCs must not only pay attention to the target language cultures and their various perspectives, products, and practices. Instead, TCs must help learners in their classes integrate the new cultural information into their already existing home, school, and community cultures. TCs must consider what each learner brings to the language and cultural learning experience. Clementi and Terrill (2013) explore *interculturality* at the intersection of "knowing myself," "exploring communities," and "engaging with the world" (p. 2), as they unpack the standards and situate the three modes of communication. Being familiar with the assets that students bring to the learning experience aids TCs in bringing their lessons to reality. Byram's (1997) model for intercultural communicative competence defines *critical cultural awareness* as "an ability to evaluate critically and on the basis of explicit criteria perspectives, practices and products in one's own and other cultures and countries" (p. 53). Joining the cultures being studied with students' home cultures becomes critical in edTPA success.

Heritage language learners bring their own unique experiences to the language classroom, and Valdés (1997) pointed to the respect necessary for language teachers to have toward their students' home language registers, vocabulary, and literacy development. While Valdés and others have explored this topic in the context of the Spanish-speaking community in the United States, less attention has been paid to the position of teaching more standard French to immigrants from French-speaking countries, such as the Democratic Republic of the Congo. Encouraging a respectful environment in which to explore varying cultural products, practices, and perspectives is paramount to any language teacher's success with heritage language learners, along with nonnative speakers of the language being studied.

Creating meaningful cultural contexts in which to situate the edTPA learning segment brings communicative proficiency development closer to the real world in which students and native speakers may interact. The most frequently used framework to view cultures in world language teaching is that of the *World-Readiness Standards for Learning Languages*.

WORLD-READINESS STANDARDS FOR LEARNING LANGUAGES

As we have discussed earlier, edTPA is a nationally available performance assessment that was designed to measure novice teachers' readiness to teach. The portfolio demonstrates TCs' ability to plan, instruct, and assess student learning from a standards-based approach. As part of the portfolio, TCs must plan a series of three to five consecutive world language lessons, known as the learning segment, based on the national standards.

As part of a collaborative effort of 11 different organizations (e.g., American Association of Teachers of French, American Classical League), the National Standards Collaborative Board recently completed its work by refreshing the national standards. Initially funded by grants from the U.S. Department of Education and the National Endowment for the Humanities, with support from D. C. Heath and Company and EMC Publishing, the national standards have become an integral part of language teachers' daily preparation. First published in 1996 as the *Standards for Foreign Language Learning*, the *World-Readiness Standards for Learning Languages* (National Standards Collaborative Board, 2015) demonstrate an unprecedented consensus among multiple educational stakeholders (e.g., teachers, business leaders, government) regarding the definition and role of world language instruction in American education (American Council on the Teaching of Foreign Languages, ACTFL, 2015). The national standards for language learning have been revised several times based on what language educators have learned from almost 20 years of implementing the Standards. The new *World-Readiness Standards for Learning Languages* create

a roadmap to guide learners to develop competence to communicate effectively and interact with cultural understanding. "World-readiness" signals that the standards have been revised with important changes to focus on the literacy developed and the real-world applications. Learners who add another language and culture to their preparation are not only college and career ready, but are also "world ready"—that is, prepared to add the necessary knowledge, skills, and dispositions to their résumés for entering postsecondary study or a career. (p. 11)

The *World-Readiness Standards for Learning Languages* are organized around the five goal areas or five Cs: communication, cultures, connections, comparisons, and communities. The standards are designed to work in conjunction with state and local frameworks and standards for all languages. These revised standards reflect the Common Core Standards, College and Career Readiness, and 21st century skills. The standards are applicable from pre-K to postsecondary levels. The *World-Readiness Standards for Learning Languages* "clarify and better illustrate each goal area and standard in order to guide implementation and influence assessment, curriculum, and instruction" (National Standards Collaborative Board, 2015, p. 80).

We recommend TCs and teacher educators become familiar with the refreshed standards. In addition to reading and understanding the *edTPA World Language Assessment Handbook*, we strongly recommend having TCs become knowledgeable about the refreshed standards too. The standards executive summary document can be accessed free of charge via ACTFL and the publication in its entirety is available from ACTFL.

MODES OF COMMUNICATION

The three modes of communication replaced the former paradigm of the four skills (i.e., reading, writing, listening, and speaking) as three parts of target language communication and proficiency. While each of the three modes (interpretive, interpersonal, and presentational) may be considered individually, their strength can be found in their interrelatedness (Center for Advanced Research on Language Acquisition, 2013a).

The Massachusetts Department of Elementary and Secondary Education (1999) states that the interpretive mode focuses on the appropriate cultural interpretation of meanings that occur in spoken and/or written form, in which the learner has no recourse to the active negotiation of meaning with the person conveying the message. The interpersonal mode involves the learner in actively negotiating meaning, whether it is participation in an oral conversation with another learner or writing and conveying messages to another person (e.g., e-mail, text). The presentational mode "refers to the creation of formal messages to be interpreted by listeners or readers without opportunities for the active negotiation of meaning" (p. 1).

When used collectively, the three modes can inform the creation of performance assessments, as discussed in the previous chapter. We recommend that as TCs plan for instruction and assessment, they review the rubrics for the tasks and the edTPA Understanding Rubric Level Progressions (Stanford Center for Assessment, Learning, and Equity, 2015b) publication in order to integrate the three modes of communication into edTPA's three tasks.

As learners are exposed to authentic materials via the interpretive mode, they can work towards the low-stakes exchange of ideas with partners through the interpersonal mode, and finally the higher stakes presentation of ideas. Integrating the three modes together, while scaffolding learners as they communicate more and more independently builds learner confidence while providing models on which to build independent communication. The interrelatedness of the modes can work to the advantage of both the teacher and the learner as authentic communicative events promote students' communicative proficiency development. Technology can offer opportunities for developing all three modes for student communication.

CORE PRACTICES

Also referred to as high-leverage teaching practices, we will briefly discuss six core practices that have been shown to have the greatest impact on student learning (Hlas & Hlas, 2012). Research suggests that such practices "may serve as a curricular framework for professional preparation in teacher education programs" (Hlas & Hlas, p. S78). Ball and Forzani (2009) operationalize such practices as those that

> are most likely to equip beginners with capabilities for the fundamental elements of professional work and that are unlikely to be learned on one's own through experience ... teaching practices in which the proficient enactment by a teacher is likely to lead to a comparatively large advances in student learning. (p. 460)

As we discuss these six high-leverage teaching practices, we recognize the importance of giving students appropriate feedback during instruction and after assessments have been administered. In Chapter 4, we briefly discussed different feedback strategies that TCs will have to learn to become accustomed to using in the classroom as they interact with students. In the following section, we discuss in more depth these six core practices that offer the highest student impact based on how the teacher makes use of each practice (Hlas & Hlas, 2012).

Anticipating Student Errors and Misconceptions During Planning

When planning and executing lessons, TCs must learn to understand how their students will react to new material and information (Even & Markovitz, 1995; Tirosh, 2000). TCs must anticipate how learners will respond to target language input, potential communication problems, and even possible misunderstandings of a cultural presentation. By carefully planning for instruction and trying to foresee how students may react to the lesson, students' errors and misinterpretations can be avoided and even used to an advantage.

When planning for instruction, many considerations contribute to TCs anticipating student misunderstandings. Taking into consideration psychophysical development patterns, school culture, previous learning experiences, and home culture(s) and relationship(s) within the target language cultures, TCs may use their own experiences as learners to help learners avoid misunderstandings. We have found that many students who make their way into teacher education programs are those who would have thrived learning languages, regardless of who the teacher was. They may have even been survivors of *drill-and-kill* pedagogical practices.

Student diversity and characteristics should inform what TCs plan in the classroom, and understanding learners as individuals can help pave the way. Regardless of their own prior learning experiences, TCs must be reminded that they are frequently the exception to the rule; they were the ones who thrived in that environment while others were not engaged by such ineffective language teaching practices. It is now their job to put themselves in the shoes of those learners who are not inherently interested in grammar and diagramming sentences, and TCs must learn to pitch their lessons to students who do not share their background or motivations for learning. Appropriate scaffolds must be used to bring students to higher levels of language learning, with appropriate comprehensible input and visuals to aid in language acquisition. Language teaching involves teachers integrating scaffolding into instruction.

Additionally, TCs must be taught not only to recognize their own learning styles, but also to recognize and work with the learning styles of their students, which is part of the Context for Learning in edTPA Task 1. As TCs prepare for Task 1, they must decide how to create and structure supports for the whole class as well as for the three focal students with specific learning needs. Hlas and Hlas (2012) recommend using a four-column lesson plan where the first column represents the planned sequence of activities that will take place. The next three columns are used to provide support for each activity by including anticipated student responses, teacher follow-up questions, and the teachers' formative assessment of student learning.

Target Language Use in the Classroom of 90% +

Comprehensible input in the target language is a highly essential component for language acquisition to occur (Krashen, 1981) as is comprehended input (Gass, 1988). Without delving into a prolonged discussion on the role of input in second language acquisition, there is little disagreement that learners must be exposed to copious amounts of the target language. The American Council on the Teaching of Foreign Languages (2010) recommends that not only teachers but also students "use the target language as exclusively as possible (90% plus) at all levels of instruction during instructional time" (p. 1). While edTPA does not stipulate in the rubrics how much of the TC's interaction with students must be in the target language, the learners must be using the target language in order to develop learners' communicative proficiency in the target language within meaningful cultural context(s). Nevertheless, we promote that our TCs learn to teach in the target language early in their teacher preparation program.

We believe that input from TCs must be directed toward communicative goals and the objectives articulated in the learning segment. All forms of scaffolds (e.g., gestures, visual supports) must be used in conjunction with comprehension checks to verify that teacher input is being comprehended, so that gaps in understanding do not occur. Comprehension checks can identify such gaps, and TCs must be aware that they need to teach their students strategies for requesting clarification when input is beyond their level of understanding. TCs should elicit talk from their students that increases fluency, accuracy, and complexity over time. Additionally, TCs should encourage self-expression and spontaneous use of the target language.

Now more than ever in the history of language teaching, there is a wealth of authentic, target language input available to teachers and learners. The Internet and instant access to newscasts, live video, and material created by native speakers for native speakers revolutionized the possibilities available inside and outside of the language classroom. International perspectives are available on the most up-to-date worldwide events. Language teachers and TCs can show this morning's Parisian television newscast, Bolivia's latest newspaper op-ed, or last night's Indian presidential candidates' debate, right from their own classroom or computer lab.

Interpersonal Communication Tasks

Based on the world-readiness standards and the 5 Cs, communication in the target language is the goal for language teaching and learning. As such, communication can be documented well in the edTPA portfolio by including various interpersonal tasks, keeping in mind that interpersonal tasks require learners to "interact and negotiate meaning in spoken, signed, or written conversations to share information, reactions, feelings, and opinions" (National Standards Collaborative Board, 2015, p. 7). Interpersonal communication can take place in a conversation (speaking and listening) or in written form (writing and reading). It is important to remember that interpersonal communication is not rehearsed language. It is spontaneously created and involves the interaction between those conversing that may go in unpredictable directions. While accuracy in the target language is optimal, the focus in the interpersonal domain is primarily on the message. As the new standards remind us, "the message to learners is not that accuracy does not matter, but rather that one should use all strategies available to understand and be understood" (p. 54).

There are a multitude of interpersonal tasks that can be used when teaching languages, and we cannot provide an exhaustive list. In our estimation, a few of the best activities are information gap activities, jigsaws, picture prompts, think-pair-share, and problem solving activities. We recommend that TCs and their instructors consult several germinal publications for models on which to base effective activities, such as Blaz (1999, 2000), *Teacher's Handbook* (Shrum & Glisan, 2015), and ACTFL's journal, *Foreign Language Annals*, to name just a few.

One critical aspect of developing those interpersonal tasks derives from the TCs' knowledge of learner development and how to develop activities that pique the interest of learners at various ages. Age-appropriate communicative events can be planned to simulate what target language speakers the same age as the students in the language classroom might be exchanging ideas about in the target language cultures. The learners themselves might already communicate about the topic with their friends in their first language.

Functional Goals and Objectives

As we have discussed earlier, the world language edTPA places emphasis on building students' communicative proficiency in the target language. As language teachers, one of our principal goals is to provide our students with the tools so that they can be effective communicators in the target language. Many times language learners have all of the vocabulary and grammar to talk about a certain topic; however, they lack the ability to put all of the words and ideas together in order to communicate their ideas. In world language teaching, we advocate strongly that TCs plan for communicative activities that have a specific purpose and that they embrace focusing on functional goals and objectives that are not based on grammar. Savignon (1983) defined a language function as the purpose of an utterance instead of some specific grammatical form an utterance takes. By focusing instruction on function rather than form (i.e., grammar), TCs can plan activities that deemphasize form and focus more on meaning. By doing so, learners can use the target language for specific purposes, thus making communicative activities much more meaningful.

In order to teach in a functional manner, TCs must learn to teach in a contextualized manner, structuring their input in the target language to focus on meaning instead of teaching grammar in the first language. Additionally, they should plan to place an emphasis on communicative goals. It is important to try to include *chunks of language*—those ways of saying things (e.g., learner hears "he tripped me up" and later states "I tripped him up") without analyzing that the verb is in the past tense.

Krashen and Terrell (1983) advanced the notion that basic communication goals can be written in terms of thematic situations and functions. As with any situation, TCs need to be ready to explain several ways to complete a task. They must also be flexible enough to anticipate a situation may look different to students than what TCs anticipate. Finally, TCs should develop rubrics that allow for students to add an element of creativity to situational tasks.

Grammar as a Concept

The traditional approach to teaching grammar may look like having a *grammar point of the day* that students focus on. Or perhaps the teacher uses a deductive approach teaching a certain grammar point and following the lecture with specific drills where mastery of the grammatical lesson is the goal. Unfortunately, when grammar is approached in such a manner, learners focus on the form and not meaning. The grammar focus ignores the pragmatic use of the language and how it is used to convey meaning in real contexts, which is at the heart of the world language edTPA.

VanPatten (1996) has shown that language learners focus attention on meaning first and then turn to grammatical understanding later. Based on the notion that comprehensible input enables learners to deduce language structures, a purely inductive approach does not guarantee that students will develop accurate understanding about language concepts (Adair-Huck, 2007).

As the profession seeks to reconceptualize grammar instruction, we advocate a story-based and dialogic approach that integrates both deductive and inductive approaches to learning, the PACE model. Such an approach allows language teacher to build students' understandings of language forms as they are found in meaningful contexts. PACE stands for presentation, attention, coconstruct, and extension. Shrum and Glisan (2015) state that the model "should be viewed as the framework for a unit of study that is carried out in multiple lessons over several days" (p. 223). See Shrum and Glisan (2015) for a detailed description of the model.

Activities Using Authentic Resources

Learners' personal preferences and interests should inform teacher choices of authentic target language input to offer to learners. Learner choice can stimulate motivation and offer opportunities for learners to share their content expertise in a language classroom. Taking into account learners' own interests, personalities, and motivations (Gregersen & MacIntyre, 2014) can help TCs personalize their teaching and the authentic input available to the learners. Gone are the days of requiring every learner in the class to take in the necessary information in the same way. Instead, technology gives language teachers and learners unprecedented access to input from all over the world.

Interpersonal communication is essential in the world language classroom. It fosters understanding in the receptive skills as well as the productive skills of speaking and writing. Such communication can take place between teacher and students as well as between and among students. Unfortunately, many of the speaking and writing tasks that teachers require of their students are presentational in nature. That is, students are asked to create (i.e., write) a conversation about a certain topic and then asked to present it. During the presentation, students either tend to read what they have written or attempt to memorize and regurgitate what they wrote.

In our estimation, language teachers must build a community of discourse. That is, "a back-and-forth communication of thought by means of a connected series of utterances shared through social interaction and collaboration (Shrum & Glisan, 2010, p. 80). Glisan recommends avoiding the use of the popular Initiation-Response-Evaluation format for teacher-student interpersonal interaction where the teacher Initiates by asking a question, the student Responds, and then the teacher Evaluates said response in the target language (e.g., very good!). Instead, Glisan suggests that teachers use the I-R-F format: initiation, asking a question in the target language, response by the student, and feedback from the teacher. Here, the teacher can even request more information by asking follow-up questions in an attempt to move the conversation forward (personal communication, July 21, 2015).

Authentic resources are a wonderful addition for students to learn more about the culture as well as perform the interpersonal task(s). Authentic texts, according to Shrum and Glisan (2010) are "those written and oral communications produced *by* members of a language and culture group *for* members of the same language and culture group" (p. 85). Those texts placed at TCs' fingertips can now inform lesson design and assessment while providing the valuable input for learners' communicative proficiency development. Having authentic input from a target language community allows teachers and learners to have a real-world model, based on a real-world genre and communicative event. That authentic example can serve not only as input but also as a template for learners to create their own target language communication.

In our methods courses, we help TCs locate and design meaningful lessons using authentic resources that can be gathered from a variety of sources such as the Internet as well as personal travel abroad. The authors, as language teachers in public schools, collected a plethora of authentic materials (e.g., bus schedules, menus, newspapers) while traveling in the Spanish-speaking world that we use in our classrooms today. We encourage our TCs to study abroad not only for language and cultural learning opportunities, but also to begin collecting authentic resources that they find interesting for their own classroom use as future educators.

TASK 1: PLANNING FOR STUDENT LEARNING

As TCs prepare for Task 1, it is advantageous for TCs to peruse Rubrics 1–4 so that they are keenly aware of the criteria used by the edTPA reviewers as they evaluate portfolios. Additionally, TCs need to review what it is that they need to do for this task. First, they must select a focus class and provide relevant context information using the Context for Learning Information sheet. Like all of the artifacts, this is a Word document in which TCs must document the required information and write it between the brackets [ ] as shown on each of the forms.

TCs must also identify a learning segment of 3–5 consecutive lessons or if they are teaching within a large time block, they need to prepare for about 3–5 hours of connected instruction (Stanford Center for Assessment, Learning, and Equity, SCALE, 2015a). They must determine a central focus for the learning segment, which "supports students to develop communicative proficiency in the target language in meaningful cultural context(s)" (p. 9). They must develop the lesson plans for each lesson taught and submit them as Part B of Task 1. Each lesson plan cannot exceed four (4) pages and if they are longer than four pages, the TC must condense or excerpt to meet the four-page limit. Lesson plans must include the World-Readiness Standards for Learning Languages (National Standards Collaborative Board, 2015), the instructional strategies and language tasks including what both the TC and the students will be doing to support diverse student needs, the instructional resources and materials, and both informal and formal assessments used to monitor student learning.

Finally, TCs must select and submit key Instructional Materials (Part C), the Assessments (Part D), and compose the Planning Commentary (Part E) "prior to teaching the learning segment" (p. 9). They must submit copies of all written assessments and/or the directions for any performance or oral assessments from the learning segment. The world language edTPA handbook reminds TCs to provide citations for the source(s) of all materials that the TC did not create. These citations should be listed by "lesson number at the end of the Planning Commentary" (p. 13).

The Planning Commentary is written by responding to the prompts in the Word document provided by SCALE, and it is worthwhile to remind TCs that they must be sure to write their comments between the brackets [ ] on the left margin after each prompt. First, they describe the Central Focus:

> A description of the important understandings and core concepts that you want students to develop within the learning segment. The central focus should go beyond a list of facts and skills, align with content standards and learning objectives, and address the subject-specific components in the learning segment. The central focus of world language teaching is developing students' communicative proficiency in the target language in meaningful cultural context(s). For example, the central focus for a world language learning segment might be talking about family and self by using adjectives, pronouns, vocabulary that relates to kinship, and verbs such as "to be" and "to have" in the target language. The whole segment can focus on the development of students' communicative proficiency in the target language, developing their skills to be able to introduce and talk about self and family through the creation of family albums, biographical writing pieces, and posters/drawings of family trees with labels. (SCALE, 2015a, p. 44)

Thus, TCs must describe how the learning objectives, written in observable L2 performance, and the standards within the learning segment address the development of students' communicative proficiency in the target language in meaningful cultural contexts with a focus on the three modes of communication. Also, TCs must explain their lesson plans and how one lesson builds upon the next and make connections between language functions and forms.

For prompts 2a and 2b, TCs describe what background knowledge they have about their students in the focal class with respect to the central focus. In particular, they are asked to discuss the diversity of their students with regard to IEPs, 504 plans, English language learners, et cetera. TCs also add information about their students' everyday experiences, cultural and language backgrounds and practices as well as their interests.

With respect to prompts 3a–d, TCs write about how they plan to support their students' communicative proficiency in the target language based on their knowledge of the students. The planning commentary will be filled with justification of instructional strategies and planned supports for the entire class, the three focal students, and groups of students with specific learning needs. In prompt 3c, TCs will explain how the planned activities promote comparisons and connections between the knowledge / experience of the students and the content found in the cultural standards. Finally, TCs write about common misconceptions and errors about the target language and/or the cultural practices within the focus and how the TC plans to address them. The final section of the Planning Commentary deals with monitoring students' development of communicative proficiency in the target language with respect to the assessments, both informal and formal. The document itself is three pages, but TCs must stay within the page limit requirement of nine single-spaced pages including the prompts.

In the following section, we examine Anna's submission for Task 1 and discuss each of the required submitted materials: Context for Learning, Lesson Plans with the instructional materials and assessments, and the Planning Commentary.

CASE STUDY

As mentioned in Chapter 3, Anna's Context for Learning reflected that she was teaching in a suburban high school setting to a Spanish II honors class. No accommodations were listed as necessary. There were no requirements or expectations that she found to influence her as she planned or delivered instruction. The class met every day for 45 minutes, using a common high school second-year Spanish textbook. There were 12 students in the class, half male and half female. The focus class had no English language learners, heritage language learners, or students with IEPs or 504 plans.

Turning attention to Anna's lesson plans, she developed three lessons over the course of 3 days, with a Spanish II Honors class for 45 minutes each day, as described in Chapter 3. Her lesson plans were created using the Clementi and Terrill (2013) lesson planning template, with Anna filling in the spaces from the Word document made available on the book's companion website, which is hosted by ACTFL (n.d.-a). By using that template, Anna was able to address a number of concepts highlighted by the edTPA portfolio, namely the World-readiness standards, modes of communication, and lesson objectives. That template also allowed Anna to maintain focus on her chosen unit theme and question, in addition to each daily topic.

The focus of her learning segment was *Life in the City*, and the products, practices, and perspectives of Spanish life. The first of her three lessons focused on common practices and perspectives across Spanish cities and differing products and practices among four Spanish cities in particular. In that lesson she focused on the interpersonal and interpretive modes of communication. On the template Anna indicated that the lesson met the remaining three standards, as well. In the first activity, Anna used a You-

Tube video to show students highlights from several Spanish cities, asking them if they ever visited a Spanish city and what already they knew about Spanish cities. She also asked them what they liked most about the video and why. Five to 10 minutes were budgeted for that first activity. The second activity, for which 15 to 20 minutes were allowed, Anna showed the students a PowerPoint presentation in which she explained the cultural aspects of the four focus cities, explicitly mentioning that she would highlight products, practices, and perspectives and distinct characteristics of each city. She listed five clusters of questions in Spanish that she would use to engage the students during the presentation, such as, "What do Spaniards in a city like to do? What activities are similar to our activities here in the United States? What are different?" For the third activity, she showed the students a sample poster that she created about one of the cities and used it as a model to explain what the students would be doing for their presentations the next day. She modeled the various parts of the poster and the presentation that were necessary for the students' final product that they would present the second day of the learning segment. She allotted 5 to 10 minutes to demonstrating the poster and presentation for the students. The fourth activity was a dictation in which she read a paragraph in Spanish that highlighted city vocabulary that students were learning in the unity. Students rewrote the paragraph in their notebooks, and the activity was budgeted 5 to 10 minutes. As the last activity, Anna reviewed the stated lesson objectives and had students write down one thing they learned about Spanish cities as an exit slip. The homework assigned was to work on the group project and prepare for the following day's presentation about their assigned Spanish city.

Anna's second lesson explored differences in products and practices in three of the four cities, focusing on what makes each city unique culturally and all three modes of communication. This lesson, too, included aspects from all five of the standards. In the first activity of the second day, for which 5 minutes were allotted, Anna introduced the group presentations, telling students that each group was a travel guide expert and that they would present information about three Spanish cities. She also distributed a handout in which the students had to indicate what they already knew about the city, list two things they learned from each presentation, and take notes on what they found interesting about the city. The next half hour was devoted to the group presentations in which three groups of four students each presented the poster created about their respective Spanish cities, with each presentation allowed 10 minutes to present. The third activity was a think-pair-share in which students wrapped up their thoughts about the presentations on the handout distributed previously. After those few minutes, the students then shared their thoughts with a peer and finally shared with the class what their partner learned from the presentations, with Anna summarizing what the students learned and reviewing the lesson objectives. This activity was budgeted 10 minutes. She assigned the students to write directions from three spots on a city map to the particular place that they researched in their city.

Examination of Anna's third lesson shows a focus on how to give directions using a map of a Spanish city using all three modes of communication while highlighting the remaining four standards. Using the Clementi and Terrill (2013) lesson plan template, she opened the lesson by explaining a station activity. She wrote that her students would be moving around the classroom visiting each group's poster and asking direction to each place on the poster. Students would be given an itinerary that outlined when they would be presenting their city and when they would be visiting other cities. After the brief explanation about how the activity worked, student had to rotate from one city to the next visiting each poster. Anna went from group to group asking questions of the students as well. After the activity, each group of students was given 3 minutes to explain why their city was the best one to visit in Spain and why. Once the presentations ended, Anna presented a writing activity in which she gave students a blank postcard to write individually about what they liked most about a city among those presented. They were not allowed to select the city that they presented. To end the lesson, Anna collected the postcards and told the students which one was the favorite city as determined by the number of cards about each city.

In addition to her three days of lesson plans, she also turned in her key instructional materials (Part C) and the Assessments (Part D). Her materials for Part C were contained in four Word document pages. She presented the materials chronologically beginning with Lesson 1. On the first two pages, she showed the dictation paragraph followed by a printed handout of the 13 PowerPoint slides with two color slides per row. In the next two pages, she showed the follow-up handout from Lesson 2 and photographs of three different Spanish city posters that her students created. The final page of the handouts was the blank postcard and the guiding questions that students needed to answer about their favorite Spanish city. As for Part D, she again displayed her assessments in four Word document pages and presented them chronologically beginning with first one. In order to avoid repetition, we refer readers to Chapter 4 for a detailed review of Anna's assessments.

Turning to her Planning Commentary, Anna took advantage of the space given on the template, writing 8 ¼ pages of the nine possible pages for the commentary. For the Central Focus 1a, she composed 111 words describing the central focus of teaching her students how everyday city life in Spain reflects the practices, perspectives and products of Spanish culture. She briefly discussed differentiating among the practices, perspectives and products of Barcelona, Madrid, and Malaga. She mentioned that the students would not be studying general cultural practices but rather what makes each city unique. She presented the purpose of the lesson, providing a culturally authentic context to develop students' ability to use Spanish by describing places, giving directions, and explaining the significance of famous places in each city.

In Part 1b, she discussed each of the learning objectives individually and chronologically by reiterating each objective and each one's focus in terms of the three modes of communication and standards. She also wrote about the meaningful cultural context for each objective. Over the course of 778 words, Anna told edTPA reviewers about her three days of lessons. In Part 1c, she explained clearly how each daily plan built upon the next in 845 words. She informed the readers that the first lesson served as an introduction to many of the language forms the students would use throughout the rest of the lessons. She gave an example of a learning task so that readers had a solid idea of her plan. In the second paragraph, she outlined her second lesson plan and talked about building upon students' previous knowledge of lessons before the three from the learning segment were taught. In the third paragraph, she presented her third lesson, telling the reviewers how this lesson built upon the first two. She wrote that the lesson gave students "another opportunity to build upon their linguistic knowledge" by recommending places to visit with the communicative activity, in which each group of students was given a few minutes to advocate in favor of their city. Her commentary focused solely on her lessons, and she did not talk about topics unrelated to the three lessons.

With respect to section 2a, Anna wrote that the students in the focus class had learned to give directions using informal commands. She then outlined how her students were able to build on previous material by learning how to create and use formal commands. She talked about her use of authentic materials (e.g., street maps) so that students could develop their communicative abilities in the target language. In 631 words, she told reviewers that her learning segment allowed students to synthesize previous learning in more culturally authentic communicative activities. Additionally, she mentioned that the learning segment built upon the students' prerequisite skills of presentational communication. She also told reviewers that the segment built upon her students' cultural knowledge of the practices, products and perspectives of Spanish culture.

In section 2b, she used 374 words to tell reviewers about what she knows about her students and their cultural backgrounds and interests. She wrote that her students were a tight-knit group and spent time outside of class socially. She felt that the activities she had planned would be well-received because the students tended to study together. With respect to the students' cultural backgrounds, in the second paragraph she outlined some of the students' demographics (e.g., ethnicity, socioeconomic status) and discussed how some had traveled abroad already. She informed reviewers that some of the students were involved in the school's extracurricular activities and gave a few brief examples. She also briefly mentioned that she felt that her students' interests and hobbies were aligned well with the first lesson.

In Section 3, Supporting Students' Communicative Proficiency in the Target Language, Anna responded to each of the four prompts in a straightforward manner. In section 3a Anna composed 387 words justifying to reviewers her understandings of her students' prior learning and personal/cultural/community assets. In the first of two paragraphs she framed her discussion in the three modes of communication and wrote about Krashen's (1981) Monitor Hypothesis with emphasis on his theory of comprehensible input. In her second paragraph, she wrote about aligning her students' interests to her instruction, mentioning that her activities were based on Gardner and Lambert's research on learners' attitudes and motivation. In the next section, 3b, she discussed the whole class first and then, in subsequent paragraphs, talked about students who appeared to be struggling as readers and were underperforming. She offered several brief examples to contextualize her rationale for the external reviewers in 309 words. In section 3c (159 words) Anna explained how her planned discussion on the first day would help students compare and make connections between the Spaniards' lives and their own. In the final section, 3d (251 words), Anna wrote that her students may have misconceptions about the cultural practices of Spaniards living in focal cities and how she planned to help students overcome any misperceptions. She mentioned a second possible misconception and then turned to identifying a common error with which her students struggle—differentiating between formal and informal commands—and how she will approach helping students overcome their difficulties in understanding the difference between the two.

In the final section of her Planning Commentary (4a), Anna described each of the three lessons in separate paragraphs with a total of 380 words. She explained briefly what each assessment is, the purpose of each assessment, and added the three modes of communication as appropriate. In 4b, composed of 207 words, she wrote about how she would adapt her learning assessments by first presenting the dictated paragraph multiple times to help students with any undiagnosed learning disabilities. She also mentioned how to differentiate a few of the activities for students. Again, she took a chronological approach by discussing the lessons in order.

We recommend that TCs frame their planning commentaries in terms of the three modes of communication, the standards, previous research, and developing student target language proficiency in meaningful cultural contexts. TCs need to write in a clear manner, briefly reminding readers of the lesson objectives and other critical information. TCs need to write each task as if it were independent of the others. Hence, critical material and comments need to be repeated and/or adapted for each task. That clarity in describing the development and selection of the activities and assessments will prevent reviewers from having to reread previous sections, artifacts, lesson plans, and other documents submitted. Anticipating the audience is a definite asset in Anna's approach to all three of the commentaries. As documented by Anna's write-up, she did not attempt to create the maximum 5 consecutive days of lesson plans. It was evident that she knew her students and could align instruction to their backgrounds and interests. She stayed within the page requirements for the portfolio and was familiar with the rubrics and expectations for developing a quality dossier of her work.

UNPACKING RUBRICS 1–4

As mentioned earlier, we strongly advise TCs and language teacher educators to examine the planning rubrics carefully well before the time the portfolio must be submitted. As described in Chapter 4, part of that familiarization involves examining the vocabulary of each rubric and its guiding questions as well as the characteristics of the median score of 3 on each rubric. We also again suggest that potential TC challenges for each rubric be actively anticipated. Below, we discuss each of the four rubrics for this task and highlight the vocabulary associated with them followed by a few yes/no questions to guide TCs and teacher educators during portfolio development.

With respect to Rubric 1, Planning for Communicative Proficiency in the Target Language, some critical vocabulary is: meaningful cultural context, language form, language function, interpretive, interpersonal and/or presentational modes of communication. The following checklist is intended to help TCs create and faculty preview edTPA portfolios:

- Are the planned tasks communicative?
- Are at least the interpretive mode and one other mode of communication being addressed?
- Is there a meaningful cultural context established?
- Do the lessons highlight language function as opposed language form?

- Are the lessons sequenced in a logical manner that aid in developing student communicative proficiency?

Anna's lessons included the interpretive, interpersonal, and presentational modes of communication across the learning segment, with communication at the center of each lesson. In her commentary, she also explicitly mentioned the three Ps of the cultures standard, lists three language functions that the learning segment addresses, and describes the meaningful cultural context that her students explored. Further, she detailed how what students learned in the first lesson contributed to what they learned in the second lesson and so forth, focusing on how the modes of communication in which the students engaged build off of one another. Throughout her entire planning commentary, she was careful to address every aspect of the prompt and explain in her description how she met the requirements of the task at hand.

Rubric 2, Planning to Support Varied Student Learning Needs, highlights additional vocabulary such as planned supports, learning objectives, individual needs of students, development of proficiency, Bloom's taxonomy and active verbs, differentiation, learning styles, multiple intelligences, anticipating misunderstandings, and performance. Questions for TCs and faculty to consider while creating and reviewing portfolios include the following:

- Are the learning objectives active and observable second language performance?
- Are a variety of students' learning styles and/or intelligences being addressed in the lessons?
- Are the objectives tied to the learning segment theme?
- Are supports for the class present?
- Are supports for individuals present?
- Do the supports listed for individuals accentuate student assets, instead of only deficits?

As explored in Chapter 4, Anna's objectives were active, measurable, and central to the whole learning segment. The supports she described in the planning commentary tie back to the students linguistic (i.e., students' knowledge of formal commands), lexical, and cultural knowledge. She described how diverse learners would be supported by a map as a visual aide during the learning segment, as well as an example presentation on which to base their own presentation created as part of the learning segment assessments. She pointed to the support that learners could offer to one another during the learner segment and how the hands-on activities that she planned benefited a variety of learners.

With respect to Rubric 3, Using Knowledge of Students to Inform Teaching and Learning, vocabulary of importance includes student and community assets, second acquisition theory, deficit thinking, and content connections to other classes. Questions to consider include:

- Is research used to justify planning decisions made?
- Is prior learning, as it relates to current planning, considered?
- Are individual students' assets included?
- Are the whole class' assets included?
- Is a deficit view presented to justify planning decisions?

Anna described her students' previous knowledge as impetus for her planning decisions a number of times throughout the commentary. She explored both their prior academic learning as well as the other assets of interest in the third rubric. She also cited research several times as reasons for the planning decisions she made.

The fourth rubric, Planning Assessments to Monitor and Support Students' Development of Communicative Proficiency in the Target Language, prompts TCs to be able to understand vocabulary such as informal and formal assessments, communicative proficiency, meaningful cultural context, performance assessment, and modes of communication. Questions to guide TCs' writing and Task 1 review include:

- Do assessments place focus on students' communicative proficiency development?
- Are the assessments planned performative in nature?
- Do assessments planned include meaningful cultural context(s)?
- Are the assessments formative in nature?
- Will there be opportunities for students to improve upon their learning as a result of the assessments planned?
- Are performance assessments planned?

Anna explicitly outlined her planned assessments for each lesson with a paragraph dedicated to each of the three lessons of the learning segment. She indicated whether the assessments in each lesson were formal or informal as well as what mode of communication each assessment helped students develop. She described specifically the meaningful cultural context in which the learners will operate in each of the assessments.

**Table 5.1.   Resources for TCs to Learn More
About Planning Student Learning**

Rubric	Suggested Resources
Rubric 1: Planning for Communicative Proficiency in the Target Language	Blaz (1999, 2006); Clementi & Terrill (2013); Shrum & Glisan (2015)
Rubric 2: Planning to Support Varied Student Learning Needs	Blaz (1999, 2006)
Rubric 3: Using Knowledge of Students to Inform Teaching and Learning	Ellis (2012); Lightbown & Spada (2013)
Rubric 4: Planning Assessments to Monitor and Support Students' Development of Communicative Proficiency in the Target Language	Blaz (2000); Clementi & Terrill (2013); Sandrock (2010); Wiggins & McTighe (2005)

RESOURCES

Several resources that faculty can use to develop background knowledge of their students with respect to Task 1 is displayed in Table 5.1. These texts and others can direct readers in their continued learning, teaching, and writing. While not an exhaustive list, it gives readers additional sources on which to draw in their instructional decisions and commentaries. Full citations can be found in the references list at the end of the book.

OUR RESEARCH

The planning task yielded the highest mean score across the three tasks ($M = 3.64$, $SD = 0.46$) for our programs' students (Hildebrandt & Swanson, 2014), which may not be surprising given the amount of planning that TCs engage in during their preservice coursework. It is rather common in general pedagogy and content-specific methods courses to have TCs create multilesson units for evaluation. That practice helps candidates get experience putting together logical and effective lessons, although not all of them are used with actual students.

Overall, our data showed that participants' lesson plans provided evidence of connections between language forms and functions within meaningful cultural contexts, but focus across all three modes of communication was lacking (SCALE, 2015a). Most participants scored 3s and 4s on the four planning rubrics as shown in Table 5.2. Of the 13 edTPA rubrics, Rubric 1: Planning for Communicative Proficiency in the Target Language had the highest mean ($M = 3.86$, $SD = 0.65$) with 15 of the 21 TCs in our previous study earning a 4 on the 5-point scale. Rubric 4: Planning Assessments to Support Students Development of Communicative Proficiency in the Target Language had the second highest mean (M

**Table 5.2.   Descriptive Statistics
of Each Performance Level for Task 1 Rubrics**

	M	*SD*	*1*	*2*	*3*	*4*	*5*
Rubric 1: Planning for Communicative Proficiency in the Target Language	3.86	0.65	0	1	3	15	2
Rubric 2: Planning to Support Varied Student Learning Needs	3.57	0.59	0	1	7	13	0
Rubric 3: Using Knowledge of Students to Inform Teaching and Learning	3.52	0.75	0	1	10	8	2
Rubric 4: Planning Assessments to Support Students Development of Communicative Proficiency in the Target Language	3.62	0.67	0	1	7	12	1

$= 3.62$, $SD = 0.67$) of the four planning rubrics, only slightly below Rubric 1. The majority of participants ($n = 12$) received a score of 4 on the fourth rubric and seven received a score of 3. On Rubric 2: Planning to Support Varied Student Learning Needs, most participants scored 4 and none scored 5; it elicited the third highest mean of the four planning rubrics ($M = 3.57$, $SD = 0.59$). The lowest mean across the planning rubrics was for Rubric 3: Using Knowledge of Students to Inform Teaching and Learning ($M = 3.52$, $SD = 0.75$), with 10 participants scoring a median score of 3 and 10 other participants earning a score of 4 or 5. Only one participant scored below the median score of 3 on all four of the planning rubrics, with scores of 2 across the task rubrics. A comparison with the national dataset from SCALE (2015e) showed that our TCs had higher means than the national average for the four planning rubrics.

CONCLUDING THOUGHTS

In this chapter, we discussed in detail the first edTPA task, Planning for Instruction and Assessment, by employing backwards design. As we have mentioned earlier, we recommend to our own programs' TCs that they first develop their edTPA learning segments' objectives and assessments. Afterward, they can begin to develop lessons and activities to plan for students' communicative proficiency development.

We again focused on Anna's edTPA portfolio to provide an example of an exemplary performance on the planning task, including her application of objectives and tying them to her instruction in the three modes of communication and the World-Readiness Standards. We also provided additional resources for teacher educators and TCs to further explore the foci of the planning rubrics and detailed our own research about our TCs' performance on the Planning task.

CHAPTER 6

INSTRUCTING AND ENGAGING STUDENTS IN LEARNING

In this chapter, we explore the second edTPA task, Instructing and Engaging Students in Learning. Assessments of observable second language performance and planning for learning were addressed in previous chapters, but now we turn to in-class instruction. This chapter focuses on the instructional process versus the planning or assessment of learning. By edTPA's definition, planning, instruction, and assessment all support student learning. The Instruction task, composed of rubrics assessing learning environment, engagement in learning, deepening thinking, and subject-specific pedagogy, is followed by the teacher candidate's (TC) analysis of their own teaching practices (Stanford Center for Assessment, Learning, and Equity, SCALE, 2015a). The emphasis of Task 2 lies in the moments of teaching, as demonstrated by the 15-minute video, and reflection on those moments of teaching, as demonstrated by the written commentary. The commentary also allows candidates to describe what they were thinking while carrying out instruction.

In this chapter focusing on the second task, we address a few critical world language instructional concepts that can promote student learning and proficiency development, such as creating a low-anxiety learning environment in which instruction is aligned to students' characteristics and assets. Additionally, we discuss error correction and provide detailed insights for video recording. Then, we explore reflective practices that aid in TC continued pedagogic development. Afterward, we attend to the specifics of Task 2 expectations and outline how our case study TC

Understanding the World Language edTPA: Research-Based Policy and Practice
pp. 103–126

approached Task 2 through her written commentary and video recorded teaching sample. Finally, we unpack the five rubrics associated with Task 2, present more resources that may be helpful as TCs work toward developing a world language edTPA dossier, and show findings from our own edTPA research. The chapter concludes with some final thoughts on preparing Task 2.

As TCs prepare for Task 2, it is important to remember the ideas for assessment and planning that we have advanced in earlier chapters. Reviewing Rubrics 5–9 helps TCs know the criteria used by the edTPA reviewers as they evaluate portfolios. Additionally, TCs need to be detail-oriented as they compose this and all parts of the portfolio. First, they must obtain permission for video recording in the classroom, including permission from parents/guardians of the students as well as any other adults that will appear in the video footage. Some schools or districts have restricted policies, so it is essential to ask about their policies before student teachers are even placed. Second, TCs should identify the lessons from the learning segment that will be video recorded early in their placement. The most recent *edTPA World Language Assessment Handbook* (SCALE, 2015a) suggests that TCs choose lessons that show TCs interacting with students in meaningful cultural contexts to develop their communicative proficiency in the target language. Videos of instruction can be either one or two video clips, of no more than 15 minutes in total, as of the latest version of the *edTPA World Language Assessment Handbook* (SCALE, 2015a). Finally, TCs must analyze their teaching and student learning by responding to the prompts in the Task 2 Word document. As with the previous two tasks, all responses must be typed between the brackets [ ] after each prompt. As before, we suggest that teacher educators guide their TCs through the rubrics before student teaching, prompting them to analyze the five rubrics, unpack what a 3 on each rubric means, and anticipate the challenges that they may face while carrying out the task.

LEARNING ENVIRONMENT

Creating a positive learning environment is critical for teaching and learning, regardless of subject content. In second language teaching, a low-anxiety environment is a necessary element for fostering student performance in and acquisition of a second language (Krashen, 1985). Huang and Eslami (2010) noted that language teachers should not "merely recognize the presence of foreign language anxiety in language learners but also help learners acknowledge, cope with, and reduce their anxiety" (p. 32). Krashen (1985) suggests that if a language learner's affective filter is elevated, language learning is prevented. However, if the student's filter is low, language learning can take place.

For decades researchers have suggested that the reduction of performance anxiety is a strong indicator of academic success (Buttaro, 2009; MacIntyre & Gardner, 1994a, 1994b; Sharma & Mishra, 2007). Anxious language learners tend to make more errors and even recognize fewer errors in a recall situation than those who are less anxious (Gregersen, 2005). Moreover, language learners with an increased state of anxiety are likely not to participate in language learning activities. That lack of participation serves to decrease the likelihood of making target language errors while protecting their social image in front of their peers and teachers. By participating less, these apprehensive language learners are less likely to develop their target language proficiency.

A review of the literature suggests that language learners are the most stressed when performing in front of the class and talking to native speakers (Swanson, Early, & Baumann, 2011) as well as when being assessed face to face by the instructor (Woodrow, 2006). There are various strategies TCs can use to ameliorate such effects; for example, using technology in the assessment of learners' abilities in the second language may lower some learners' apprehension during a one-on-one assessment. The emergence of computer-assisted language learning, blended with new instructional paradigms about teaching and language acquisition, has helped transform the profession (Hai-Peng & Deng, 2007).

Additionally, TCs can help reduce student anxiety by explaining briefly from time to time how languages are acquired, pointing out that learners must become risk-takers and concern themselves with communicating ideas, instead of the number of errors being created. Formative assessment can be a critical part of instruction as language learners begin to foster a strong sense of efficacy in language learning. TCs can also recognize and celebrate student achievement as they work in the classroom, sharing with students their expectations concerning content learning, student achievement, and social behavior (Wilen, Bosse, Hutchinson, & Kindsvatter, 2004). TCs' sense of humor can likewise help create a learning environment that is low anxiety yet conducive for language acquisition (Swanson, 2013). Further, classrooms in which students feel safe in expressing concerns or asking questions are conducive to learning and language acquisition; TCs that foster mutual respect with and among students can form an environment in which tolerance, a sense of common identity, and community are promoted (Wilen et al., 2004).

From the first day with students, TCs need to develop an educational atmosphere in which students feel comfortable taking risks as they build their target language proficiency. We advocate that TCs get to know their students as they work with them, and even before if possible. By knowing their interests and background knowledge, TCs can plan more effectively to build off of student assets, improve their instructional abilities, and help students reach their potential.

LEARNER CHARACTERISTICS

Approximately 50 years ago Joan Rubin (1975) published an article that changed the way we view learner characteristics. In *What the 'Good Language Learner' Can Teach Us*, Rubin wrote about what good language learners do. She argued that there is more benefit from studying the habits of successful language learners than there is from studying learners who are not as successful and/or stop language learning altogether. Of the many characteristics she discussed, we will discuss a few briefly.

The first of Rubin's good language learner characteristics that we will address is students' motivations to acquire a new language. There are various reasons students enroll in language courses, and fostering and improving student motivation are critical to language learning (Dörnyei & Ushioda, 2013). Research supports the notion that students of teachers who promote learner autonomy tend to have more success academically than those whose teachers are more controlling of student learning (Deci, & Ryan, 2002). In addition to motivation, Griffiths (2009) addresses language learner age and offers evidence from her own research suggesting that overall, younger is better. She also discusses the role of students' learning styles, and personality.

We believe that it is in TCs' best interests to foster an environment that promotes learner autonomy. Developing a student-centered approach to teaching and learning allows students maximum opportunities to use the target language. TCs should facilitate learning by providing comprehensible input and creating activities that allow students to be the ones using the target language the majority of the time in class. We advocate for getting to know the learners by incorporating a variety of instruments, such as learning style inventories and multiple intelligences surveys into class. Asking students directly about their interests and preferences can avoid the trial and error approach that others may take in getting to know their students. Later, when composing the edTPA commentaries, TCs can refer to theory as they describe their rationale for planning, instruction, and assessment.

Comprehensible input, or $i + 1$ (Krashen, 1981, 1985), should be the foundation of the contemporary language classroom with authentic materials, by native speakers for native speakers, as a primary source of second language. Tailoring that input to a level that stretches learners but does not stretch them too far into frustration is a skill central to learning to be an effective teacher. Teacher produced language, too, provides opportunities for learners to hear language just above their current level, at $i + 1$ instead of $i + 30$. Finding authentic sources that are aligned to learners' interests either as individuals or by developmental level can motivate those learners to pay attention and want to learn about the topic at hand.

Having a *learner-centered classroom* offers TCs the opportunity to better engage their learners in their own learning by providing a respectful environment, in which learners participate more and have higher learning outcomes (Richards & Bohlke, 2011). Student motivation is central to all teaching (Dörnyei, 2001), and when TCs understand their students' needs and goals, their participation and cognition styles, and their need for community, they can set the right conditions to spark interest and support student learning (Richards & Bohlke, 2011).

ERROR CORRECTION

As we noted in Chapter 4, teachers need not be afraid to correct students' errors (Ellis, 2009). There are a variety of strategies that teachers can use to provide error correction such as clarification requests, repetitions, and recasts. As conceptualized by Ellis (2001), second language instruction can be categorized into meaning-focused instruction and form-focused instruction. Meaning-focused instruction does not involve direct, explicit attention to language form. However, form-focused instruction in general views the new language as an object that can be studied through discrete lessons "targeting specific grammatical structures and rules" (Loewen, 2007, p. 1).

Given that the new paradigm of language teaching is the communicative language approach, an integrated approach that incorporates attention to language structures within a meaning-focused activity or task should be employed. As Loewen (2007) noted, recasts, the teacher's reformulation of a student's incorrect utterance while maintaining the central meaning of the utterance, can work well. Recasts serve both as a clarification request and a correction. The teacher can continue to prompt conversation and understanding by dialoguing with learners and remaining in the target language. Some researchers advocate in favor of using recasts (Ellis, Loewen & Erlam, 2006; Russell & Spada, 2006). However, others believe that recasts are so implicit that learners might fail to notice their errors. Instead of using recasts, they advocate in favor of prompts or elicitations as a form of feedback. In a prompt circumstance, the teacher attempts to get the learner to self-correct instead of giving the person the correct answer. Using an elicitation, the teacher tries to elicit the correct response from a student by asking questions or by asking students to reformulate their utterance. Again, emphasis is placed on communication and not on learning rules or grammar.

Nevertheless, we advocate that TCs use error correction strategies as a means to promote language acquisition in a communicative manner. During instruction, errors will be made that require TCs to address grammar errors so we suggest that TCs become adept at using a variety of corrective feedback strategies, both implicit and explicit.

VIDEO CONSIDERATIONS

Permission Forms

At Georgia State University, leaders in College of Education and Human Development developed the Parent/Guardian edTPA Release Form with assistance from the legal department. The form is two pages. On the first page, the TC fills out the top portion providing the parents/guardians with the following information:

1. the name of the teacher education program;
2. the name of the mentor/cooperating teacher;
3. the name of the principal in the school where the TC is placed for student teaching/internship;
4. the name of the school; and
5. the date.

In four brief paragraphs, the parents/guardians are informed that the TC is a teacher candidate in the program at Georgia State University and that the university is implementing edTPA. A brief explanation about edTPA follows informing the parents/guardians that it is a requirement for teacher certification in Georgia. In the second paragraph the letter explains the video recording of the TCs instruction in the classroom and that children may appear in the video. It also states that the video will be uploaded to a private and secure course management system. Furthermore, parents/guardians are told that the TC must submit samples of student work and that no students' names will appear on any materials that are submitted. Finally, it states that faculty, cooperating teachers, and TCs may see the video and student work samples for training purposes. It reminds parents/guardians that the videos and materials will be viewed under secure conditions and that the videos and student work will never be posted on publicly accessible websites nor will the identity of children, schools, or districts be revealed.

The second page contains the release form on which parents/guardians can either grant or not grant permission to video record or reproduce their child's (children's) materials from class. There is also a permission form near the bottom for students who are more than 18 years old. Both forms have lines, signatures and dates. The forms have been translated into eight different languages (e.g., Chinese, Spanish).

Each district or school in which individual TCs are placed may have specific restrictions on video recording instruction and students, with some districts outright banning it. This ban can exist despite the state sharing information about edTPA and its role in contributing to the licensure of new teachers. Careful planning with districts well before the placement is finalized should ensure that last minute withdrawals don't take place because of the district forbidding video recording. Permission for video recording instruction in other settings, like community centers or Saturday language schools, must also be provided by the directors and/or other stakeholders if used for a mini-edTPA assignment. Some community centers grant permission outright, while others will ask how videos will be used or ask that you not video record particular children. To encourage respect and continuity, this permission should be renegotiated each time one works with the organization and each time leadership roles in the organization change.

Planning to Video Record

On the first day of placement in schools, we recommend that TCs hand out the permission form in the necessary home languages and begin collecting them the next day for the selected focal class. We remind our TCs to email parents/guardians at the start of the semester in order to collect as many signed forms as possible before planning to video record. In the past, some of our TCs have offered students extra credit points to get the forms returned in a timely manner. Nevertheless, some parents/guardians will not grant permission so TCs must be reminded that when video recording takes place, that only those students can be shown in the video. Thus, the students who cannot be video recorded must be moved out of the video recording frame(s), but they must remain in the class for instruction. When recording, TCs will need to rearrange class seating arrangements and be sure to teach to the entire class so that no one is left out, while only having those students whose parents /guardians allow their children to be in the instructional video frame.

Considerations about the type of camera must be taken into account. As we were pilot testing edTPA in our programs, we found that cellular phones were not always the best cameras to use. We believe that there are varying degrees of quality cameras in phones and TCs are wise to test different video cameras before recording for edTPA purposes. At Georgia State University, our language lab coordinator investigated various manufacturers of video cameras and bought 10 cameras and tripods for our TCs to use during field placements.

After much investigation, we were satisfied that the cameras have better video cameras and better microphones than many of the cellular phones. They have SD cards and are compact in size. Our TCs can choose to use one of the cameras or use a different video camera. It is their choice. While we do not advocate or promote one manufacturer over another, we strongly advise language program faculty to work collaboratively with their departments to investigate ways to help offset costs for TCs with such equipment while helping TCs develop a tremendous edTPA dossier.

Video Camera Placement

Once TCs have arranged the focal class' seating arrangement, we recommend that they pilot test the placement of the camera. Learners need to be instructed that the class will be video recorded and that proper behavior should be demonstrated. TCs can place a camera and tripod in a desired location and film part of a lesson to determine how the video appears on a computer and how well the TC and the students can be heard. Using a tripod can eliminate the shakiness of a handheld device and allow easier filming for the trusted adult in charge of taping. Ideally the camera will blend into the background of the class if positioned correctly, even on days when taping doesn't take place. It is very important that the external reviewers be able to watch the instructional videos without any problems (i.e., the video is clear) and be able to hear the TC and the students (i.e., the audio is understandable). If reviewers are unable to watch/listen satisfactorily, it is very likely that the evaluators will not score the instructional rubrics and give a Conditions rating for each of the rubrics. With such a rating, TCs may have to resubmit the work at an additional cost. Therefore, pilot testing the location of the video recording device and the device itself is critical.

We strongly suggest that cooperating teachers or other adults carry out the TC video recording. Having a student video record takes the student out of the lesson and limits his or her participation. TCs and the person filming must become familiar with the device with which they are going to work and practice filming and reviewing the video/audio.

When the days arrive to begin video recording instruction, we suggest that TCs:

1. Make sure the equipment is working properly; test the camera and video quality before actually taping;
2. Check the camera's battery supply so that it has a sufficient charge for recording the lesson;
3. Make sure there is sufficient memory on the camera to record a lesson;
4. Check the camera frame so that the desired area of the classroom is visible when; recording making sure to not include those students who do not have permission to be in the video(s);
5. The room is adequately illuminated so reviewers can see the students and TC; and
6. The audio is set properly so that students and TC can be heard well.

Prior to Editing Video

There are several considerations that must be taken into account before editing any video clips. First, we suggest that all video clips be placed in a specific folder called, edTPA Master Video clips, on both the computer and on an external hard drive (e.g., jump drive). Then, we ask TCs to make copies of those clips and rename them according to edTPA specifications. Finally, when editing takes place, we instruct TCs to use only the copies of the originals for editing purposes. By following such protocol, if errors take place in the editing process, those video clips can be deleted and a copy of the master file can be made and then used for editing the second time. Once the final video clips are produced, we strongly suggest that TCs place multiple copies on the computer as well as on the external hard drive in a folder subfolder called Submitted edTPA Video clips along with the rest of the portfolio documents (e.g., commentaries).

Choosing Video Clips

We recommend to our candidates that they video record every lesson of the learning segment so that they have ample evidence from which to choose later on. Oversampling will make the burden easier; if later on the chosen segment is deemed unsatisfactory, there is another readily available to submit instead of reteaching and refilming, which could delay licensure or graduation. And upon submitting the edTPA, it is better to have too much evidence than not to have enough and be scrambling for adequate video recorded lessons.

Selecting the best video of the learning segment may take a little while as TCs weigh what each video clip is demonstrating. As student learning and proficiency development is of such importance in the world language edTPA, we advise our TCs to choose videos in which students are interacting to create authentic communication with one another. After all, while it may seem that the video recorded lesson is there to show what the TC can do, this perception is mistaken. edTPA focuses on student learning and having the video recorded sections reinforces that learning and proficiency development is occurring, which will serve the TC well when the portfolio is later scored.

In both of our programs, TCs develop a mini edTPA dossier during their practicum coursework. They become very familiar with the handbook and other edTPA documents. Additionally, they become familiar with video recording and editing video. With respect to video editing, TCs may only edit the footage for length, as the submitted video must be one or two video clips of no more than 15 minutes of video in total. The video is used to show reviewers that the TC demonstrates how he or she interacts with his or her students in a "positive learning environment to develop their communicative proficiency in the target language in meaningful cultural context(s) with a focus on at least two modes of communication" (SCALE, 2015a, p. 21). TCs must include the interpretative and at least one other mode of communication. To that end, TCs must be made aware that they can cut video, but they cannot splice video together. They cannot add credits, transitions, etc. to their video clips. The only exception to the no-editing policy is for student anonymity, which permits student faces to be blurred.

On campus TCs may be able to find a variety of resources on campus to aide them as they compose their video recorded teaching sample. For example, video recorders and tripods may be able to be checked out from the campus library or a center in the college of education. Language resource coordinators in language departments may also be able to provide hardware assistance or help clipping video recordings to meet the exigencies of the current handbook. Making resources like these easily available to TCs may alleviate external stresses associated with composing the portfolio, including eliminating the need to buy superfluous hardware or software.

In the *edTPA World Language Assessment Handbook*, there is a section with which TCs must become familiar, Instruction Task 2: Artifacts and Commentary Specifications. It details for TCs what they need to submit, a list of the supported file types for video (e.g., .mov, .mp4) and the planning commentary (e.g., .doc, .docx), the maximum length of the video clips and commentary, and additional important information (SCALE, 2015a). At Illinois State University, the preferred video formats are *.avi* and *.wmv* for PC users. For Mac users, the preferred format is .mov. However, other formats are accepted for edTPA: .lv, .asf, .qt, .mov, .mpg, .mpeg, .avi, .wmv, .mp4, and .m4v. Nevertheless, it is good practice to consult the most recent *edTPA World Language Assessment Handbook*, as handbooks may be updated periodically.

If the size of the video clip(s) is too large per edTPA accepted video size, the video clip(s) can be compressed. There are a variety of programs that can be used, and the developers of edTPA have two guides for compressing video that TCs can use depending on if the TC is using a PC or a Mac:

- PC: http://www.edtpa.com/Content/Docs/ VideoCompressionGuidePC.pdf
- Mac: http://www.edtpa.com/Content/Docs/ VideoCompressionGuideMac.pdf

It is important to remember that if a video file is too small, audio may be lost. Thus, it is wise to check the audio after compressing files to make sure that the audio is still audible. If after compressing the video(s) the audio is not functioning properly, we suggest deleting that file, returning to the master video file(s), and starting the compressing procedures again. Also, we remind TCs that if they are working in iMovie or Windows Movie Maker, the video(s) should be exported as a video file instead of a project file.

During the edTPA pilot testing phase at Georgia State University, the technology integration was redesigned so that TCs can spend more time planning to shoot video, video recording, reviewing the video clips, compressing video, and editing video among other assignments. TCs also video record their instruction during the practicum course after they have the signed permission forms from parents/guardians. Program faculty member spend time discussing what edTPA allows and does not allow. We recommend that program coordinators and faculty members include video creation and editing as part of their programs if it is not in the curriculum at present. We recommend that TCs begin working with video at the early stages of their programs so that they feel comfortable working with it when it counts.

REFLECTIVE PRACTICE

Individual and collective learning needs feature prominently throughout the edTPA process and form the foundation from which proposed instructional changes should take shape. With the goal of developing students' communicative proficiency in the target language, TCs respond to a number of prompts to outline changes based on the video recorded evidence. To be successful, proposed changes must reach beyond the surface level such as classroom management and simple reteaching. Grounding suggested changes in second language acquisition theory rewards TCs and forms another firm foundation on which to base instructional decisions.

Student target language usage and proficiency development are at the center of edTPA expectations, and TCs are wise to develop and carry out lessons in which learners have a number of opportunities for prolonged practice. Richards and Bohlke (2011) prompt teachers to ask themselves the following questions about each lesson they develop:

- What kind of language-learning opportunities did the lesson provide?
- How many opportunities were there for students to practice meaningful use of the language?
- Who had most of the opportunities for language use during the lesson—the teacher or the students?
- Did all of the students participate in the lesson, or did some students have more opportunities for participation and practice than others? (p. 6)

These questions provide a meaningful way for TCs to think about their students' responses and language growth afforded by the lesson.

Giving and taking constructive criticism gives TCs a vocabulary of growth and can foster the mentality of ongoing reflective practice. The TELL Project is one framework of "characteristics and behaviors that model teachers exhibit" and is composed of "7 [sic] domains designed to address a teacher's need to Prepare for Student Learning, Advance Student Learning, and Support Student Learning" (http://www.tellproject.org/framework/): environment, the learning experience, collaboration, planning, performance and feedback, professionalism, and learning tools. The project website offers a self-assessment for TCs or in-service teachers to use to continue developing professionally, with a focus on student learning. An attractive feature of the website, too, is a statement of how each item on the self-assessment and each area of the domains are related to the American Council on the Teaching of Foreign Languages/Council on the Accreditation for Educator Preparation, Interstate Teacher Assessment and Support Consortium, and National Board for Professional Teaching Standards standards, as well as the Charlotte Danielson (2011) and Robert Marzano (2007) frameworks. Those tools may be useful for developing reflective assignments in the methods class-room and for reflecting on video recorded lessons.

Thus far in the chapter, we have explored issues related to the learning environment, learner characteristics, and error correction, along with practical considerations for video recording lessons and tools for developing TC reflective practice. In the rest of the chapter, we turn to our case study of a successful edTPA portfolio and unpacking the five instructional rubrics, followed by several resources for further exploring the rubrics' topics.

TASK 2: INSTRUCTING AND ENGAGING STUDENTS IN LEARNING

As we have discussed in the previous two chapters, TCs are wise to review the rubrics for each task before developing their portfolios. Per the most recent handbook (SCALE, 2015a), TCs must think about what the learning environment should look like, what kinds of language tasks the TCs will use to engage students, and what plans are for eliciting and building on students' responses in order to develop communicative proficiency. TCs must also examine how they will connect new content to students' prior knowledge and use evidence from instruction in order to examine and change their teaching practices to meet students' needs.

The 2015 *edTPA World Language Assessment Handbook* (SCALE, 2015a) informs TCs that they need to obtain the appropriate permissions from parents/guardians to film students in the classroom. Additionally, the document explains that TCs must examine their lesson plans from the learning segment and identify challenging learning tasks in which students and the TCs are actively engaged. It also states that the accompanying video clips should provide a sample of how the TCs interact with the students to develop target language proficiency. Finally, the handbook gives details about the video clips and how TCs must be shown interacting with students in at least two modes of communication, interpretive and inter-personal or presentational.

With respect to the Instruction Commentary, the developers of edTPA require no more than six single-spaced responses from TCs that include the prompts. TCs can provide up to two additional pages of supporting documentation such as transcriptions of inaudible comments from the video. Those additional pages do not count toward the six-page limit. TCs must use the Word document provided by SCALE and, as with the other tasks, TCs must compose their comments and between the brackets [ ] on the left margin after each prompt.

CASE STUDY

With respect to Task 2 (SCALE, 2015a), according to her commentary Anna turned in two .wmv formatted video clips, one from Day 2 and one from Day 3 of her lesson plans. Per the *edTPA World Language Assessment Handbook*, Anna obtained parental permission for video recording, examined her lesson plans for the learning segment, determined to target the students whose parents/guardians gave permission for their children to be video recorded, and began to respond to the commentary prompts writing her responses between the brackets [ ] on the commentary form. Her first video clip was seven minutes long, while her second video clip was slightly less than eight minutes.

In Section 2 of the commentary regarding the promotion of a positive learning environment, Anna wrote that she demonstrated (1) mutual respect for, (2) rapport with, (3) responsiveness to her students, and (4) challenged students to engage in learning. She mentioned certain time frames of the two videos (e.g., Clip 1, Minutes 1:15–3:12) in which she felt she accomplished what was asked in this section. Specifically, she noted in separate paragraphs totaling 454 words how she promoted a positive learning environment by addressing each of the four aforementioned requisites for promoting a quality learning environment.

Next, in Section 3a, Engaging Students in Communication in the Target Language, she explained (in 471 words) how she engaged her students in developing their communicative proficiency via two modes of communication, the Interpretive and Presentational. Again, noting specific points in the video (e.g., Clip 2, Minutes 5:54–7:34), Anna addressed how her students were developing their communication skills in the interpretive domain, for example, as they listened to her instructions for their homework and as they listened to their peers give their presentations in Spanish. She wrote about how she scaffolded instruction and contextualized her thoughts in theory citing Krashen' (1981) notion of *comprehensible input* when talking with her students. With respect to students developing their communicative proficiency in the presentational mode, she discussed how students rotated around the room and not only listened to each group's presentations, but also had to present to their peers about their Spanish city. She supported her statements by referring reviewers to time stamps of the two videos.

In Section 3b, describing how instruction linked students' prior learning to new learning, Anna composed 638 words in four paragraphs by informing the reviewers that she synthesized prior learning about the language function of informal commands with new knowledge they acquired about Spanish cities into one culturally authentic scenario. Again, she cited exact time stamps of her videos (e.g., Clip 1, 3:12–6:47 mins), which reviewers could follow along with her description. Specifically addressing the criteria from the rubrics, she wrote about how she gave students multiple opportunities to use their previous linguistic knowledge in a new context, that is, giving commands. She directs the reviewers' attention by informing them that students can be heard giving and receiving directions while using the cities' maps.

In her commentary, she complimented her students by telling the reviewers that her students were hardworking and courteous individuals. She wrote about their cultural and personal assets (e.g., high grade point averages, most of the students are Christian) and cited examples in the two videos by specific clip and time marker as mentioned earlier. She even referred to a specific student in the video who was making a personal connection to new learning by talking about her Catholic upbringing. Again, she referred to a specific moment in the video that reviewers could find by video clip number and minute. She also made reference to another student who, like most students in her class, traveled internationally and had already visited Madrid.

In the next section of her commentary, Deepening Student Communicative Proficiency in the Target Language during Instruction, Anna again carefully followed the instructions and referred to examples found in her two video clips. In Part 4a, she wrote five paragraphs (469 words) to talk about how she elicited and built upon student responses to promote thinking and develop students' communicative proficiency in Spanish. She mentioned specifically that she had students take notes during the presentations in order to help them stay on task. She also explained that she developed an interpersonal activity so students could discuss the questionnaire she gave students. She also mentioned how the Spanish City station activity helped promote her students' interpersonal skills by having them respond to their peers' questions in an impromptu format. She provided specific places in the video clips for reviewers to see what she was describing.

In Section 4b, she explained in 326 words how she supported her students' development of communicative proficiency with respect to language forms, language functions, and meaningful cultural context(s). Discussing what took place in her first cited video clip, she stated that her students were presenting their research on Madrid. She mentioned that her students in one of the groups described certain places in the city: the cathedral, the Prado Museum, the Bank of Spain or the Plaza de Toro. She followed by stating that by doing so, her students were developing the language function of answering informational and clarifying questions through the question and answer session. She went on to tell the reviewers more about the activity and how it helped build student proficiency. Then, she referred to her second video clip, which showed the students in an interpersonal activity. She explained that students did not rehearse their language and were negotiating meaning in a cultural context. She took time, briefly, to specify which language forms were being addressed (e.g., prepositions of position, commands). In her final two paragraphs, she mentioned two more specific instances in which her activities developed her students' communicative proficiency with respect to language forms, language functions, and meaningful cultural context(s). She cited video timestamps at the beginning of each of the paragraphs (e.g., Clip 1: 2:46–5:13 mins).

With respect to Section 4c, her explanation of how instruction promotes comparisons between students' personal, cultural, or community assets and the cultural perspectives, practices, and products of the target language (SCALE, 2015a), Anna's explanation was rather short, only 151 words. Again, she selected and referenced a specific clip. She talked about how students had to answer and discuss the follow-up questions to the group presentations. She wrote how her students in the video are answering the follow-up questions based on their own backgrounds, opinions, and personal interests.

In the final section of the commentary, Analyzing Teaching, she answered Section 5a by writing two paragraphs citing specific video selections and telling reviewers about what changes she would make to her instruction for the entire class (paragraph 1) and for students who she felt needed more support (paragraph 2). In 233 words, she told the reviewers that her students had difficulty coming up with a hypothetical situation where students had to tell how to get from one place in the city to the next. She felt that the students lacked spontaneous creativity and perhaps by allotting extra time her students would have been better prepared for the activity. She felt that in light of the fact she did not offer students much written or oral feedback during the two lessons cited in the videos, she should have included time for her students to peer edit each other's homework. Then, she wrote about how she would have modified the third lesson.

In the final part of Section 5, Section 5b, she used 372 words broken into two paragraphs to write about how these changes would improve student development of communicative proficiency in the target language. She supported her explanation by citing evidence of student learning as well as theory and research. In this final write up, she did not cite any specific video clips. She mentioned that she should have had students develop at least three scenarios before having the students complete the station activity. Citing a cognitive perspective to processing information, she argued that having more time to process what is being required for the task, students can better recall prior knowledge and then begin to formulate answers. Also, she mentioned Bloom's taxonomy and how important it is for students to build understanding at the lower levels before trying to work in the higher levels (e.g., Create). She ended the section by writing about the importance of peer editing. She again cited Krashen's (1981) input hypothesis and suggested that comprehensible input in the target language is essential for language acquisition, even if it comes from peers.

It is important to remember that Anna selected a Spanish 2 Gifted class for her learning segment, evaluated under the 2013 handbook (SCALE, 2013c). She explained that her three focus students were gifted individuals and did not mention students under 504 plans or an individualized education program because of the requirements of the 2013 handbook. Under the 2015 edTPA guidelines,

> At least one of the focus students must have specific learning needs, for example, a student with an individualized education program or 504 plan, an English language learner, a reader who is struggling in their first language, a student at a different level of language proficiency, a student who is underperforming or with gaps in academic knowledge, a heritage-language speaker, and/or a gifted student needing greater support or challenge. Note: California candidates must include one focus student who is an English language learner. (SCALE, 2015a, pp. 27–28)

Given that the students in her focus class are classified as *gifted*, she described her three focus students in terms of language learning difficulties although not officially diagnosed as such. While Anna remained within the guidelines set forth by edTPA developers, we urge program faculty to help TCs get placements in diverse settings so that TCs have the opportunity to become proficient working with a more heterogeneous student population. By working within such a rich classroom environment, TCs can learn more ways to differentiate instruction.

UNPACKING RUBRICS 5–9

As TCs develop their portfolios, it is important for program faculty members to remember that per edTPA guidelines, they cannot assist TCs when it comes to developing lesson plans, selecting video clips, writing commentaries, et cetera. Refer to Chapter 2 for details. TCs must work independently. So, as we discuss each rubric, we offer questions that TCs should consider as they prepare for instruction. With respect to Task 2 and its rubrics (5–9), there are some critical vocabulary with which students must become familiar. While some of these terms may have been introduced early in a teacher preparation program, we feel it is wise to review it with TCs again as they begin to develop their edTPA portfolios.

Additionally, we advise readers to familiarize TCs with the foci. We also suggest working with TCs to examine each rubric for the performance necessary to earn at least a score of 3 on each of the five instruction rubrics as well as the rubrics' guiding questions. In the following section, we will highlight possible important vocabulary for each of the rubrics and pose some useful questions for TCs and the supervisors as they compose and review edTPA portfolios.

In addition to the commentary, this task has the unique requirement of a video recorded lesson to demonstrate that the TC is prepared to teach. This video recorded section of the portfolio gives the TC the opportunity to show reviewers what student are doing during the lesson. The TC is wise to choose a lesson in which students are showcasing language that they have created and we offer the following checklist to aide TCs in choosing an effective video:

- Does the video show what students are doing in the video?
- Are all students on-task?
- Are all students engaged?
- Are all students communicating in the target language?

With respect to the five instructional task rubrics, Rubric 5, Learning Environment, focuses on vocabulary such as student engagement, positive learning environment, rapport, mutual respect, and challenging. Its focus is on students' abilities to use the target language. The following questions can be used to examine the work submitted for evaluation or as part of an in-class assignment prior to student teaching:

- Does the TC show his or her students respect?
- Does the TC show rapport with students?
- Do students show the TC respect?
- Do students show each other respect?
- Can the classroom environment be deemed positive?
- Has the TC developed a low-risk learning environment?

As presented in Anna's commentary, she developed respect for herself and for her students in a variety of ways. After each presentation, she encouraged the class to applaud the efforts of the students. As she moved around from presentation to presentation, she used direct eye contact with students as she interacted with them. She provided encouraging comments as her students worked through the learning segment. She stated that her students showed her respect by listening to her as she provided directions, instruction, and feedback. In her video clips, it was obvious that she had created a positive learning environment that challenged students but was not one filled with anxiety. Students appeared to enjoy the activities shown in her videos.

With respect to Rubric 6, Engaging Students' Target Language Communication, the important vocabulary for TCs is: three modes of communication, meaningful cultural contexts, language function, language form, prior student learning, personal assets, cultural assets, community assets, deficit thinking, cooperative learning, and communicative proficiency. As we work with our TCs, we use the following questions to guide their thinking:

- Does the commentary address assets instead of deficits?
- Does the TC focus on student or community deficits?
- Are there opportunities for students to move from the interpretative to another mode of communication?
- Is the TC lecturing?
- Are students producing target language in collaborative ways?
- Is the new learning linked to prior knowledge?
- Is the new learning linked to student assets?
- Is language form linked to language function?

In Anna's case, she talked about her students' personal assets such as high grade point averages, high motivation to acquire a new languages, and their sincere dedication to their schoolwork, for example. In her commentary, she never mentioned once any student deficits or even framed any of her comments from a deficit perspective. She discussed and showed how she moved from the interpretive mode to the presentational mode as well as the benefits to the students from having researched and presented on a city in Spain. Additionally, she discussed how she linked her students' prior learning to new learning and how she linked commands (language form) to language function (getting around a Spanish city). In her video clips, she was interacting with the students and not appearing to take a teacher-centered approach to instruction. Her students were engaged in cooperative learning tasks in a meaningful cultural context.

Turning to Rubric 7, Deepening Student Communicative Proficiency in the Target Language, the critical vocabulary includes language forms, language functions, meaningful cultural context, student responses, forms of corrective feedback, initiation-response-evaluation, and initiation-response-feedback. As we work with our TCs, we ask them the following questions:

- Is real-life communication taking place?
- Are students communicating about real-world topics?
- Is teacher feedback to students focused on the message instead of grammatical and lexical accuracy?
- Is teacher evaluation focused on the message instead of the form?
- Does teacher evaluation go beyond labeling student responses as correct and incorrect?
- Is the TC drawing more information out of students instead of merely evaluating their utterances?
- Are students talking to one another, as opposed to talking only to the teacher?

It was evident in Anna's portfolio that her students were discussing and presenting about real-world topics using communication strategies that they would use if they were in a Spanish-speaking country, in this case, Spain. Her students were actively negotiating meaning in a meaningful cultural context and appearing to have fun in the process. She facilitated instruction instead of using a teacher-centered approach. Her evaluation and feedback to students was focused on form and on communication. She did sprinkle in some comments about grammar, but the focus was not placed on it. The students were actively participating with each other, and her station activity seemed to have worked well. The audio on the video clips was adequate and the reviewers most likely did not have difficulty watching the video and following along with her commentary.

With respect to Rubric 8, Subject-specific Pedagogy, we remind our TCs to focus on the *World-Readiness Standards for Language Learning* that are not as amply addressed in the other rubrics. In particular, TCs would be wise to be able to define the following vocabulary and include them, like the others, in their commentaries: comparisons, connections, 3 Ps of culture (i.e., products, practices, and perspectives), communities, and prior student knowledge. Before TCs complete this task, like the other two tasks, we remind them to keep the following questions in mind:

- Are two of the three Ps of the cultures standard represented in the lessons?
- Do the lessons make connections between new information being taught and students' previous experiences and knowledge?
- Is the comparisons standard present in the lessons?
- Is the connections standard present in the lessons?

In Anna's case, the three Ps were present and she discussed them as she told what her students were doing. The lessons made clear connections between prior knowledge and the new information that she was presenting/teaching. She actively compared and made connections, and she even took the time to mention the standards by name and number. As we prepare our TCs in our programs, we encourage them to use the important vocabulary found in each task in their commentaries so the reviewers are not left guessing how the standards were addressed in instruction.

With respect to the final rubric in Task 2, Analyzing Teaching Effectiveness (Rubric 9), TCs must demonstrate an understanding of their students' individual and collective learning needs along with the use of second language acquisition theories to guide instructional choices. These questions can be used to guide TCs for this rubric are:

- Are the proposed instructional changes based on evidence as opposed to opinions or supposition?
- Are proposed changes grounded in students' needs?
- Are individual students' needs addressed?
- Are the collective needs of the class taken into account?
- Are proposed changes grounded in second language acquisition theory?

Anna's commentary clearly framed her changes based on evidence. She reflected on her students' needs as a class and as individuals. She did not discuss a wide variety of second language acquisition theories as she discussed her proposed changes, but she did let reviewers know that theory guided her thoughts. She referred to the necessity of input but did not reference any particular theorist or theory by name.

Overall, Anna's edTPA dossier was well-prepared and clearly written. Her video clip selections were appropriate in terms of content, length, and file format. She followed all of the guidelines, and her scores would have been deemed sufficient to pass the edTPA requirement in California (35), Georgia (29), Illinois (31), Iowa (35), Minnesota (29), New York (35), and Washington State (30).

RESOURCES

In Table 6.1, we have highlighted some resources for program faculty to guide their thinking as they work with TCs. These selections as well as others can help TCs as they develop their portfolios. See the references for complete citations of each resource.

**Table 6.1. Resources for TCs to Learn More
About Instructing and Engaging Students in Learning**

Rubric	*Suggested Resources*
Rubric 5: Learning Environment	Krashen (1981, 1985); Richards & Bohlke (2011)
Rubric 6: Engaging Students' Target Language Communication	Glisan & Shrum (2015); Richards & Bohlke (2011); Sandrock (2010)
Rubric 7: Deepening Student Communicative Proficiency	Lyster & Ranta (1997); Richards & Bohlke (2011); Shrum & Glisan (2015)
Rubric 8: Subject-Specific Pedagogy	Shrum & Glisan (2015)
Rubric 9: Analyzing Teaching Effectiveness	Lightbown & Spada (2013); Richards & Bohlke (2011)

OUR RESEARCH

Overall, the 21 TCs in our pilot study (Hildebrandt & Swanson, 2014) earned a mean score of 3.33 (*SD* = 0.56) on the edTPA 5-point scale across the five instruction task rubrics. The mean for instruction was higher than the mean across the assessment rubrics, but it was not as high as the mean across the planning rubrics. As shown in Table 6.2, Rubric 5, Learning Environment, had the highest mean among the instruction rubrics (*M* = 3.71, *SD* = 0.72), indicating that those TCs provided a low-risk environment in which learners could express themselves. None of the participants scored below three points on the 5-point scale on Rubric 5. However, nine participants scored a 3 and another nine received a score of 4. Three participants earned the highest score of 5 on that rubric.

Data analysis showed that Rubric 6, Engaging Students' Target Language Communication, was the instruction rubric with the second highest mean score (*M* = 3.43, *SD* = 0.67), with 91% of participants earning a score of 3 or 4. None of the participants earned the highest or lowest score on this rubric. In general, the participants were able to help learners link prior learning to new learning, but many were unable to lead language learners in deepening and extending communicative proficiency in the target language (SCALE, 2015a).

On the next three rubrics lower means than the previous two were found. On Rubric 7, Deepening Student Communicative Proficiency in the Target Language, one third of the participants were able to prompt and build on students' responses to develop students' communicative proficiency (SCALE, 2015a). A mean of 3.24 (*SD* = 0.83) was found with 76% of participants earning a 3 or 4 on the rubric, and one participant earned the top score of a 5. Participants earned the lowest mean score on Rubric

**Table 6.2.   Descriptive and Frequency Data
for Each Performance Level on the Instruction Rubrics**

	M	SD	1	2	3	4	5
Rubric 5: Learning Environment	3.71	0.72	0	0	9	9	3
Rubric 6: Engaging Students' Target Language Communication	3.43	0.67	0	2	8	11	0
Rubric 7: Deepening Student Communicative Proficiency	3.24	0.83	0	4	9	7	1
Rubric 8: Subject-Specific Pedagogy	3.05	0.92	0	4	10	5	1
Rubric 9: Analyzing Teaching Effectiveness	3.24	0.70	0	3	10	8	0

8, Subject-Specific Pedagogy ($M = 3.05$, $SD = 0.92$), across the four instruction rubrics, indicating that the participants found it difficult to provide opportunities for students to make connections to and comparisons between their students' existing knowledge and experiences and the new cultural practices, products, and perspectives examined (SCALE, 2015a). One participant earned the highest score possible on the rubric while 5 participants were rated as a 4, 10 as a 3, and 4 were rated as a 2 on the rubric. With respect to Rubric 9, Analyzing Teaching Effectiveness, a slightly higher mean ($M = 3.24$, $SD = 0.70$) than Rubric 8 was found, which showed that some of the TCs had trouble using evidence to evaluate and modify instructional strategies to meet students' needs (SCALE, 2015a). None of the participants scored at the bottom or top end of the performance spectrum, and almost half of participants ($n = 10$) received the median score of 3.

A comparison with the national dataset from SCALE (2015e) showed that our TCs had higher means than the national average on the five instructional rubrics.

CONCLUDING THOUGHTS

In this chapter, we have detailed the second edTPA task, Instructing and Engaging Students in Learning, by continuing with the backwards design approach. As discussed earlier, one of the keys to developing a quality edTPA portfolio is the TCs learning objectives and assessments. Afterward, it is critical to teach to those objectives and show that students are building their proficiency in the target language in meaningful contexts. It is essential that TCs review the five rubrics for Task 2 and keep the criteria for a median score of 3 on each rubric in mind as they develop their commentary and what they want to show in their video(s). Care must be taken as TCs select video clips so that their best work is documented. Clarity in the commentary is critical so that the reviewers can easily understand what the TCs are describing.

As soon as possible TCs must secure parent/guardian permission for video recording students, well before beginning writing. We advocate that TCs start the process the first day of class with students, laying the foundation for a smooth edTPA experience. Then, as they are teaching the lessons in the learning segment, we strongly suggest that TCs video record every lesson in its entirety so they have a variety of video from which to select their maximum of 15 minutes of video clips.

As shown in the case study, Anna began to secure parental permission the first day she was in the classroom. She also established a positive learning environment. As she developed the lesson in her learning segment, she recorded each of her lessons and then watched them, trying to decide which video clips to select for her portfolio. She reviewed her coursework on methods and second language acquisition and identified theories and theorists that could be referenced in her write up. She is a reflective practitioner and thought carefully about her lessons and how she could improve as a Spanish teacher. Even though she developed her edTPA portfolio at a time when her scores were not consequential for her certification, she carefully and thoughtfully prepared a portfolio that would have passed the edTPA cut score in Illinois.

Now that we have discussed in great detail the three edTPA tasks, in the following chapter we turn to activities that world language program faculty can include during TCs coursework. We discuss the transition of our programs as we began to thread edTPA throughout our courses and field experiences.

CHAPTER 7

ACTIVITIES FOR THE METHODS CLASSROOM

Thus far, we have discussed how world language teacher education program faculty and teacher candidates (TCs) can become more successful edTPA portfolio creators. Additionally, we have presented many ideas to keep in mind as TCs prepare and construct their dossiers for external review by edTPA reviewers. In this chapter, we present in-class activities that program faculty can use in world language teacher education courses to help TCs prepare for edTPA. We believe that our own TCs' successful edTPA results have been enhanced by reshaping our curricula and integrating various learning opportunities into our world language teacher education courses. From the moment TCs matriculate in our programs and take their first course, their preparation to complete edTPA successfully begins and continues throughout the program. We did not completely reconstruct our entire teacher education programs around edTPA, but we have integrated it substantially in our coursework, early field placements, and obviously in TCs' final field placements.

Without a doubt, there are a number of activities that teacher educators have in their methods-teaching toolbox that could be used to meet the exigencies of edTPA. Further, by highlighting the edTPA skills addressed in each activity, TCs may be able to develop a more robust schemata concerning edTPA and later draw on that schemata as they complete the portfolio during student teaching, when the stakes are higher.

In this chapter we describe several activities to use before TCs begin to prepare their edTPA portfolio for external review. From the time our TCs

Understanding the World Language edTPA: Research-Based Policy and Practice
pp. 127–156
Copyright © 2016 by Information Age Publishing
All rights of reproduction in any form reserved.

arrive in their first world language education class, they are introduced to the vocabulary used in the world language edTPA. They explore a multitude of theoretical and practical information about teaching and assessing world languages in meaningful cultural contexts in these courses. They are taught the value and need for focusing on building students' communicative proficiency development in the target language using the three modes of communication. TCs become familiar with major pedagogical themes, such as the central tenets of communicative language teaching, second language acquisition theory, the national standards, and curricular design, to mention a few. They become aware of the costs to become a language teacher and the programmatic and state requirements that they must fulfill in order to continue through our programs successfully. edTPA is a major part of our programs and we try to help our TCs prepare for it from the first day we meet them. We strongly suggest that program faculty members help their TCs understand edTPA early to enable them to perform successfully on this new teacher assessment.

Some of the following activities serve as opportunities to explore a number of edTPA topics at the same time, while others focus on a particular skill or rubric. We will begin with more generally useful activities and later move to the activities for each of the 13 world language edTPA rubrics.

BLOOM'S TAXONOMY/LEARNING OBJECTIVES MATRIX

In Chapter 4, we presented the notion of backwards design and writing effective and measurable instructional learning objectives. We advocate using the Revised Bloom's Taxonomy (Krathwohl, 2002) as a framework to guide K–12 students to higher levels of language learning and production. TCs can describe in their commentaries their rationale using Bloom's Taxonomy as a guide to show external edTPA reviewers that their instruction is indeed leading to higher levels of learning, built around active and measureable objectives.

As an in-class activity to teach TCs how to develop effective objectives, we use textbooks that are adopted and used in the schools in which we place TCs. Per our college's permission forms and with TC consent, we use previous edTPA portfolios for training purposes, with the author's identity concealed. Thus, we use exemplars from former students' edTPA submissions. We also use the revised taxonomy (Table 7.1) shown below, which readers may want to use in their own classes to aid TCs in their analysis and creation of active and measurable objectives, to assess knowledge of the various types and at a variety of cognitive levels.

**Table 7.1.   The Revised Bloom's Taxonomy
and Placement of Learning Objectives**

Knowledge Dimension	Remember	Understand	Apply	Analyze	Evaluate	Create
Factual						
Conceptual						
Procedural						
Metacognitive						

Note: Bloom's Taxonomy: Aligning Objectives, Assessment, and Instructional Activities (Adapted from Airaisan & Miranda, 2002, p. 253).

Analyzing our Case Study

In our own classes, we use this template as a starting point to have students critically analyze the simplified lists of verbs available through many websites and published resources. TCs read the Krathwohl (2002) article the week before the in-class lesson when the class discusses what Bloom's taxonomy is and how it can be used in our classrooms. We introduce them to the two dimensions of the revised taxonomy: the Knowledge Dimension and the Cognitive Process Dimension. Then, we share exemplars from a previous TC's externally reviewed Context for Learning document in order to enable TCs to know more about the school and the students in the sample dossier. Once TCs have a thorough understanding of the taxonomy and the sample Context for Learning, we show via the projector the learning objectives from Day 1 of the lesson plan, taken from the learning segment developed by one of our former TCs who excelled on edTPA during the pilot study.

As a paired learning activity, we give each pair of students a blank copy of the taxonomy and ask them to fill in where they feel each of the learning objectives should be placed within the taxonomy. For example, they are to use to template and write O:1 where the first objective aligns with the taxonomy, O:2 for the second objective, and so forth. TCs are encouraged to discuss their rationale for the placement of each objective. We explain to our TCs that in our experience as teacher educators, we find that learning objectives typically contain one verb, but in this case where the objective contains more than one verb, a critical analysis needs to take place in which the task and student second language performance or activity is deconstructed in order to arrive at the proper level of the revised taxonomy.

As example of this activity, below are Anna's learning objectives, as stated on her lesson plans, followed by a Table 7.2 where the objectives are placed into the framework. We examined Anna's lesson plans in tandem with the activities planned and carried out, along with her assessments, in order to ascertain the most accurate portrayal of the intended practices.

Day 1 Lesson Plan Objectives

1. Identify the practices, products and perspectives of Spanish city life by listening to a cultural PowerPoint presentation. (O:1)
2. Identify distinct cultural practices and products of Granada, Barcelona, Madrid and Málaga by listening to a cultural PowerPoint presentation. (O:2)
3. Discuss the differences and similarities between American and Spanish city culture. (O:3)
4. Apply their knowledge of Spanish city culture into a group presentation project that examines several places within a specific Spanish city. (O:4)
5. Rewrite the dictated paragraph. (O:5)

For the first day of instruction in the learning segment, Anna focused on cultural practices, products and perspectives. With respect to Bloom's taxonomy (see Table 7.2), her objectives were mainly found in the Conceptual domain with varying levels of cognitive processing. For Objective 1 (O:1), the task could be placed either at the Understand level or in the Analyze level because identification is typically an Understanding process whereas listening can be considered an analytic process. By the way the objective was constructed, it is unclear at which level of the cognitive process dimension the objective should be placed. Nevertheless, we believe that listening and identifying practices, products and perspectives of Spanish city life (an interpretive activity) is a lower level cognitive task. The level of thinking being addressed can be classified as Identifying, which is subsumed under the Understanding level. That is, they are not engaging in an analysis of the products, practices, and perspectives of Spanish city life. Per Krathwohl (2002), "determining the meaning of instructional messages" (p. 215) is categorized under the Understand level.

We place her second objective (O:2) in the same category and level for the same reasons. Even though she tasks the students with identifying distinct cultural practices and products of the three cities, the learners are interpreting and classifying the information, which places the objective in the Conceptual domain at the Understanding level of cognitive processing. Turning to the remainder of her learning objectives, the final three objectives were at the Conceptual Knowledge level in varying levels of the

Table 7.2.   Learning Segment Day 1

Knowledge Dimension	Remember	Understand	Apply	Analyze	Evaluate	Create
Factual	O:1					O:5
Conceptual		O:2		O:3, O:4		
Procedural						
Metacognitive						

Note: Bloom's Taxonomy: Aligning Objectives, Assessment, and Instructional Activities (Adapted from Airaisan & Miranda, 2002, p. 253).

cognitive process dimension. Her third objective (O:3), in which she assigned students the task of comparing and contrasting American and Spanish city culture by engaging in class discussion, asked students to analyze the similarities and differences between the two cultures, which requires students to differentiate and organize (Krathwohl, 2002). Her fourth objective (O:4) is rather elusive as the verb Anna used (i.e., apply) in her objective could be categorized as Apply under the cognitive process dimension. However, closer examination of her lesson plans showed that her students were answering her questions about the cities as a class after she presented her PowerPoint. Volunteers were solicited to answer the questions. Thus, the objective can be placed at the Analyze level in the Conceptual knowledge domain. Her final objective (O:5) required students to rewrite a paragraph that she had just read to them. It tests their memories and does not ask them to create any new information; thus, we place this objective in the Factual domain at the Create level.

With respect to her second day of instruction, Anna's learning objectives (below) moved from the more simplistic tasks of identifying practices, products and perspectives to more complex tasks in the higher levels of Bloom's taxonomy.

Day 2 Lesson Plan Objectives

1. Describe famous places within a Spanish city in a group presentation using their research notes.
2. Explain the cultural significance of famous places within the Spanish cities of Madrid, Málaga, and Barcelona.
3. Describe the geographic location of Madrid, Málaga, and Barcelona and the relative location of famous places within those three cities using an authentic street map.

4. Identify distinct cultural practices and products of Barcelona, Madrid and Málaga by listening to the cultural presentations of their peers.

5. Apply their knowledge of Spanish city culture by writing a postcard that summarizes places they would like to visit from Madrid, Málaga, or Barcelona.

Her first three objectives asked students to describe and explain famous places (see Table 7.3). These learning objectives are part of a presentational activity, and students had time to prepare and rehearse their descriptions and explanations so we place it in the Factual domain at the Create level of cognitive processing.

Her fourth learning objective, much like the first two learning objectives from the First Day lesson plan, asked students to identify information in an interpretive task so we place the objective in the Conceptual Knowledge dimension at the Understand level of cognitive processing. Her final learning objective asks her students to write a postcard, which is a classified as a Conceptual task at the Create level.

On her third and final day of instruction, her four learning objectives (below) continued to bring students to higher levels of cognitive engagement. None of the tasks on this day are found in the Factual domain.

Day 3 Lesson Plan Objectives

1. Describe cultural practices and products of Madrid, Málaga, and Barcelona in an informal group presentation.

2. Ask for directions to various places within Madrid, Málaga, and Barcelona.

Table 7.3.   Learning Segment Day 2

Knowledge Dimension	Remember	Understand	Apply	Analyze	Evaluate	Create
Factual						O:1, O:2, O:3
Conceptual		O:4				O:5
Procedural						
Metacognitive						

Note: Bloom's Taxonomy: Aligning Objectives, Assessment, and Instructional Activities (Adapted from Airaisan & Miranda, 2002, p. 253).

3. Give directions to various places within Madrid, Málaga, and Barcelona using the informal command verb forms.

4. Reflect on their learning by writing a postcard that highlights what they learned about their favorite Spanish city.

As shown in Table 7.4., her learning objectives have migrated to the Create levels of the revised version of Bloom's taxonomy in several different dimensions of knowledge, mainly procedural. Using a stations activity, Anna's students presented information as part of a group project and participated in an unrehearsed interpersonal conversation by negotiating meaning in terms of asking for and giving directions to get around in several Spanish cities. They also reflected on their learning by writing a postcard in which they explained what they had learned about their favorite city.

It is evident that Anna's learning objectives were not teacher centered. She continually tried to bring her students to higher levels of language learning. In our methods classes, we take the time to show TCs the revised Bloom's taxonomy and show how they can document that their instruction is building toward the goal of communication. In terms of edTPA, they can show how their objectives are helping to construct and build students' communicative proficiency in the target language within meaningful cultural context(s) (SCALE, 2015). We recommend to our TCs to think about ways to describe their objectives in terms of Bloom's taxonomy in their instructional commentary, briefly at least, in order to show how their objectives are bringing students to higher order thinking skills via the taxonomy. Due to the limited space in the commentaries, we urge them not to include the tables as shown here, but rather to describe how their objectives are classified on the taxonomy, showing that each day's instruction builds upon the previous day's objectives. In summary, this exercise aids TCs in understanding that instruction is less about decontextualized drills and more about the promotion of using higher order thinking skills to acquire the new language.

Table 7.4.   Learning Segment Day 3

Knowledge Dimension	Remember	Understand	Apply	Analyze	Evaluate	Create
Factual						
Conceptual						O:1
Procedural						O:2, O:3, O:4
Metacognitive						

Note: Bloom's Taxonomy: Aligning Objectives, Assessment, and Instructional Activities (Adapted from Airaisan & Miranda, 2002, p. 253).

The activity described above can be used as a framework for TCs and teacher educators to discuss and plan unit goals and lesson objectives, as well as their assessment. Further, it can serve as a tool to align lesson objectives with lesson activities and assessments. It can be an eye-opening experience when TCs can see where their lesson objectives align or don't align with planned in-class activities and assessments.

USING ACTIVE AND MEASURABLE OBJECTIVES IN THE METHODS CLASS

Most of us in teacher education are able to instruct others how to develop active and measurable objectives for language classes. Less frequently, however, may be the explicit modeling that should accompany the pedagogical preaching. We too are guilty the "do as I say, not as I do" approach to teacher education at times, but edTPA has prompted us to ground more of our TC's in-class and out-of-class work and assessments in Bloom's taxonomy. As time goes on, we hope to analyze more explicitly our own instruction, as we did Anna's above, and design sequential activities to scaffold TC's knowledge creation across the levels of cognitive development.

In the meantime, however, we have begun to highlight how TCs will demonstrate their understanding (Wiggins & McTighe, 2005) of concepts in class by tying activities to the American Association for Colleges of Teacher Education (ACTFL)/Council for the Accreditation of Educator Preparation CAEP standards (Foreign Language Teacher Preparation Standards Writing Team, 2013). Each methods class begins with a Power-Point slide with a quote related to the topic of the hour, projected as TCs enter the room. The first author's favorite, used while talking about performance assessment, is popularly attributed to Albert Einstein: "Everybody is a genius. But if you judge a fish by his ability to climb a tree, it will live its whole life believing that it is stupid." TCs spend the first five minutes completing a daily reading quiz that assesses their knowledge of important vocabulary. The agenda for the class follows with a verbal overview from the instructor. The third slide contains the means by which their understanding will be elicited, followed by the ACTFL/CAEP standards being addressed in the class period. Table 7.5 is a sample slide from a 2.5 hour methods class.

DAILY READING QUIZZES

As mentioned above, French, German, and Spanish TCs at Illinois State University (ISU) complete a daily reading quiz at the beginning of each methods class. After the quiz, the instructor frequently asks TCs to visit

Table 7.5.   ACTFL/CAEP Standards

Teacher candidates will be able to ...

- Compare and contrast models of coteaching. (ACTFL/CAEP 6)
- Describe the inverted pyramid of proficiency levels. (ACTFL/CAEP 4)
- Rewrite ineffective objectives. (ACTFL/CAEP 5)
- Categorize objectives into types of knowledge and levels of thinking skills. (ACTFL/CAEP 5)
- Create a standards-based lesson for assigned week at Unity. (ACTFL/CAEP 3, 4, 5)

the class wiki and begin reading the latest resource posted while the remaining TCs in the class finish the quiz. Generally a short supplementary reading based on the theme of the day, these resources can allow TCs to see the newly acquired information from the reading in a new context. Further, as we teach our TCs, any minute wasted during class is one fewer minute of learning that can take place.

The 5–10 point daily quizzes focus on the Remembering level of Bloom's taxonomy with Factual information highlighted. This practice is based on the observation that, even when they are seniors, TCs at times need external impeti to complete readings. Without the general vocabulary from the readings, in-class discussions and activities prove challenging in any content area. The quiz vocabulary comes from the day's assigned readings and are generally made up of matching items that require recognition. There is even a quiz on the edTPA handbook glossary. Immediately after the last TC finishes the quiz, the class reviews the quiz together to enable everyone to have a foundation in the vocabulary necessary for an informed discussion and more impactful in-class activities. With the readings completed, the whole class has a better experience meaningfully encountering the topics at hand.

USING COMICS

The act of creating visual representations of newly learned, complex information provides an opportunity for TCs to actively process and synthesize information presented in class and via readings. As the dominant sense for most of us, vision can solidify complicated material, especially during the acts of creation and presentation. For example, creating posters of comics that explain the differences between poor and promising assessment practices, drawn on large Post-It Notes, allows TCs to demonstrate creatively what they have learned, as well as to witness their classmates' learning through brief presentations. This activity can also be used to elucidate other complicated topics encountered in the methods class,

Table 7.6.   Instructions for Comics Activity

Open the class wiki and read the article linked on the Announcements page.

In groups of three, use the markers and Post It notes provided to create a comic in which you answer these two questions:

- What were some poor assessment practices that you have experienced?
- What are some promising assessment practices that you can use in your future class-room?

You can use the style of either model comics or any other cartoon artist you like. Or feel free to create your own from scratch!

such as Krashen's monitor model (1981), the three Ps of the Cultures standard, or sociocultural theory (Vygotsky, 1978).

As an example, Table 7.6 shows instructions and sample questions projected at the front of the room and written on the class wiki. After their daily reading quiz, TCs spent a few minutes reading a couple of cartoons from the archives of PhD comics (http://phdcomics.com/comics.php) and the Oatmeal (http://theoatmeal.com/). There are a number of artists whose work could be substituted for those two examples. The purpose of the activity is to have TCs gain a sense of how cartoonists make visuals about complicated topics in an entertaining and simplified way. If contemporary cartoons from target-language speaking sources can be found, all the better. Aromatic markers can evoke TCs' nostalgia for elementary school and inspire a novel learning experience in the college classroom.

TWEET IT

Each of the three edTPA tasks contains a rubric requiring TCs to cite research in order to earn at least a three on that rubric (i.e., Rubrics 13, 3, and 9). To earn fours or fives on those rubrics, TCs must connect their decisions made to SLA research. Undergraduates in general can find it difficult to interpret research and may not understand the connection between theory and practice in the classroom. Therefore, exposing them to SLA theory and connecting that research to classroom practice as early as possible in the program are advantageous.

Using an interface with which most TCs are familiar can aide their comprehension of these educational and SLA theories, which will in the end assist them not only in their edTPA portfolio, but in their future teaching career in general. Twitter holds a prominent place in worldwide culture and can be a useful tool in the classroom. In addition to investigating what current SLA researchers are saying and sharing on Twitter, TCs

Table 7.7. Instructions and Examples for Tweet It! Activity

Summarize the most important concept(s) of your preferred second language acquisition theories in a 140-character tweet, as if posted by one of the primary proponents of the perspective (e.g., Omaggio Hadley, Krashen, and Turnbull).

Examples:

- Noam Chomsky: Ever notice how kids just get it? #UG #LAD #CPH #takethatskinner #bsskinner
- Lev Vygotsky: Chillin with @Piaget chattin about that interaction hypothesis. #engagingconvos #innateability #learningenvironment #SLAtheories
- B.F. Slimmer (Skinner's Twitter handle, of course): Language acquisition is dictated by imitation of adults. We repeat what we hear. #morelikegnomechompsky @in8ist4eva

can take on the role of an individual SLA researcher, living or dead, to summarize important SLA concepts concisely and with humor. The 140-character format necessitates concise statements, prompting Twitter-appropriate language and abbreviations. That union of academic content with nonacademic discourse can help TCs internalize the theories about which they are writing. Further, hashtags provide a fun way of making additional points and even taking jabs.

Table 7.7 provides sample instructions for the activity, along with examples created by former TCs in our classes. The tweets do not have to be posted on Twitter to be effective, but if the instructor is so inclined, the class could create a collective Twitter account and tweet throughout the semester on what they learn. Of course, the instructor would be wise to vet any tweets before posting to ensure as professional of a tone as possible. As we know, audience if everything.

TECHNOLOGY CLASS IDEAS

Each day new technologies emerge, many of which are particularly useful for second language learning. As these new digital tools become available, TCs need the opportunity to become familiar with them. While we do not advocate in favor of any particular app, platform, or software, we do encourage TCs and teacher preparation faculty to explore emerging technologies, Web 2.0 platforms, and free and open source software for innovative ways to improve language acquisition and teaching. Creative use of free resources in the methods classroom can provide a powerful model to complement TCs' previous experiences with technology, both as a student and an instructor.

With particular interest in helping our TCs develop a high-quality portfolio, and more importantly, become highly effective language teachers, we have modified our technology integration course to accommodate edTPA at Georgia State University. To that end, we have TCs learn to create quality videos. We purchased a number of high quality video cameras and show TCs the basics of video recording. We start with walking them through the camera's manual. They learn to check the camera's basic functions and how the camera works. In particular, they learn how to check the battery and audio levels, as well as the amount of memory available on the memory card. They also learn how to frame subjects in the viewfinder and how to attach the camera to a tripod, along with other basic functions.

There are so many details to consider when creating video and providing it for official edTPA scoring. In our programs, we prioritize reviewing the *edTPA World Language Assessment Handbook* fully and discussing at length the requirements for video(s). TCs are taught about camera angles and how to set up a class for video recording where some students' parents/guardians have not given permission to be included in videos. As further steps in their preparation for Task 2's video, Georgia State TCs practice shooting video and transferring it from the memory card to their computers. They learn to make copies of the original videos and the importance of using a copy of the video for editing purposes. We also take the time to show them file management techniques, such as creating separate folders and developing file names that clearly describe what the video is and its purpose. While it may be argued that many of today's TCs are video enthusiasts, there is a great difference between a video shot as entertainment for a Facebook or a Vine posting and one for a high-stakes assessment (i.e., edTPA).

Editing the video clip(s) for length is currently permitted by edTPA and enabling TCs to choose the best clip(s) can enhance their chances for edTPA success. For that reason, we show TCs how to edit video per edTPA guidelines. That is, they practice how to make cuts in full length videos using iMovie and Windows Movie Maker so they can have continuous video clips that do not exceed edTPA's 15-minute rule. Also, TCs are taught how to insert captions in the video, just in case some of the audio is not audible, and how to blur the faces of students whose parents/guardians did not approve of their students appearing in the videos, both of which are permissible via edTPA guidelines in the handbook. We do not take the time to show them how to cut and splice video together because edTPA guidelines do not allow for such edited video. According to the *edTPA World Language Assessment Handbook* (SCALE, 2015a), a video clip must be unedited and continuous without an interruption in events. Additionally, TCs must submit no more than two video clips that do not exceed 15 minutes total in running time.

In addition to learning how to work with video, we strongly recommend that TCs become effective users of the Microsoft Office software such as Excel and PowerPoint. Excel can be used for data analysis pur-poses, and it creates interesting graphics from data. Additionally, we teach our TCs to use PowerPoint as a means to scaffold instruction in interesting ways. However, we kindly suggest that TCs use PowerPoint sparingly because so many teachers, regardless of content area specialty, use Power-Point on a daily basis and, at times, ineffectively. We caution our TCs against including confusing graphics and slides with too much text, prac-tices that can turn a teacher's oral presentation into an unanticipated reading exercise at a distance.

Finally, we prepare our teachers for scenarios when technology is not available or does not work when needed. We cannot remember how many times we have prepared PowerPoint presentations, videos, and interactive web 2.0 tools only to have the technology not perform as planned or we arrive at a location only to find out that technology is not available in the room(s). Thus, we teach our TCs to prepare contingency plans in the case of such unforeseen circumstances. Some contingency plans may involve steps such as downloading a video from YouTube ahead of time, instead of relying on the video stream, or printing out copies of the article from the target language newspaper, instead of relying on the digital version being available. Guaranteeing flawless access to authentic input is never a given, but having a backup plan can assist TCs as they bring content cre-ated by native speakers for native speakers into their classrooms.

MINI-edTPA PORTFOLIO AT A LOCAL COMMUNITY CENTER

To encourage success on the consequential edTPA portfolio, TCs need structured opportunities to practice creating, recording, and analyzing lessons and the learning of real children. During their practica is a fine time to begin preparing TCs for the exigencies of edTPA, as they can begin analyzing their teaching practices and the accompanying student learning in a real world setting. As mentioned in Chapter 2, TCs in our programs build a mini-edTPA portfolio to gain experience with planning, instruction, and assessment. We also find it critical for them to learn how to film, select, and edit video clips of themselves working with students in a field placement. We want our TCs to feel comfortable with all aspects of edTPA before they have to design, build, and turn in their portfolios for external review. A mini-edTPA assignment prompts TCs to create evi-dence-based lessons, explaining decisions made and the K–12 language learners' language proficiency development in written form, using the critical vocabulary and concepts contained in the assessment. Creating a mini-edTPA portfolio during a methods or practicum class also provides

TCs an opportunity to get to know the handbook and accompanying templates before having to pay the $300 fee.

Therefore, at Illinois State University, language TCs complete a semester-long service-learning project in which they spend at least 25 of the practicum class' 50 required clinical hours at Unity Community Center, a local multicultural Out of School Time center that serves 45 K–12 students from lower income families in the Normal community (Unity Community Center, 2015), many from immigrant families who speak Spanish or French at home. While many TCs from a myriad of ISU teacher education programs volunteer at the University of Illinois' Extension Unity Community Center, the center also needs consistent high quality programming and linguistic assistance for communication with parents. More information about the collaboration between ISU's language TCs and Unity can be found in Hildebrandt (2014).

During the first half of the semester, TCs volunteer at Unity to get to know the K–fifth graders that they will be teaching the second half of the semester. The instructor guides the integration to the center with weekly reflections and get-to-know you activities for the youth and TCs, guiding TCs to approach Unity youth through a culturally sustaining pedagogy (Paris, 2012) or asset model, as opposed to the all too frequent deficit model, as discussed in Chapter 4. Also during the first half of the semester, TCs learn about the *World-Readiness Standards* (National Standards Collaborative Board, 2015), lesson planning, classroom management, and second language acquisition, among other topics. TCs also read and discuss chapters from books about service learning (Kaye, 2004) and coteaching (Villa, Thousand, & Nevin, 2013).

World language TCs in Illinois work toward a K–12 teaching license, but few elementary schools have Foreign Language in the Elementary Schools programs in rural central Illinois. Therefore, TCs in the Department of Languages, Literatures, and Cultures have few opportunities to engage younger students in learning a second (or third) language. As part of their practicum, TCs create lessons together as a class, based on the unit and lesson plan templates found in Clementi and Terrill's (2013) *The Keys to Planning for Learning*. As an individual or group assignment, depending on the number of TCs in the class, TCs create possible thematic units using the unit template and focusing on the essential question posed by the unit. Then, during class, each TC writes their essential question on the board and the class considers each one, with the instructor acting as discussion facilitator. Over the course of 15–20 minutes, the class determines what would be the most age-appropriate, meaningful thematic unit for K–fifth graders at Unity Community Center, combining questions and unit ideas, as appropriate. During the fall of 2015, for example, TCs decided on the essential question of "Where in the world are Unity youth?" With one French TC and 12 Spanish TCs, they built a 7-week long unit based on the premise of going to the focus country for a celebration or event, which ranged from Fest Noz in Bretagne, France to a Shakira concert in Colombia. TCs developed a fun and interactive game for the seventh week's review, with each team developing an 8-minute long engaging activity to assess vocabulary retention informally. Table 7.8 shows the week-by-week breakdown for the unit. Using the rule of thumb of five to seven new vocabulary words or chunks per lesson, TCs were able to divide the task of creating materials, with each team responsible for creating materials for one aspect of the lesson (e.g., map, introduction song, weather and clothing visuals).

As part of their preparation for teaching at Unity, TCs in the class must develop all materials and lesson plans before the first lesson at Unity. They agree upon measurable objectives and performance assessments for each week of instruction, creating and building off of one another. The planning task of the mini-edTPA is due the week before the first Unity lesson, although TCs may make modifications after the initial submission based on the lessons taught before theirs. The instruction task is due the

Table 7.8.   Unit Outlines for Fall 2015 Teaching at Unity Community Center

	Oct. 15-French	*Oct 22-Spanish*	*Oct. 29-Spanish*	*Nov. 5-Spanish*	*Nov 12-Spanish*	*Nov. 19-Spanish*	*Dec. 3 Review*
Team							All, stations
Where? Map	Bretagne, France	Argentina	México	España	Puerto Rico	Colombia	
Weather	Il fait beau	Nieva	Hace buen tiempo	Hace buen tiempo	Hace calor	Hace sol y calor	
Clothing 1	un short	abrigo	vestido	camisa	gafas de sol	gafas de sol	
Clothing 2			sombrero	capa	sandalias	traje de baño	
Celebration name	Fest Noz	Navidad	Día de los muertos	El Encierro	El día de los reyes	Concierto de Shakira	
Celebration object	Les biniou (mot celtique)	Fuegos artificiales	máscara	toro	regalo	baile	
Celebration month	L'été	diciembre	noviembre	julio	enero	febrero	

week after they teach and the completed assessment task is due 2 weeks after the lesson is taught.

After the practice portfolios are submitted, the instructor can provide varying levels of feedback, as resources dictate. For example, simply completing the portfolio in a good faith effort may earn the TC all of the points for the assignment, or each task or rubric may contribute a predetermined number of points to the overall grade and be scored based on the handbook rubrics. Once again, we strongly suggest that methods instructors and student teacher supervisors undergo edTPA evaluator training, even if they do not ultimately end up evaluating portfolios in an official capacity. The instructor may comment on each portfolio individually, which proves challenging at the end of the semester. Or they may read all of the portfolios and offer constructive feedback at the class level based on the trends observed across the portfolios. The amount of feedback offered is up to the discretion of the instructor, but we caution readers that providing feedback on the practice portfolios is a time-consuming and challenging task, particularly for large methods classes. Further, without reviewer training, instructors may inadvertently misapply rubrics and mislead TCs as to their preparedness for the consequential portfolio later on. The resources developed jointly by Illinois State University College of Education and Stanford University, mentioned above, also serve as means to assess formatively miniportfolios in the methods or practicum class.

Initially funded by a generous grant from the ISU Office of the Cross Chair in the Scholarship of Teaching and Learning, this language teacher education program at Unity was one of 11 recognized the inaugural year of the ACTFL global engagement initiative (ACTFL, 2015) and has been lauded as a program of distinction by Unity for the last 3 years. The program's success has garnered other local attention when it was featured in the local newspaper and various campus publications.

RESOURCES DEVELOPED AT ILLINOIS STATE UNIVERSITY

Along with Stanford University and its SCALE headquarters, Illinois State University has been a leader in edTPA material development and edTPA implementation at the university, college, and programmatic levels. Among the first universities to do so, ISU hired a full-time edTPA Coordinator to aid TCs, instructors, student teacher supervisors, and program directors, among other stakeholders at ISU and beyond. This level of initial engagement enabled ISU faculty to become engaged in the early steps of the assessment's development.

Content-specific tools developed at ISU include "Thinking Organizers: Tools for Candidates to Organize and Record Their Thinking" for 22 content areas, ranging from agricultural education to world language (Palmer, 2015a). Readers who create an online edTPA Resource Library account, as mentioned in Chapter 2, and refer to the link in our references can access the 22-page Word document that includes "Thinking Organizers and Helpful Hints" for each of the three edTPA tasks. Using the URL in the references of this book will enable readers to download the documents, which were not available by searching the online library for thinking organizers.

In their two-page introduction, the thinking organizers are described as an "avenue through which candidates can record their thoughts, reasoning, and evidence of practice" and "have easy access to that information when they are ready to write their commentaries" (Palmer, 2015a, p. 1). The world language thinking organizer dedicates eight pages to planning, six pages to instruction, and five pages to assessment. Those documents guide TCs through each commentary prompt, using frequent visual organizers and the critical vocabulary of the *edTPA World Language Assessment Handbook* (SCALE, 2015a). These task-specific tools may aid TCs in creating the habits of mind that can bring them success in their edTPA portfolio creation and teaching career. The introduction also states that "instructors can use the tables in formative experiences leading up to the summative edTPA portfolio creation" (Palmer, 2015a, p. 1).

A commentary review sheet for each of the three tasks (Palmer, 2015b) prompts users, whether TCs or instructors, to determine if the commentary has included critical components. For example, one section addresses the central focus, while other asks users to determine if lesson objectives align with each of the three modes of communication. This document also provides a column for users to write comments concerning the given criteria. Toward the end of the six-page Word document for planning (Palmer, 2015b), another table asks users to answer additional questions based on specific edTPA rubrics in a section called "Looking ahead." The instruction commentary review sheet again follows the order and verbiage of each task's commentary prompts, along with a self-check list with yes/no questions concerning video clips and their content and based on the technical and content-specific exigencies of the second task. That document is five pages long. The assessment commentary review sheet (Palmer, 2015c) also numbers five pages, follows the assessment task prompts in order, and ends with three yes/no questions about feedback to students. These documents can be acquired by emailing Elisa Palmer at Illinois State University.

Finally, a content-specific completion checklist in a spreadsheet is available for a variety of uses by world language teacher education programs and TCs. This spreadsheet, containing three columns and 102 rows, is organized by edTPA component (e.g., Context for Learning, lesson plans, and instructional materials), logistical criteria (e.g., font size, document titles, lesson plan length), and whether the criteria was or was not met.

These resources, developed at ISU, certainly provide additional lenses through which to view the edTPA assessment handbook and can offer detailed ways to guide TCs through the labyrinthine journey of submitting the edTPA. Conversely, the sheer number of additional materials, if used all at the same time, could overwhelm candidates. We recommend finding a number of moments along TCs' suggested program of study to introduce the various organizers. We also recommend that readers update their professional digital library with the thinking organizers, commentary review sheets, and completion checklist using the most recent version of the handbook, as subtle content-specific changes can take place from one year to the next.

ACTIVITIES BY edTPA RUBRIC

When we began reframing our curricula with edTPA in mind, we used a backwards design approach, looking at the Task 3 rubrics first and brainstorming ideas for each of its four rubrics. In this section, we discuss briefly a few ideas to help teacher educators prepare TCs to compile an edTPA portfolio. As mentioned earlier, we frame our instruction in two publications: the *edTPA World Language Assessment Handbook* (SCALE, 2015a) and the *Understanding Rubric Level Progressions* (2015b). For each activity, we use these two publications to guide TC learning so that they become very familiar with the portfolio and state licensure requirements.

Task 3

For Rubric 10, Analysis of Student Communicative Proficiency in the Target Language, we remind TCs that the guiding question deals with TCs' ability to analyze student work and identify patterns of learning across the class. In our methods courses, our TCs evaluate deidentified student performance data to find trends in learning on assessments and the accompanying scores, using Excel to create reports. For example, our TCs develop an interpretive task and administer a true/false assessment that assesses students' understanding of the piece (e.g., reading). Then, the student data are input into Excel and the TCs calculate means and standard deviations as well as examine the items' reliability coefficients. Excel is a great software for displaying findings graphically (e.g., bar graphs). Data can be analyzed at a class level as well as at an individual student level, based on the revised Bloom's taxonomy dimensions and knowledge types. Quantitative description can and should be connected to quantitative and qualitative findings documented, as required in the real life portfolio submission.

Another activity that has worked well takes place during the practicum when TCs are in schools observing veteran teachers and teaching shorter activities or 1- to 3-day lessons. TCs select a short reading that is aligned with the unit that the students are currently studying. Then, using the story, they are asked to work with their cooperating teacher and create an assessment based on the story. Afterwards, the TCs must evaluate students' responses in terms of item response theory to see if their questions are reliable and valid as well as determine what students answered correctly and incorrectly. Afterward, we have TCs write a brief summary and peer review it for clarity.

Much like Rubric 10, the guiding question for Rubric 11, Providing Feedback to Guide Student Development of Communicative Proficiency in the Target Language, deals with giving feedback to students to identify what students are doing well and where they need to improve with regard to the learning objectives. We have found that TCs can learn to construct feedback by using data from their practicum. We show them exemplars from former TCs who have completed edTPA. As mentioned earlier, our TCs have given us permission to use their work for training purposes, and the TCs do not receive a copy of the work. Exemplars are shown using projectors and are used for discussion purposes. A second activity that works well using former TCs' portfolios is where TCs examine the feedback given by former TCs in the program and determine how they would have given feedback. We have found that TCs can learn a lot by examining externally reviewed portfolios. We discuss the need for specific qualitative feedback about their performance on the assessment(s) that is developmentally appropriate because teacher certification in Georgia is pre-K to Grade 12 and Illinois is K–12.

A third activity can be where TCs watch peer videos of instruction during their practicum after reading the learning objectives for the lesson. Afterward, they share ideas about missed opportunities for extending student discourse per initiation-response-evaluation versus initiation-response-feedback strategies (see Chapter 5). Instead of focusing on giving an evaluation immediately after a student's response (initiation-response-evaluation), TCs must be taught to extend student discourse and focus on communication instead of delivering constant corrective feedback, which may lead to a decreased sense of efficacy in language learning (i.e., confidence to use the target language). Student motivation may be adversely affected as students become less willing to take linguistic and cultural risks and raise their affective filter. Further examination of video samples can aid TCs in framing feedback in terms of accuracy, student progress focusing on form and function, and building students' proficiency in the target language.

Turning to Rubric 12, Student Use of Feedback, we strive to have our students learn how to deliver corrective feedback in a positive manner that shows how the focus students are to use the specific and not generalized feedback in order to improve their proficiency in the target language. For example, one activity that has shown good results is when TCs are given a couple of minutes to write as many positive phrases as possible in the target language with regard to positive feedback to students. Then, as a small group, TCs can create a list of positive words and phrases that can be used with language learners. Then, the TCs can create a master list from all of the groups so they have a large set of great phrases that can be used orally or on written work to compliment student achievement. In a recent activity carried out in our classes, one group was able to generate a list with more than a dozen positive reinforcement phrases (e.g., ¡Qué bueno! ¡Maravilloso!) that could be used in oral or written feedback, along with personalized comments concerning students' language proficiency and interculturality development.

Then, we teach TCs how their first response when giving corrective feedback should be positive followed by the correction the TC wants to make. Then, a second positive comment can be made in order to show learners that they are trying and that they are improving their accuracy in the target language. For example,

> *Very nice organization of your description. Keep in mind that there are several people to whom you are talking and not just one. Your variety of adjectives was wonderful.*

As shown above, the first and last comments are positive and the specific corrective feedback is nestled between the two. We have enjoyed conducting this activity with TCs because we have noted the lack of breadth of positive phrases that our TCs possess. It is important not to work from a deficit perspective when working with second language learners and the use of positive feedback in conjunction with corrective feedback works well. We have also noted that TCs tend to give rather vague feedback instead of giving feedback that connects language forms and functions.

Another activity that aids this is showing former TCs' feedback to students. We show examples from an outstanding portfolio and then show examples from a portfolio that was scored lower. We have the TCs use the *Understanding Rubric Level Progressions* (SCALE, 2015b) document to determine the differences in feedback as well as scoring. As the reader may discern, the use of externally reviewed portfolios can be a great learning tool with TCs who will have to develop an edTPA dossier.

With respect to the final rubric of Task 3, Using Assessment to Inform Instruction, the guiding question concerns TCs' ability to use conclusions drawn from data analysis, along with relevant SLA research and theory, to advance ideas about the next instructional steps. Again, we strive to keep SLA research at the forefront of our discussions as we get TCs to move consistently and constantly from practice to theory and from theory to practice. Additionally, we use externally reviewed edTPA portfolios as a resource. For example, because we have TC permission to use their port-folios for training purposes, we show our TCs the assessment results from a former TC's learning objectives and results from data analysis. Then, we ask the current TCs what should be the teacher's next step(s) toward improving instruction. Typically, we begin the activity as a paired activity and ask the TCs to work together to develop a few ideas of how they would approach the situation. Then, we move to a class discussion and base the discussion in SLA theory as we look at the learning segments' les-son objectives and determine (1) the next steps for instruction and (2) how to articulate those steps in a narrative format that fits within the guidelines for the commentary.

Task 1

Following our backwards design approach to edTPA, next we present briefly a few ideas to help TCs as they plan for instruction. The guiding question for Rubric 1, Planning for Communicative Proficiency in the Target Language, centers on how TCs' lesson plans in the learning seg-ment build around a central focus, which according to SCALE (2015a) should surpass a simple list of skills and facts. Readers will find a lesson plan template developed by our colleague Dr. Victoria Russell (Valdosta State University) in Appendix A of this book and as a Word document online (http://pbswanson.edublogs.org/edtpa-book/). That template may be helpful as TCs begin to prepare their lesson plans. As noted in her les-son plan, planning and instruction should be aligned with the content standards and learning objectives TCs set out to help learners meet. In our estimation, TCs must focus on integrating the Communicative Lan-guage Teaching approach into planning and instruction. Thus, in our methods courses, and others, we integrate second language acquisition theories into everyday classroom discussions and practices. We dedicate a portion of the methods class to theory through readings from Lightbown and Spada (2013), for example. At Illinois State University, focus is placed on *how* to teach languages during the first half of the semester and the *why* we need to teach in this manner during the second half of the semes-ter.

At Georgia State University, we spend less time discussing unit plans and have increased focus on the learning segment, as defined by SCALE (2015a). We spend time on conceptualizing and writing 3 to 5 days of instruction, as demonstrated through detailed lesson plans, that are logically connected and sequenced, with each lesson building on the previous one. We discuss how to connect form to function, how to integrate the three modes of instruction in the classroom, with special attention to developing activities in the Interpretive and at least one other mode within the learning segment. During class, we discuss what not to plan for, such as the of grammatical rule memorization and/or multiple-page vocabulary without context. We focus on the goal of communication and the central tenets of Communicative Language Teaching, working with our TCs to move away from the Grammar-Translation method of instruction in which many of the TCs were taught and in which they may have thrived, while their classmates struggled. Additionally, we place emphasis on helping TCs realize that many of them learned languages well in ways that others do not. That is, TCs may have participated in an *apprenticeship of observation* (Lortie, 1975) that worked against their particular or favored learning style and countered current SLA theory taught in methods courses.

With respect to Rubric 2, Planning to Support Varied Student Learning Needs, the guiding question focuses on how TCs' lesson plans will support students in relation to their characteristics, which includes the TCs' understanding of their students' learning needs and learning styles. A suggested activity is to have TCs take a learning inventory (e.g., multiple intelligences, learning styles) and practice writing learning objectives using the ABCD model (explained earlier). This activity helps TCs learn to explain their learning objectives in relation to a framework so they can show how they are supporting varied learning needs. Additionally, TCs can analyze the learning objectives in textbooks in a paired activity and determine if those objectives (1) lead to observable second language performance by students and (2) can be explained via a learning model. Many times we have found that TCs do not continue writing learning objectives as observable second language performance and it is worthwhile to show students how to juxtapose their own ideas against theory. The revised Bloom's taxonomy is a great tool to use with preservice teachers as they are learning to create learning objectives for their students.

Next, the methods class(es) can be a very valuable venue in helping TCs learn more about the students they will be teaching. Rubric 3, Using Knowledge of Students to Inform Teaching and Learning, requires TCs to get to know their students, while avoid a deficit mentality toward their students (Lynn, 2014). That is, TCs may view poor academic performance in terms of students' backgrounds and lack of familial support to cite one example. Such thinking can lead to low expectations and TCs not acknowledging student strengths and qualities. Thus, TCs must show that they are using the knowledge about their students when planning for instruction.

An activity that has been helpful is where TCs study the largest employers in the area, the median salary of families, and the report cards of local school districts available online from state departments of education. From this information, TCs begin to understand more about their students, the economic climate in the area, and how students are faring on local and state assessments. It also helps TCs understand the demographics of the students they are going to meet in schools in terms of race, gender, and grade, enrollment by disability, graduation rates, and the total number of schools in the districts. After the TCs gather and share the information, we discuss economic differences between communities. It gives them a better understanding of the socioeconomic background of the students they will be teaching. It also helps TCs move from a deficit perspective to a more asset-based frame of mind.

A second activity asks TCs to think of a high school learner they have met during their practicum. Individually, each TC must list the student's assets and determine what characteristics make the student unique. They are encouraged to list the academic and social strengths of that student, while developing a list of supports that could be offered to the student in order to help him or her acquire the target language. Then, students are paired and each presents his/her ideas. Afterward, the TCs are paired with a new partner and exchange the information again. A master list of ideas is then created as a class.

Turning to the final Task 1 rubric, Planning Assessments to Monitor and Support Students' Development of Communicative Proficiency in the Target Language (Rubric 4), in-class activities can prompt TCs to evaluate former TCs' feedback, and even advance their own ideas for feedback based on deidentified student performance assessments. Rich discussions can follow as TCs determine what theory(ies) guide(s) the assessments. Additionally, TCs can learn a great deal about collecting and analyzing data, as well as what those data show, perhaps for the first time in their teacher education studies.

TCs can also investigate proficiency assessment development by examining learning objectives created by previous TCs. Over the years we have collected a library of textbooks that are used in the schools in our areas. TCs learn to develop meaningful performance objectives and base subsequent performance assessments on those objectives in the methods classroom. We encourage TCs to use integrated performance assessments and take time to show TCs how to create interesting and meaningful assessments and to measure performance with rubrics clearly aligned with stated objectives. We urge our TCs to use a summative performance assessment for their consequential portfolio to highlight active and measurable objectives reflected in as many environments as possible, from beginning general teacher education courses to our methods and practicum courses. We feel it is quite late in a teacher education program to show students how to write objectives and create performance assessments in a methods course. We want our TCs to have multiple opportunities over the course of their studies to learn how to develop this critical skill.

We advise teacher educators to remind TCs to video record the performance assessment, when carried out with students whose parents/guardians have granted permission to video record, and submit that video as part of their edTPA dossier in Task 3. We have recently learned at Georgia State University that even though it is unclear in the handbook, if a TC fails to submit the video recorded performance by students, the external reviewers will not assess this portion of the portfolio. Instead, the TC will receive condition codes requiring them to resubmit part of the portfolio for external review, costing time and money. For example, if a TC does not have the performance assessment video recorded and the entire portfolio is based on that performance assessment, the TC may have to resubmit other work samples for Task 3 or resubmit an entirely new portfolio. Those events may further delay timely program completion, licensure, and employment, and even necessitate a new student teaching placement.

Thus, we strongly urge teacher educators to continually remind TCs of this requirement. We highly recommend that TCs video record all teaching moments of the learning segment so they have a complete video library to use when selecting video segments for their dossiers.

Task 2

The guiding question for Rubric 5, Learning Environment, focuses on the type of learning environment the TC establishes and how the learning environment fosters respectful interactions in the classroom. We recommend that TCs become familiar with the concepts of respect and rapport as defined by edTPA before they compose their commentary and select their videoclip(s) for this task. For example, in a methods class, TCs can create a list of positive characteristics necessary for a respectful and effective second language learning environment, as observed during field placements and other learning opportunities (e.g., Annenberg videos). During this activity, TCs can deconstruct what makes a positive learning environment in terms of the physical and affective. When TCs unpack *fun*, *engaging*, and *comfortable*, among other adjectives that are initially offered as positive characteristics, they begin to understand the multifaceted physical and affective features that encourage (or discourage) learning.

TCs can also supplement the ideas listed based on their own experiences as second language learners or informally poll second language learners about what makes a great learning environment for them. We believe teachers many times fail to ask their own students about what is working for them and what they feel would improve their learning. By helping TCs become aware of the learners and their learning styles, preferences, opinions, and anxieties, TCs can learn more about developing a respectful and successful learning environment. We have included in Appendix B a resource developed by the Project LINC, a federally funded grant to investigate "research-based support for inclusive teaching in a diverse classroom, covering the converging needs of foreign language instructors, students with disabilities, and non-tenure-track faculty" (Project LINC, 2015, Welcome, para. 1). The Foreign Language Autobiography (Hildebrandt & Edwards, n.d.) opens by asking students about their language learning history and their fears about taking the current class. As part of the activity, language learners list the characteristics of a good and bad class and teacher, whether foreign language or not, in two separate tables.

On the second page, students complete the statement "For me, foreign language is like ..." often eliciting meaningful analogies that can serve as a jumping off point for a later class discussion or a personal conference with the student. The autobiography inquires about the student's level of anxiety upon entering the class, their goals for the class and semester, and their passions. The final section lays out instructor hopes for the semester about students' learning and skill development, followed by short reading about taking risks in the classroom, using the analogy of a race car. Finally, students provide any comments prompted by the reading and any additional information that the instructor should know. This tool was created for the college language classroom, but could be easily adapted to better fit other levels. The autobiography can be a helpful resource for beginning language learning students and TCs to reflect on the learning environment, along with the conditions that influence student proficiency development.

In Appendix C the reader will find an activity that can give TCs a chance to simulate classroom management, as part of or independently from a microteaching in front of classmates. "Party Quirks" can take place during a general or content-specific methods class and is modeled off of the sketch of the same name on the sketch show *Whose line is it anyway?* We recommend looking on YouTube for clips of the Party Quirks sketches. On the show, one of the four troupe members is the host of a party to which each of the other three troupe members are invited. The host answers the door to guests who must carry out an assigned role, such as "a chicken with attitude." The host of the party must determine what that secret, assigned role verbally for the guest to stop the behavior.

The Party Quirks activity simulates a high school freshman class in the first quarter of the school year. Each TC in the methods class has a student role that they acquire, either by assignment or choice. The student roles are described on slips of paper cut from the descriptions in Appendix C, along with the necessary behavior that the "teacher" must carry out in order to stop the behavior. We generally prefer to have volunteers for the role of teacher so that we don't overwhelm those TCs who may not be comfortable with that portion of the role play, particularly without a model. The "teacher" teaches the class a basic, impromptu lesson on a topic of their choosing, while the "students" carry out their behavior described on their clip of paper.

The target behaviors that the "teacher" must carry out are described in assigned readings, such as Wong and Wong (2009), and during guided classroom discussion. One sample student role is: "You whisper with your neighbor about the upcoming dance. You are not distracting to the whole class, but your attention is obviously NOT on the lesson." The only "teacher" behavior that will cause the "student" to stop is "proximity— teacher must be within 2 feet of you for at least 10 seconds." The activity gives TCs a chance to put into practice some of the critical teacher behaviors that will help establish an effective learning environment as they become more and more responsible for managing student behavior in their clinical settings.

Rubric 6, Engaging Students' Target Language Communication, and its guiding question require TCs to provide video evidence of having engaged students in communicative proficiency development in meaningful cultural context(s). We remind TCs that their written commentary should provide additional context for the video clip(s), as scorers will have no other evidence beyond that provided for each task. As we have suggested before, using former TCs' video clips in the methods class, with permission of course, can give TCs a better handle on the exigencies of edTPA. The ideal videos for this purpose would be those in which students are engaged in proficiency-based activities, instead of focusing exclusively on form. Choices in video selection should be based on that criteria as well as whether the TC connects students' prior knowledge and experiences to the learning segment's stated objectives. Positive and negative examples can be shown, although highlighting the TCs' assets along with areas of growth should be a natural part of the discussion.

As with all of the rubrics, we remind TCs to consider the guiding question when encountering Rubric 7, Deepening Student Communicative Proficiency in the Target Language. TCs must demonstrate, via the video clip(s), how they elicit and build on students' responses to guide learning during entire class, small group, and individual discussions with students. One fruitful activity we have used asks TCs to collect data about communication patterns in the early field placement observations. TCs can analyze those data to detect patterns, such as who does the majority of the talking in class, how students are introduced to interpersonal activities, whether the teacher relies more heavily on initiation, response, evaluation or initiation, response, feedback in a particular setting, and with whom teachers and students are generally communicating. Those patterns found can then be explored to inform how they influenced student behavior, their communication efforts, and ultimately their learning. As always, we must model our appreciation of the hosts and remind TCs that they are observers, not evaluators, and that it takes courage to open one's classroom to others. After collecting and analyzing the data, TCs can base their in-class discussions on those data instead of on their opinions and perceptions. We have found that such TC observations of in-service teachers enhance TCs' beliefs about language teaching.

As with the previous rubric, TCs can explore Rubric 8, Subject-specific Pedagogy, as part of the methods class through observing in-service teachers and engaging in data-based pedagogical discussion. Providing language-specific examples from a variety of cultures can help TCs identify the three aspects of the Cultures standard. As a Spanish-specific example, TCs can examine what a *tortilla* is as cultural product and the art of tortilla making as cultural practice. They can learn more about the varying types of tortillas in different countries and cultures (e.g., Spain, Mexico, Andes, U.S. tortilla chip).

In addition to analyzing target language cultures, TCs must inform their teaching with the characteristics that learners bring to the classroom. As an introductory methods class activity, TCs can list the multitude of cultures to which they belong. Instructors can use their own self-identified cultures as examples. For example, the first author lists some of her various cultural identities: a Wisconsinite, a Hildebrandt, a university professor, a Spanish speaker, a feminist, a cat-lover, a knitter, a Stephen Colbert fan, a Neil deGrasse Tyson admirer, and an optimist, to name a few. Instructors can also find a variety of visual resources to enhance these activities by Googling *circles of my multicultural self*. By exploring their own cultures and identities, TCs can come to appreciate the multifaceted nature of their students' cultures and connect lessons to those various cultures. As an extension activity, TCs can identify the cultural products and practices and the accompanying perspectives of their self-identified cultures. Finally, they can brainstorm the various cultures to which practicum or internship students belong and develop a list of the products and practices that exist within each of those cultures. TCs can be encouraged then to research the cultural perspectives that inform the listed products and practices and share that information with their classmates. We strongly recommend that the instructor carefully monitor these discussions to ensure that stereotypes do not inadvertently become perpetuated.

If TCs are unsure of what school(s) they will be student teaching in, they can create a profile of the school(s) in which they would like to be placed and research information about that school and its district's learners. We urge our TCs to visit schools in which they would like to be placed for their final field experience, that is, student teaching, as early in their teacher education studies as possible. Further, we are aware of a number of local highly effective language teachers who are committed to proficiency- and standards-based instruction and assessment and with whom we encourage our TCs to work.

Rubric 8's guiding question concerns how TCs connect target language cultures' practices, products, and perspectives to students' academic and personal backgrounds (SCALE, 2015a). TCs become better prepared for student teaching when they are knowledgeable about the school's student population and the individual teacher and students with whom they will work. That foundational work can, in turn, help them develop quality edTPA dossiers. By preparing future teachers in such a proactive manner, we help TCs build a stronger sense of teaching efficacy. Bandura (1997) found that one's sense of efficacy is most malleable during early learning opportunities. Additionally, by working with their language teacher educators and various in-service teachers, our TCs continue to build a strong foundation of self-efficacy that will help them overcome obstacles and impediments to learning (Bandura, 1997), encourage them to experiment with new instructional methods in order to meet the needs of their students (Cousins & Walker, 2000; Guskey, 1988), and increase their commitment to teaching (Coladarci, 1992). All of these outcomes can, we hope, will help reduce the shortage of language teachers the United States is presently experiencing (Swanson, 2008, 2012).

The final Task 2 rubric is Rubric 9, Analyzing Teaching Effectiveness, whose guiding question centers on how effectively TCs examine the teaching and learning in their video clip(s) and make suggestions about what could have been done differently in order to support the needs of the students (SCALE, 2015a). Any proposed changes should relate to the learning segment's central focus. TCs must delineate potential instructional changes for the entire class, based on the video recorded evidence showcased. However, changes can also be proposed for parts of the learning segment that were not included in the video clip(s) referenced in the commentary (SCALE, 2015a).

As previously mentioned, Illinois State University TCs teach beginning language lessons to youth served by a local community center as an ongoing service learning/civic engagement project. During the first half of the semester, TCs learn how to develop world language specific lessons and assessments and collectively develop the outline for a thematic unit. They create lesson plans in groups of two or three, depending on the size of the class, and workshop those lessons with their classmates. During the second half of the semester, TCs coteach lessons to Unity youth. Once TCs get back to campus from Unity each week, they collectively reflect on the teaching and learning that took place that evening, first focusing on what went well and why and then moving on to what didn't go so well and how they can improve the next lesson(s), based on those observations. The instructor will be wise to preface the discussion each week with a reminder to be respectful, to offer constructive criticism that can be used for future growth, and to acknowledge the courage it takes to subject one's teaching to analysis, particularly as a novice teacher. The instructor should further remind the TCs who taught that week that their classmates are offering constructive criticism of their work and that feedback is meant to improve their teaching, not reflect on them as a person. Immediate group reflection provides a model for TCs to depersonalize feedback and to use it instead to improve their teaching practice. Before class the next week, TCs compose a delayed reflection paper individually on what their favorite and least favorite parts of the lesson were and why. Approximately midway through the Unity teaching experience, TCs are asked to explain what they have learned at Unity. At the end of the semester, they are asked again what they learned, along with suggestions to help make the Unity program better.

At Georgia State University, TCs video record themselves teaching lessons and then write a critical reflection on the lesson. Peers are assigned to critique the lesson of a classmate and discuss ways to improve the lesson's delivery following a similar format of what went well, what needed improvement, and ideas for changes to improve the lesson.

CONCLUDING THOUGHTS

This chapter has focused on ideas for readers to use immediately in class with their own TCs or to prepare for their own edTPA portfolio submission. In our methods courses and throughout our programs, we use the *edTPA World Language Assessment Handbook* (SCALE, 2015a) and the *Understanding Rubric Level Progressions for World Language* (SCALE, 2015b) as required texts. In both of our programs, TCs rely heavily on Shrum and Glisan's (2015) book, *Teachers Handbook: Contextualized Language Instruction*. It is the gold standard in K–12 language instruction, and has been a tremendous resource for our TCs over the years. While we integrate other authors' work in our programs, we feel that program faculty must include the edTPA handbook and rubric level progression publication early in teacher preparation programs. By integrating such resources early into teacher education programs, TCs can begin to internalize the required edTPA vocabulary and the various exigencies presented by the portfolio and the 13 rubrics.

As program faculty members develop other activities, we encourage them to share their ideas via scholarly and pedagogical publications, as well as by presenting their ideas at local, regional, and national conferences, which is where we encountered Dr. Russell's lesson plan template. Sharing knowledge is critical, especially now that edTPA has become a consequential measure of beginning teacher effectiveness in so many states.

As we began to pilot test edTPA several years ago, it became clear that we needed to modify our programs in order to help TCs prepare for it as a consequential teacher certification assessment. Over the intervening years, other researchers and teacher educators in the field have begun to voice opinions about edTPA and its implementation. In the following chapter, we further discuss our experiences with edTPA, summarize our ideas presented throughout the book, and provide suggestions for making edTPA a better reflection of world language teacher effectiveness.

CHAPTER 8

CONCLUDING THOUGHTS

During our 2012 American Council on the Teaching of Foreign Languages (ACTFL) Convention breakfast meeting, we discussed collaborative research ideas, ultimately deciding to investigate the then new edTPA for world and classical languages. As classical language programs have so few teacher candidates (TCs), we committed to focusing our research on the world languages edTPA and our own TCs' performance on it, per approval from our institutional review boards. At that time, our two programs were pilot testing the assessment, and TC edTPA performance was not yet consequential for teacher licensure or certification in our states. At the time of this book's writing, passing edTPA score is mandatory for a teaching licensure or certification in our states, along with several others (American Association for Colleges of Teacher Education, AACTE, 2016). As the pilot testing phase concluded, we were glad to have incorporated edTPA into our curricula and fleshed out ideas to restructure our programs. We were fortunate to have tremendously talented and diligent colleagues with whom to work as edTPA was integrated into our teacher education programs.

In the preceding chapters, we described what edTPA is and how program faculty can incorporate the exigencies of edTPA in their programs. Afterward, we discussed the Context for Learning and each of the three edTPA tasks. In the last chapter, we described methods class and early field experience activities we have used and which were created with each of the 13 world language edTPA rubrics in mind. In this chapter, we document some general concerns related to edTPA as raised in the literature, followed by other world language-specific challenges that face TCs,

Understanding the World Language edTPA: Research-Based Policy and Practice
pp. 157–191
Copyright © 2016 by Information Age Publishing

instructors, and program leaders. We cite concerns that the most recent *edTPA World Languages Assessment Handbook* (Stanford Center for Assessment, Learning, and Equity, SCALE, 2015a) has raised in our own minds, and we share thoughts on edTPA collected from world language teacher educators from around the country. In an effort to remain constructive, we advance suggestions for making edTPA a better reflection of world language teacher effectiveness.

As we continue preparing language teachers for K–12 settings, we hope that SCALE will consider our observations and recommendations in order to better align the world language edTPA with the profession's expectations of language teacher preparation programs and TCs. We pose this constructive criticism to improve edTPA, particularly as this externally reviewed and costly assessment becomes more prevalent in additional states and teacher education programs alike. As edTPA scores become consequential in more states, continued feedback and improvement of edTPA becomes even more critical. We close the chapter with the next steps we anticipate taking as edTPA gains a foothold in Illinois, Georgia, and other states.

GENERAL CONCERNS SURROUNDING edTPA

edTPA certainly offers a more robust evaluation of new teacher abilities than some earlier measurements of new teacher knowledge, performance, and effectiveness. As Au (2013) writes, "it is leagues better than any pencil-and-paper test could be" (p. 22). We are compelled, however, to share some edTPA concerns raised in the literature and to add to the ongoing professionwide conversations. We begin our discussion with general edTPA concerns, including the dangers of outsourcing teacher evaluation to for-profit companies, the potential depersonalization of teaching and teacher education, and how edTPA addresses multicultural education. We go on to explore measurement issues, student teaching placement and timeline challenges, and technology concerns. We close this section with a discussion of using edTPA in licensure/certification decisions, along with the problems facing programs and TCs when remediation and retakes are necessary. We later move on to world language-specific concerns.

Deprofessionalizing Teaching and Teacher Education

Relegating new teacher assessment to corporations is of great concern a number of researchers and teacher educators. With edTPA becoming an increasing force in new teacher evaluation, licensure, and certification, these issues of teacher and teacher educator professionalization must be addressed.

The corporate encroachment into education (Madeloni & Gorlewski, 2013) and outsourcing teacher evaluation to corporations like Pearson (Au, 2013; Cochran-Smith, Piazza, & Power, 2013; Dover, Schultz, Smith, & Duggan, 2015; Winerip, 2012) cause anxiety among teacher educators. Madeloni and Gorlewski (2013) contended that edTPA was "designed to answer questions posed by corporate education reformers instead of the questions of teacher educators" (para. 16), while Dover et al. (2015) cautioned against "market-driven educational commercialism" (para. 3). Croft, Robbins, and Stenhouse (2013) describe the "testing industrial complex" (p. 72) that promotes "excessive high-stakes testing; false political narratives about improving education; and transfer of curricular and financial governance from individual to local, local to state, and state to national/private entities" (p. 73), with edTPA used as an example.

A large corporation intruding into teacher education and potentially profiting from TCs worries us and others (Madeloni & Gorlewski, 2013). At a present cost of $300 per dossier submitted for review edTPA adds an additional expense to the already costly endeavor of teacher certification and licensure. TCs in Georgia already pay more than $800 for repeated clinical background checks, standardized state content and pedagogical tests, ethics assessments, and additional fees (Hildebrandt & Swanson, 2014). Those costs have deterred many from entering and staying in the teaching profession in Georgia (Owen, 2015). Further, when candidates are not successful the first time they submit edTPA, they must rewrite, and perhaps refilm, task(s) on which they were unsuccessful the first time and resubmit at an additional cost of $100 per task. Today's cost is $300, but we predict it will rise along with the costs of other TC assessments. This cost, in addition to university tuition and fees, becomes alarming for potential teachers who will enter the teaching profession at approximately $36,000 (Hildebrandt & Swanson, 2014). Further, the specialized and expensive equipment needed to video record lessons can also challenge TCs, teacher education programs, and colleges of education.

This challenge to teacher education extends to copyright issues, with SCALE protective of rubrics and rubric language. TCs, teacher educators who participate in local scoring, and edTPA reviewers are required to sign nondisclosure agreements which outline the limited access to edTPA handbooks and the required confidentiality for videos, TC-developed materials, and K–12 students. Institutions that participate in edTPA may share handbooks and other protected edTPA materials only via secure means.

Institutions of higher education and their TCs bear much responsibility for protecting K–12 students and their privacy, but these agreements may stymie teacher educators' willingness or perceived ability to share resources developed to help TCs engage with edTPA. When in doubt, some state or institutions may decide to take a conservative route and not allow any edTPA materials to be used for TC education or program development. That secrecy and the local decision not to use former TCs' materials in any way, shape, or form, limits the availability of models, as will be seen below. Teacher educators can at times find it difficult to share ideas and thoughts on edTPA, as rubric language is copyrighted by SCALE and many fear legal action if they cross a perceived fuzzy appropriate use line.

One agreement concerning edTPA portfolio use (Illinois State University, n.d.) details limits that teacher educators must respect, particularly regarding the confidentiality necessary when working with TC portfolios. An exception is made for "educational purposes, conducting assessment development, program improvement and professional development with and only in compliance with the release forms obtained" (p. 1) by the TC. Individual universities or states may have their own version of nondisclosure agreements, and we urge readers to locate their local version and work under the auspices described within. With that said, teacher educators may need to educate university officials and state legislators about SCALE's expectations, particularly if their decisions made are more conservative than the general confidentiality and security statement (SCALE, 2015f).

That four-page guide, entitled *Confidentiality and Security of edTPA Candidate Materials and Assessment Data* (SCALE, 2015f), "applies to Pearson and SCALE handling of materials and data for candidates who register for edTPA" (p. 1). It also provides a wider context for program leaders to set edTPA policy and practices, while respecting the privacy of their TCs and K–12 students. Topics include video confidentiality guidelines for candidates and faculty, proper permissions from parents/guardians of K–12 students, technical logistics concerning TC materials developed, and storage of and access to materials and edTPA scores. It also explores *authorized access*, which outlines acceptable means of TC support. In that section, the document states that "Prior to submitting assessment materials for scoring, candidates may request authorized faculty reviewers at their educator preparation program to provide feedback on their edTPA materials (including video recordings) prior to submission" (p. 2). It goes on to caution that "Candidates should follow their campus directions for receiving feedback" (p. 2). Finally, the document states that "edTPA assessment materials, without candidate or other identifying information, may be used for edTPA program development and implementation, including scorer training" (p. 4).

As can be seen, stakeholders at all levels can be overly cautious in their decisions to not use previous edTPA portfolios, commentaries, videos, or scores, partly to avoid "getting in trouble" or experiencing legal ramifications. In the same way that stakeholders can consult the acceptable candidate support document created by SCALE (2014a), they can explore the resources explained in this section to confirm appropriate levels of support for candidates and programs alike. These documents should comfort readers and help alleviate fears of litigious action.

We were equally concerned that our own research not cross lines established by nondisclosure agreements; after extensive conversations with other teacher educators and careful examination of the nondisclosure agreements, we arrived at the conclusion that our work falls within the acceptable use of edTPA materials. Beyond the titles of the rubrics themselves and the central edTPA tenets (e.g., meaningful cultural context, communicative proficiency development, etc.), we have been careful not to give away too much information and to respect the nondisclosure agreements we have both signed. Of course, test security is a legitimate concern, but we encourage stakeholders to take full advantage of the resources that they are entitled to use to support their TCs and prepare their programs for edTPA implementation.

Depersonalizing Teaching and Teacher Education

Counter to the American tradition of local educational control, standardized assessments like edTPA, by their very nature, depersonalize teaching and standardize the teacher preparation processes, thereby diminishing local teacher educator influence and ignoring local expertise (Cochran-Smith et al., 2013; Dover et al., 2015; Schulte, 2012; Tuck & Gorlewski, 2016). Standardizing teacher education may even limit teacher education programs and institutions in preparing precisely the types of teachers needed for particular local environments (Sawchuk, 2013). That decreased local control of teacher preparation and evaluation practices goes against the historical influence of local context. Madeloni and Gorlewski (2013, para. 14) claim that "standardization erases relationships" and that edTPA may "exploit the privacy of students and teacher candidates" (para. 15), with data prioritized over people.

The rise of tutoring services and the *cottage industries* of tutoring and scoring edTPA (para. 3) further add to a culture of "marginalizing local experts" (Dover et al., 2015, para. 2). Madeloni and Gorlewski (2013) have argued that the hiring of scorers on a *piecework basis* and paying $75 per portfolio "reinforces the ranks of casual, temporary, outsourced labor" (para. 17). Moreover, scorers' working conditions may be problematic, with brief training periods, a heavy workload, and low per hour rates of pay (Dover et al., 2015).

Additionally, some have questioned Pearson's power to influence personnel decisions at universities. Madeloni and Gorlewski (2013) cautioned that "voices of dissent have been silenced by intimidation and job loss" (para. 19) after refusing to participate in early efforts to pilot edTPA. They go on to highlight the *culture of coercion* (para. 22) created when nondisclosure agreements are required to train for scoring edTPA portfolios, which they claim "restricts academic voice and freedom" (para. 22).

Years before edTPA was unveiled, highly trained faculty members at colleges and universities throughout the country prepared TCs in the three focus areas of edTPA (i.e., planning, instruction, and assessment). TCs developed portfolios that contained longer sequences of planning (e.g., unit plans), video recorded lessons, and K–12 learners' work samples with assessments and feedback on those assessments. In fact, our programs' portfolios resembled edTPA to a large extent, as they were based on the Teacher Work Sample (Renaissance Partnership for Improving Teacher Quality, 2002). TCs learned to differentiate instruction and even had to prepare materials for job interviews as part of the portfolios (e.g., resumes, philosophy of teaching statements). While they were a student teacher or intern, we could offer suggestions on lesson plans, unit plans, assessments, et cetera. If a TC was having difficulties with planning, for example, we could intervene and help before the TC taught the lesson. We could work within Vygotsky's (1978) zone of proximal development. We could do that as part of our work preparing TCs and without charging each one $300.

Encountering Multicultural Education

An extension of edTPA's impersonalization extends to issues of multicultural and social justice teacher education (Au, 2103, 2015), with Tuck and Gorlewski (2016) contending that "edTPA presumes that the 'problems' associated with educating Black and Brown learners can be addressed by raising the standards for their future teachers" (p. 205). They further raise the concern that edTPA results will be influenced by variables beyond teaching effectiveness, including native language, racial identity, socioeconomic status, and resources available.

Another problematic feature of many standardized tests, including edTPA, is their inattention to diversity both in piloting and implementation phases. Some have raised the concern that TCs who participated in the initial field tests are predominantly White and native speakers of English, thereby representing a low level of diversity (Dover et al., 2015). In the United States there is already a critical lack of teachers of color and from lower socioeconomic class backgrounds, and some fear that edTPA may limit those teachers' opportunities as other standardized assessments have done in the past (Au, 2013). New York state, as a relatively early edTPA adopter, has witnessed much discussion surrounding its implementation and attention to diversity. Tuck and Gorlewski (2016) examine the consequences of edTPA policy that ignores race and racism in the state of New York, contending that "settler colonialism and anti-Blackness are interwoven into this tool of education policy," meaning edTPA (p. 198). Lynn (2014), conversely, asserts that edTPA may be able to contribute to more equitable and improved educational outcomes for all students, particularly for minority males who have been historically underserved. the AACTE Resource Library distributes his two-page statement as one of The "edTPA handouts to share with stakeholders" (AACTE, 2015).

Further, TCs may be limited in what lessons they present, deeming "safer" topics as more in line with what they think will help them succeed on the assessment. For example, in a social justice oriented teacher education program, Au (2013) found that TCs did not address power and equality in their edTPA portfolios, choosing instead to sterilize their teaching to fit the exigencies of the assessment. The National Association of Multicultural Education (2014) reinforces the contention that edTPA does not effectively encourage TCs to engage in critical multicultural education, stating that the organization

> rejects any incursion of outsourced, private, corporate interests into this sensitive and critical human work [of teaching], deeming it contradictory to our commitment to critical multicultural public schools that are responsive to the voices of the communities they serve, and seek to develop a socially and economically just world. (p. 1)

Sato's (2014) of edTPA's underlying conception of teaching posits that edTPA does not fall into the transformative epistemology of teaching, whose "outcome … is to shape and reshape the person in ways that leave both teacher and student in a different state of being as a result of the instructional relationship" (p. 4). Instead, she explains, its focus on disciplinary learning limits its representation of teaching.

The concerns outlined in this section highlight how edTPA may not address the American educational system's underlying inequities faced by teachers and learners at all levels. They also highlight the need for educational policy and teacher evaluation tools to empower teachers and learners as they address societal challenges by constructive means, including multicultural education.

Measurement Issues

A number of issues present themselves when examining edTPA through an educational measurement lens. Certification and licensure tests, like edTPA, assume that effective teaching outcomes are unchanging, agreed upon by everyone, and able to be seen and measured (Tuck & Gorlewski, 2016, p. 205), which prompts a number of measurement challenges.

While many tout edTPA as a valid and reliable assessment of teacher candidate performance, doubt exists about the correlation between teacher candidates' edTPA scores and student achievement (Lewis & Young, 2013). Questions of how edTPA scores compare to scores on other measurements of teaching also arise (Lewis & Young, 2013), and as of yet edTPA's concurrent validity is uninvestigated. At present 38 states and the District of Columbia are using edTPA in various ways, yet little is known about how it compares to existing measures. Additionally, there is a shortage of research to show that edTPA provides new and improved information regarding novice teacher effectiveness. The stated 58% to 78% pass rate (Dover et al., 2015), depending on cut score, is considered "relatively low" (para. 5).

Given that edTPA is such a new assessment, comparative data are scant, consequential validity is unknown, and sufficient data were lacking before widespread implementation (Dover et al., 2015). It is impossible to know what the washback will be of having edTPA as a primary source of information across so many states and contexts. Further, as a summative assessment, edTPA does not offer opportunities for feedback or coaching (Dover et al., 2015). And pressed timelines force TCs to submit materials from their first weeks of the clinical experience when they are not as familiar with the educational environment and their teaching skills are not as honed (Dover et al., 2015), as will be seen in subsequent sections of this chapter.

Additionally, there may be challenges to edTPA's content validity, as demonstrated by the misalignment of what edTPA measures and what teacher education emphasizes, a case we will explore in the world languages edTPA section. As a standardized measure of new teacher readiness and effectiveness, edTPA represents a "single, high-stakes snapshot" (Dover et al., 2015; para. 4) that "is neither educator preparation nor a comprehensive assessment of candidates' readiness for the classroom" (para. 12). Some point to the potential narrowing of teaching events chosen to offer up for evaluation, with TCs choosing to teach lessons that fit the edTPA design (Dover et al., 2015; Sato, 2014). The influences of the student teaching placement, cooperating teacher, and the socioeconomic status of students in the placement further complicate whether TCs are able to demonstrate the rather advanced teaching skills demanded by edTPA (Dover et al., 2015).

Construct validity is whether an assessment is "actually measuring the content that it purports to measure" (Sato, 2014, p. 12), and edTPA's construct validity evidence is limited at this time. As noted above, little information exists as to how edTPA compares to other beginning teacher assessments. Further, when completing edTPA, TCs must engage in a type of technical writing that they rarely encounter in their undergraduate studies. Concerning National Board certification portfolios, Bond (1998) finds that these types of writing-heavy assessments "rely heavily upon examinees' ability to write about what they know and how they teach" (p. 248). That reliance on technical writing abilities may punish those with less linear and skilled writing, which are critical to fully explaining the TC's thought processes fully while planning, teaching, and assessing student learning.

A threat to the consequential validity of edTPA also makes some users uncomfortable. That is, limiting how the scores are used beyond their initial purpose can be challenging. Au (2013) points to the prospect that value-added measurements, linking edTPA and K–12 student standardized test scores, could become part of teacher education program evaluation, despite the fact that edTPA was not created for that purpose. With the pressures that teacher education programs already face from states, this prospect is deeply troubling to program viability, funding, and needs. These concerns influence the assessment's validity and demand increased attention from SCALE and caution from state legislators.

Student Teaching Placement Challenges

edTPA prompts a number of student teacher placement challenges. First, qualified and effective cooperating teachers may be difficult to find under the best of circumstances. In more instances that we care to mention, principals have offered up inservice teachers as cooperating teachers because those teachers need to update their teaching practices and, the principals believe, the TC will provide the necessary positive model. While many K–12 teachers use current world language pedagogical best practices and second language acquisition theories to inform their teaching, others follow a behaviorist "drill-and-kill" path or another outdated approach. A TC whose cooperating teacher implements up-to-date practices that positively impact student learning will have an advantage over a TC who, for example, does not teach using the target language or relies exclusively on worksheets to *teach* a language. We imagine each content area will recognize these challenges in their own student teaching placements, along with a myriad of other issues.

Despite the need for the best teachers to be cooperating teachers, who can blame them for not wanting to host a student teacher? Au (2013) explains that some "cooperating teachers are resisting taking student teachers specifically because the edTPA feels too intrusive and is driving the student teaching experience" (p. 24). Evaluation of in-service teachers' effectiveness, via performance reviews and student outcome measurements, may be adversely affected by having a novice teacher teaching their students. According to Amrein-Beardsley, Collins, Polasky, and Sloat (2013), a number of states already use value-added measures, which are "methods to capture the value a teacher adds to student learning from one year to the next (i.e., a teacher's value-added)" (p. 3), used to inform teacher evaluations. With *Race to the Top* funding, the federal government encouraged states to use these methods as part of their accountability measures, using large-scale standardized exams as groups of students progress from one grade level to the next in order to determine the individual teacher's impact on student learning, "as compared to teachers with 'similar' students" (Amrein-Beardsley et al., 2013, p. 3). Such measures impact teacher evaluation practices and outcomes, as well as pay scales, and potentially pit teacher against teacher. Even in world languages, an untested content area under federal educational policy, these practices can have impressive influences on teacher evaluation, personnel decisions, and pay.

Video recording teaching, as part of edTPA's second task, can prove challenging beyond the technical issues raised below. Even as states adopt edTPA and its accompanying video recording requirements for licensure or certification decisions, districts may have policies that prohibit that very act. For example, the Illinois State Board of Education released a letter to school partners detailing its commitment to edTPA and mentioning its "video recorded instruction component" (ISBE, 2013, p. 1). The letter's author goes on to ask districts to review their "policies for the use of video in [their] classrooms to determine whether current district procedures for obtaining parental permission are adequate" (p. 1). Further, it suggests that districts and schools assist in the edTPA process "by working with candidates to secure parental permission" (p. 1). We applaud the board of education's communication requesting that school districts allow their students to be video recorded, but at present there is not a requirement for districts to permit video recording. The video recording necessity can, therefore, limit even more the number and quality of potential student placements. Further, obtaining parental permission to video record adds an additional level of complexity to the student teaching experience.

Timeline for edTPA Completion

The time necessary to complete the edTPA portfolio can further complicate TC student teaching placements and TC performance. The length of the student teacher's placement in the school can greatly influence the familiarity that the TC can gain about the educational setting and students. TCs' edTPA performance may be impacted by some states' mandates that TCs student teach at each academic level for which they seek licensure or certification. Those mandates generally result in placements that last less than one semester and they have less in-depth knowledge of student teaching placements, curriculum, and students. Thus, if a state designates licensure in world languages as K–12, a TC could be placed for equal time in each of the three settings: elementary, middle school, and high school, challenging placement officers and language education programs. If the state's certification is for Grades 7–12, the TC may be required to spend half of the time in the middle school and the other half in a high school setting. Such requirements make compiling an edTPA dossier even more burdensome because of the time needed to complete it and the in-depth knowledge of students and setting required. In Georgia, certification is pre-K–12 but the TCs at Georgia State University spend their entire student teaching experience in the same school at the same level. And, these individuals work diligently for the first 9 weeks or so to complete the edTPA portfolio, upload their evidence, and await their scores. If they had to complete the portfolio in half the time, the results may not meet the state's expectations for licensure.

As we discuss with our TCs, they should consider beginning their edTPA work when the K–12 classes begin and not when their institution of higher education classes start. For example, classes in the fall at Georgia State University usually commence the third week of August. However, K–12 classes begin in late July or early August. With the timeline to complete the portfolio, TCs are encouraged to begin working in schools as student teachers when school begins, giving them an extra 3 weeks to prepare their portfolios. In fact, TCs in Georgia must have a "first days of school experience," so all TCs in field placements must report for preplanning and attend the first 3 days of school in their placement schools. During pilot testing, we found that our TCs needed to complete the dossier in about 8 weeks to have results before graduation. If revisions to any of the tasks are required, TCs need time to revise their work and resubmit it for evaluation, at an additional cost, before the semester ends. TCs must pass all three tasks of edTPA in order to be eligible for licensure in most states.

While TCs in both of our programs have passed edTPA successfully in almost every case, there have been a few instances in which a TC received condition codes on the assessment task and had to resubmit work. Thankfully, these individuals had filmed every teaching moment within their 3- to 5-day learning segment, as recommended, and only needed to revise the commentary and upload a video showing students taking the final performance assessment. Nevertheless, serious issues now arise with respect to the timeline needed to complete the portfolio. First, much like other TCs throughout the US, the majority of students in the foreign language teacher education program at Georgia State University have part-time or full-time jobs along with student loans. In fact, more than half of the university's students (59%) are Pell Grant recipients (Georgia State University, 2015, p. 3). Student teachers in this program typically quit their jobs when college classes begin and donate their time at schools for 14 weeks. However, with our encouragement to have an additional 3 weeks to develop a passing portfolio, they now must quit their jobs several weeks earlier than usual and incur even more debt in order to begin when the K–12 schools begin in the fall.

Although one might argue that the university should request longer placements for all student teachers, Atlanta school districts are not willing to consider such requests. Longer placements would afford TCs the maximum amount of time necessary to create a portfolio worthy of a passing score, but logistics can stand in the way. These timing challenges become even more daunting for those TCs who plan to student teach in the spring semester. If they do not have passing scores on the three tasks by the time the school year ends, they may have to request a new placement and complete a new student teaching experience the next academic year. These supplemental placements adversely impact TCs' timeline to graduation and further tax placement officers.

Since modifying the Georgia State University World Language Teacher Education curriculum, TCs complete a mini-edTPA portfolio during the practicum semester before student teaching as part of their overall course grade. The mini-edTPA dossier, evaluated internally, gives the instructor an idea of where the TC is at in terms of meeting edTPA's exigencies. If a TC's portfolio is determined to be below the standard needed to pass edTPA, we feel that these individuals are not ready to tackle the real edTPA and encourage them not to risk the $300. Thus, in order to help develop a highly effective language teacher who will be vocationally satisfied and more likely to remain in the profession, we strongly recommend that these TCs devote another semester to a second practicum placement in order to develop their teaching practices, honing the skills necessary to elicit a passing edTPA score. Such occurrences have been shown to add time to graduation, but TCs' scores on edTPA are among the best we have seen.

Noting that some TCs may not be ready for edTPA, we strongly recommend that programs have a remediation plan in place for TCs to work closely with program faculty members. For example, if a TC started in the fall semester (i.e., August-December) and did not receive a passing edTPA score, we would encourage the TC to remain in the school with the same focal class to keep working on passing edTPA. If a program is unable to assign an Incomplete grade until the TC finally passes edTPA, the TC will most likely have to pay additional tuition and fees, while unable to earn money during that time. If the TC can be given an Incomplete grade, then the TC is not considered part of any class, meaning that he or she will not figure into a faculty member's teaching load. So, while the TC is spared spending additional tuition money, the faculty member is left to work with the TC in addition to his or her regular workload. We fear that some TCs will become unable to cope with the uncertainty of certification and will drop out of our programs, after spending years seeking certification. This outcome would exacerbate the already significant shortage of language teachers in most states. At Georgia State University, TCs who cannot pass edTPA can still graduate with a degree in the language (e.g., BA in Spanish). These individuals could be hired on provisional certification by school districts and complete edTPA later while working. However, at Illinois State University, TCs must pass edTPA to earn a teacher education degree.

Finally, it is worth noting that teacher strikes can affect the timeline as well. For example, at the time of this writing, two Illinois school districts' teachers have expressed that they may strike in the spring of 2016. These work stoppages, while within teachers' rights, can adversely affect TCs' edTPA timeline. Further, otherwise mundane occurrences in schools or districts can also affect the timeline. For example, if three consecutive snow days occur during the time when TCs are supposed to be teaching their edTPA learning segment, those TCs will need to complete additional work to ensure that their teaching reflects the lessons planned and the video recording scheduled or rework the lessons and assessments altogether.

Retake and Remediation Policies

When preparing for edTPA, programs must address the possibility of retake and remediation policies for TCs who do not pass the assessment the first time. The possibility of not passing edTPA should prompt TCs to video record each time they teach a lesson to the focus class. Additionally, TCs should collect more than one set of student evidence for the assessment task. At present, there is a charge of $100 for each task that must be resubmitted for evaluation. At Illinois State University, the edTPA retake policy had to be worked through university curriculum committees and integrated into Gateway 3, the final component of teacher education programs. edTPA's high stakes implementation sparked early curricular changes to make it easier for TCs who do not receive a passing edTPA score to move to the nonteacher education Spanish, French, or German degree programs and remain on time for graduation. Such curricular maneuvering was critical in the spring of 2015 as education programs across campus were encouraged to align more closely their teacher education and nonteacher education majors. Thus, we recommend aligning language teacher education program requirements with those of target language majors, so that TCs can join or exit the programs as needed with the least amount of disruption to their graduation timelines.

Additionally, teacher education faculty should design a remediation plan in advance for student teachers and interns who do not pass edTPA the first time. At Georgia State University, we are looking at adding a one-credit class to the offerings for TCs, which may save them money and provide the necessary assistance for revising their portfolios. Moreover, it will then count as part of the teaching load of the faculty member in charge of student teachers and interns. At present, the faculty member must work with these individuals without compensation and without the mentoring counting toward the teaching load, which is problematic.

Technical Issues

Finally, submitting edTPA portfolios to Pearson systems can provoke technical issues at an already stressful time. Even with explicit directions for uploading the portfolio for external review via LiveText, it can take several hours to get the portfolio uploaded correctly. As TCs quickly learn, a substantial number of artifacts must be titled correctly and uploaded. Further, the videos must be a certain size and format, as previously discussed. Precarious Internet connections can further complicate matters and increase everyone's stress level. In one instance in 2015, it took more than 5 hours for TCs to receive permission from Pearson and upload their portfolios via Wi-Fi. Therefore, we strongly recommend uploading portfolios on computers that are connected to the Internet via an ethernet connection. Additionally, we recommend that TCs work in pairs before uploading their portfolios to check each other's file names, file sizes, et cetera. In our experience frustration can be decreased by having checked the portfolio prior to upload. Also, we recommend that TCs meet with program faculty to upload edTPA portfolios as a group, receive in-person guidance from a program faculty member, and celebrate their achievement afterwards. Over the years, Illinois State University faculty have developed an edTPA approved video formatting guide and another for submission in LiveText (Palmer, 2015c). It is recommended that programs develop such lists for their TCs.

Implementation and Use
in Licensure and Certification Decisions

Earlier we discussed edTPA's impact on program completion timelines and its economic implications for TCs who work as they study. In addition to extending time to program completion, employment can also be delayed. In Georgia, for example, school districts are reluctant to hire uncertified teachers on provisional certification due to state and federal requirements. Already in the state there is a language teacher shortage and school district personnel continually reach out to program faculty when teachers are needed throughout the year.

edTPA is a high-stakes assessment that many TCs in our program find intimidating when they hear about it. When our colleges made the decision to pilot test it, many faculty members expressed concerns about future enrollments in teacher preparation programs, and in our programs we have seen steep declines in TC enrollments. However, we cannot conclude that there is any one reason to explain why TCs have left our programs. We have conducted informal research and find various factors, one of which is the increased cost of becoming a teacher. We have also found that a number of our TCs are leaving our programs in favor of alternate routes to teacher certification, where educational rigor is of concern (e.g., unaccredited programs, ill-prepared faculty teaching classes). Nevertheless, in a recent publication, Owen (2015) reported survey results in which teachers in all content areas ($N = 53,066$) in Georgia listed the number of and emphasis on obligatory tests as the number one reason for teacher attrition in the state.

These general concerns are indicative of the intricate policy and economic contexts in which edTPA requirements are situated. These issues undoubtedly influence edTPA implementation practices across content areas. The following section elucidates world language edTPA issues that merit discussion.

WORLD LANGUAGE-SPECIFIC CONCERNS

When first unveiled, edTPA was touted as a content-specific assessment that uses "shared rubric constructs that define effective teaching" (SCALE, 2015e, p. 22). That is, several edTPA rubrics are common across content areas. Relying so heavily on shared rubrics and constructs to measure effective teaching across such diverse teaching domains diminishes the assessment's content specificity. These commonalities cause us to question how edTPA aligns with the language teaching community's and teacher education programs' expectations for beginning language teachers. We caution that some edTPA expectations are not well aligned with the current state of language teacher education and its best practices. We challenge SCALE to explore the world language-specific concerns and make edTPA more congruent with language teacher education program practices and priorities.

Target Language Usage

Content handbooks and a variety of other resources developed by SCALE point to edTPA's emphasis on student learning, which we also believe to be a critical aspect of teacher preparation and evaluation practices. SCALE stresses that the primary concern is student communicative proficiency development (SCALE, 2015a), but student learning in language classrooms is predicated upon appropriate target language input, both verbal and written, created by language teachers (Elder, 2001) or demonstrated by authentic target language culture resources (Hall, 1999). Therefore, language teacher education programs generally prepare TCs to use the target language at least 90% of a given class period—a standard that TCs may not have experienced from their own K–12 language teachers. This practice was highlighted by ACTFL (2010) in its statement entitled "Use of the target language in the classroom." edTPA examines student target language communication exclusively, while taking teacher target language use less into consideration for scoring portfolios.

Tailoring input to the appropriate linguistic level of the student audience becomes one of the most challenging and important of novice language teachers' developing pedagogical practices. Teacher-created target language input can be maximized when the teacher speaks and writes the target language at understandable yet challenging levels, thereby fostering student communicative proficiency without overshooting students' ability to negotiate meaning (Krashen, 1985). Despite this emphasis in world language teacher education programs, the profession still has a long way to go before using the target language in the language classroom is a given. However, effectively preparing TCs to use appropriate levels of input for students can cultivate classrooms in which target language use is the expectation for the teacher and learners alike. We fear that edTPA's diminished attention to teacher target language use may reinforce the already troubling lack of teacher target language use in the United States context (Ceo-DiFrancesco, 2013).

As we began to analyze TC performance during our universities' edTPA pilot testing, we noticed that some TCs were teaching predominantly in English, as demonstrated in their instructional video recordings. Some of those TCs' instructional performances were deemed worthy of 3s or above on the world language rubrics, despite not using the target language as the primary vehicle for instruction. In one case, a TC made statements in Spanish and immediately translated each statement into English throughout her instructional video; that TC secured higher scores than we had expected on each instructional rubric, particularly given the lack of target language use. As we compared scores on those five rubrics from one TC to another, we noticed that some TCs who used very little target language during instruction scored rather well on the rubrics. In some instances, they received higher externally reviewed scores than those TCs who taught exclusively in the target language.

An examination of the externally reviewed scores revealed that TC target language use is not explicitly reflected in the rubrics and, therefore, may not be considered by reviewers. Unfortunately, target language input from the TC is not part of the criteria in any of the rubrics or in either the lesson plans or video recorded teaching segment. edTPA requires reviewers to focus on the TCs' documentation of student learning rather than evaluating teacher behavior. TCs who taught in the target language were treated the same as those whose videos showed them hardly using the target language with the students, despite the time and effort dedicated in language teacher education programs to finely tune TCs' comprehensible input (Krashen, 1985). While the rubrics do not stipulate that TCs must use the target language during instruction, second language acquisition theorists and professional organizations, like ACTFL, strongly advocate in favor of language teachers using the target language during instruction. The language teaching profession, in general, advocates teaching in the target language, providing students with as much target language input as possible, particularly through their own speech and authentic materials created by native speakers for native speakers.

In 2015, we presented a workshop at the ACTFL convention and the participants were a bit taken aback when comparing student teacher target language use in a couple of sample videos that former student teachers graciously allowed us to share. The same was true for the two of us. One TC used only French when communicating with students, but earned 2s and 3s on the Instruction task rubrics. The other TC used Spanish approximately 25% of the time, translating almost everything that she said into English or asking students "¿Qué significa?" The second candidate received 3s and 4s on those same rubrics. We did not examine the narrative each candidate wrote, but the performances we saw seemed very much out of sync with what we are teaching teacher candidates to do and what the profession advises. We feel that target language use by the TC would be a good addition to Rubric 8.

Teacher language use provides students with comprehensible input, complemented by authentic materials. It also provides students with real world modeling in the form of someone that they know using the language on a daily basis. In the *World Language edTPA Assessment Handbook* (SCALE, 2015a), there is no assessment of teacher target language usage. We caution that such lack of agreement between language teacher education program emphases and edTPA evaluative foci calls into question edTPA's content specificity. We believe that explorations of any potential disunity present in other content areas would be worthy of investigation.

Meaningful Cultural Context

Additionally, some express concern about the definition of *meaningful cultural context(s)*. Kramsch (1993) advanced the notion that culture in language learning is not an expendable fifth skill, attached to the teaching of speaking, listening, reading, and writing. She contended that culture is in the background from the first day of instruction, ready to unsettle the good language learners when they expect it least, challenging their ability to make sense of the world around them. Thanasoulas (2001) added that language teaching is culture teaching and someone involved in teaching language is also involved in teaching culture simultaneously. Thus, stipulating that the learning segment must include meaningful cultural contexts may strike some as superfluous.

A laudable feature of edTPA across content areas is its attention to student characteristics, knowledge, and assets. That emphasis on students as unique individuals in diverse home and community cultures is refreshing. However, we are troubled by the relative deemphasis on *target language* cultures. Although the products, practices, and perspectives of the two cultures standard (National Standards Collaborative Board, 2015) are only highlighted in world language edTPA prompts and rubrics once each in the instructional task, we believe that the recent publication of the *World-Readiness Standards for Learning Languages* (National Standards Collaborative Board, 2015) offers a unique opportunity for the world languages edTPA handbook to make improvements. We hope that the information above will help inform those changes to better reflect what we know students need from TCs so they can learn how to use world languages and respect other cultures.

Concerning TC target language use and the construct of meaningful cultural context, we are optimistic that edTPA expectations for TC performance will align more closely with language teacher education expectations in upcoming handbooks. In mid-February of this year, several SCALE personnel participated in an hour-long conference call with six language teacher educators from across the country. This call, facilitated by ACTFL, provided an excellent opportunity for both groups to negotiate next steps that can maintain edTPA's spirit of student learning while reinforcing language teacher education emphases.

Lack of Models to Support Program Faculty and TCs

Another aspect many have noted as a concern is the lack of world language-specific models. Backwards curricular design suggests that educators must start with the end in mind. Thus, models and exemplars would be helpful in making edTPA exigencies more transparent to program faculty. As we began pilot testing edTPA, we did not have any exemplars in world languages or classical languages. We were not sure what a proficient portfolio contained or what a portfolio that needed revision did not contain. We attended non-content-specific edTPA workshops directed by SCALE personnel, with general examples that did not apply to world or classical languages. When we would ask questions specific to language TC evaluation, the trainers could not answer them. While SCALE training may be different and more focused today on specific content areas, the fact remains that there is a dearth of models and exemplars for world and classical languages. Colleagues in states now pilot testing edTPA are reaching out to us and other colleagues requesting model portfolios and exemplars, which we cannot lend because of confidentiality clauses. We strongly recommend that SCALE share model world and classical language portfolios, along with their official scores, so that language teacher education faculty can view and deconstruct the scoring rationale. It would be helpful if the external reviewers' notes were made available as well to guide faculty members as this high-stakes assessment becomes consequential in more states.

World Languages edTPA External Reviewers

Further, the credentials of external reviewers and the "opaque rating process" (Meuwissen & Choppin, 2015) make some uneasy. During conversations with other language teacher preparation faculty, it is unclear many how potential external reviewers are evaluated and then chosen as reviewers. SCALE (n.d.-b) state that "50% of scorers hired are faculty/supervisors and 50 percent are teacher leaders" (p. 1); however, evidence is lacking as to reviewers' qualifications. During informal conversations with two external reviewers, they both noted that they were not required or asked to present a demonstration of their planning, instructional, or assessment abilities. They were not asked about their planning for instruction regimen, their ability to teach in the target language 90% of the time at all levels, or their knowledge of assessment in general or integrated performance assessments in particular. Neither of them had ever had a student teacher during the course of their careers as public school teachers; nor had they ever mentored a practicum student. However, both are members of ACTFL, are employed in the field, and are certified to teach languages.

To be precise, we are concerned that ineffective language teachers may be serving as external reviewers. By ineffective, we mean, for example, that those teachers may:

1. teach about languages in English (e.g., grammar-translation method) instead of teaching students to acquire a second language;
2. focus instruction on grammar and vocabulary instead of proficiency;
3. fail to plan for instruction on a daily basis;
4. frame instruction on a textbook instead of developing learning objectives based on backwards design and bringing students to higher levels of learning;
5. use antiquated assessment practices (e.g., multiple choice grammar and vocabulary tests);
6. employ a *drill and kill* approach to instruction rather than implementing activities that build student proficiency in the new language.

These out-of-date techniques call into question some inservice teachers' ability to evaluate TC planning, instructional, and assessment practices, despite the intentions and verbiage of the edTPA rubrics.

We have been approached by language teachers with whom we do not place our student teachers and asked about becoming an external edTPA reviewer. When asked about their motivation to help the next generation of language teachers, a common response is that they can make a little extra spending money. While teacher salaries are low and definitely need to be increased across the nation, we feel that there must be a rigorous system in place to vet external reviewers. They should be exemplary teachers who embody and use the best practices in second language acquisition, as described in recent research. We do not feel another teacher exam is needed, but great care must be taken when employing reviewers. Teachers who do not teach in the target language and do not employ a proficiency-based model of planning, instruction, and assessment should not be allowed to serve as a reviewer, especially for this high-stakes, costly assessment. Teachers who do not use practices in their own classrooms should not be evaluating the next generation of language teachers, who are now accountable to the higher standards.

At present, qualifications for current or retired classroom teachers include having at least a bachelor's degree, extensive professional development, and classroom teaching experience among other criteria (Pearson, 2014). Pearson, on the website of edTPA reviewer qualifications, states that it is highly preferred if applicants have familiarity with performance-based assessments. However, we wonder how *extensive professional development* is defined. Often language teachers who hold only a bachelor's degree and have attended only general professional development events, instead of world language-specific events, still have difficulty recognizing and demonstrating best practices in language teaching. School district budgets in our two states have been drastically reduced over the years and much of the professional development offered explores pedagogical practices that are not specific to world languages. Additionally, even if the professional development is content-specific, it is presented by district personnel who may not have a high degree of that specific content knowledge. We have witnessed a number of professional development opportunities presented by a department chair or older veteran teacher who does not follow best practices in their own classroom. Several events that we have seen were led by teachers certified well before 2000, who are close to retirement, and who have limited knowledge about recent second language acquisition research. Via casual conversations, we learned that these individuals generally teach language via the four skills of reading, writing, listening, and speaking, despite the standards initial release nearly 2 decades ago (National Standards in Foreign Language Education Project, 1999). Both that early document and the most recent edition (2015) reinforce a communicative framework of three modes of communication, which are central to world language edTPA. In several cases, the individuals providing professional development were not even members of state, regional, or national language teacher associations.

Research on world language teachers in the United States and Canada shows that about half of the language teachers hold a master's degree (Swanson, 2012). The percentage is roughly the same for world language teachers in Georgia (Swanson & Huff, 2010) and for American teachers in general, with slightly more than half (50.1%) having at least a master's degree (Coopersmith, 2009). Thus, the probability of having a reviewer with only a bachelor's degree is approximately one in two. School district leaders value faculty members with advanced degrees, and research on teaching makes it clear that having a graduate degree in the field leads to better educational outcomes for learners (Swanson, 2012). Thus, we suggest that stricter and content-specific criteria be developed for edTPA external reviewer selection.

Moreover, including retired teachers in reviewer pools is problematic. For example, a person who retired in May 2015, after 30 years teaching in high schools, would have been prepared to teach in the mid-1980s, when the grammar-translation method was popular. The national standards for language learning were not developed and second language acquisition theory and research were just beginning to make strides. Assessment at that time was limited to mainly so-called "objective" measures (e.g., multiple choice) and few were evaluating communicative proficiency development from a framework of performance assessments. Continuing to assume that professional development funds were limited in content areas like world languages, professional development was most likely for general education contexts, such as classroom management and the Madeline Hunter (1982) approach to instruction. Textbooks focused heavily on grammar and rote drills. Communication in the target language was not the focus; knowledge of the grammatical rules and vocabulary were the curricula de jour. It is common knowledge that teachers, much like other professionals, tend not to read research journals or even join their national associations. Among the tens of thousands of world language teachers in the United States, only 12,500 are members of the American Council on the Teaching of Foreign Languages (ACTFL, 2016).

Overall, more needs to be known about external reviewers, with increased transparency about the selection process and reviewers' credentials warranted. In particular, it would be helpful to have input on the acceptable qualifications to become a reviewer, particularly within specific content areas. While Pearson (2014) has outlined minimal general qualifications, we suggest that external reviewers should be required to show a high level of understanding and implementation of second language acquisition research, as demonstrated by their own pedagogical and assessment performance in the classroom. Ideally, National Board certified teachers would be prioritized to evaluate edTPA portfolios, but the relatively low number of National Board certified teachers of world languages other than English (Hildebrandt & Eom, 2011) makes that ideal difficult to realize.

These content-specific challenges have been explained with the intention of raising SCALE's attention prior to the assessment's next revision. We acknowledge that the development and preparation necessary to take edTPA national is a colossal undertaking and that revision of the assessment can take place if justified. We feel that revision is merited and we call for meaningful changes to future editions of the *World Language edTPA Assessment Handbook*.

We hope that stakeholders in other content area teacher education programs will articulate examples of incongruities between their expectations for TCs and those of their edTPA handbooks. The following section gives voice to our colleagues from across the country who grapple with how best to prepare their TCs for edTPA and future teaching careers.

VOICES FROM THE FIELD

As edTPA unfolded in our respective states, it became widespread across others as well. In order to better understand the nuances of this high-stakes assessment across geographical context, we talked with others in the field to share experiences. For this section, we invited several of our colleagues to share their perspectives.

Dr. Anne Cummings Hlas, associate professor of Spanish and foreign language education at The University of Wisconsin–Eau Claire, was asked to address concerns related to edTPA. She notes that while there are benefits, controversies also surround edTPA. First, its adoption by states that already require many TC and program evaluation measures seem to assume our current system is not working. Further, it suggests that a solution to this problem is to outsource the teacher licensing process to a for-profit company. Moreover, the rigid common architecture at edTPA's core originated from mathematics, but it has not been properly vetted as a tool to evaluate world language teacher effectiveness. More information on predictive validity studies within languages, in particular, seems necessary.

Within the assessment itself, the tasks and requirements expected from teacher candidates to pass edTPA seem to require more skill with writing a reflection and following formatting than knowing one's content. For example, in Rubric 8: Subject Specific Pedagogy of the world language edTPA, TCs must specifically provide opportunities to discuss the three Ps of the Cultures standard (i.e., practices, products, and perspectives). The inclusion of these specific features can be viewed at times as forced rather than purposeful.

A sweeping national teacher assessment such as edTPA carries a heavy burden in assessing whether teacher candidates really do demonstrate the knowledge and skills needed to teach. As such, scoring of these portfolios requires transparency. Unfortunately, the feedback provided to TCs and teacher education programs is not helpful with accountability at center stage. National assessments, similar to edTPA, lead to many questions that will need to be addressed in the years to come, such as:

- How does increasing TC assessment demands promote teacher quality?
- Which is preferable, to see more standardization or more flexibility in assessing teacher candidates?

- What types of research support the implementation and administration of edTPA?
- What is the relationship between edTPA and TC knowledge after 5 years of teaching? Ten years?

Dr. Sarah Jourdain, an assistant professor of French and pedagogy with tenure at Stony Brook University in New York, offers another voice to our discussion. She serves as the director of foreign language teacher preparation at her institution, and she believes that the kindest way to describe edTPA implementation in New York State, particularly for world language teachers, is "less than smooth" (personal communication, January 25, 2016). She noted that in 2012, the New York State Board of Regents adopted the edTPA as a high stakes, summative assessment for teacher preparation. That practice runs contrary to many other states that have folded edTPA into their teacher preparation programs as one measure of formative assessment, the purpose for which it was originally intended. Beginning in 2014, New York State TCs have been required to submit their edTPA portfolios to Pearson for assessment by external evaluators. These external scores determine whether a TC obtains certification or not. However, after edTPA's implementation and the resulting outcry from teachers' unions and college administrators, New York State put into place an edTPA safety net. That policy modification stipulated that any TC who does not pass the edTPA may instead take the New York State teacher certification exam, which was in place prior to edTPA's implementation in the state. The safety net is scheduled to expire very soon.

Dr. Jourdain mentioned several other impediments to TC edTPA success. First, world language teacher educators have not been provided with any models of what successful edTPA submissions might look like. Models are available in most other subject fields, but there are not any for world languages. In addition to a lack of sample edTPA planning commentaries, lesson plans, videos, etc. in world languages, the New York State Deputy Commissioner of Education sent an official directive in July of 2015 warning TCs not to share any of their edTPA materials with anyone (D'Agati, 2015). Many teacher education faculty members understood that edTPA portfolios were not to be shared with teacher preparation faculty either. Dr. Jourdain noted that as of October 28, 2015, there has been some softening of this position. It now seems that teacher educators in that state may now request that their graduates share with them some successful components of their own edTPA dossiers. Teacher educators may analyze and discuss those samples with their current TCs, while emphasizing that no plagiarism of past submissions is tolerated. Naturally, these actions presuppose that there are TCs who have passed the edTPA and who are willing to share their materials with program faculty.

Further, Dr. Jourdain mentioned that there are issues with the video recording requirements in the New York State edTPA roll-out. Although edTPA is mandated by the state for TCs and it requires TCs to submit video footage of their teaching, no provisions were put into place to require that school districts who accept a student teacher also allow that student teacher to video record in the classroom. Teacher education faculty members strive to work these details out prior to placement. However, in her program she recently encountered two school districts that accepted her student teachers, allowed them to begin student teaching, and subsequently informed her that the student teacher would not be allowed to video record. She stated that this scenario leaves her TCs and faculty members in a very unpleasant, unprofessional situation. What should her program faculty tell TCs? Should they tell the TCs to cross their fingers and hope that their second placement will allow video recording? Or does the program coordinator pull them out of their placement and scramble to find a new one in a district that allows video recording? By enacting the former option, program faculty unfairly reduce the amount of time that teacher candidates can use to compile their edTPA materials as they are unable to start their portfolio until their second placement. By selecting the latter option, and since finding new placements is both difficult and time-consuming, the number of days is reduced in which TCs can student teach, potentially jeopardizing their ability to successfully complete the mandated number of days of student teaching.

She notes that there are many aspects of edTPA that are quite beneficial for teacher candidates—encouraging backward design in planning, fostering students' higher order thinking skills, evaluating via performance assessment, and reflecting on professional development, to name a few. She stated that "our TCs had been doing much of what is in the edTPA prior to its statewide implementation in New York, but our faculty had been assessing its components. Now, teacher candidates must pay $300 to have these materials assessed by an external evaluator." She finds that "rather than valuing the expertise of teacher education faculty, New York State's implementation of edTPA diminishes our role." Additionally, she mentioned that rather than helping TCs become better teachers, time must be spent guessing about the expectations regarding what should be submitted and how it will be assessed. She confesses that "the whole situation would be laughable if only people's careers and the quality of education provided to our children were not on the line" (personal communication, January 25, 2016).

Next, we consulted with Nancy Ferrill, a 6-year veteran administrative professional and University Student Teacher Supervisor at Illinois State University's Department of Languages, Literatures, and Culture. She has worked with edTPA since the university began to pilot test it and discussed six issues with edTPA. First, she mentioned that she understands edTPA's theoretical purpose of measuring TCs' ability to teach, but she finds it quite different in practice. One of her main concerns is that edTPA requires TCs to split their focus between learning to be a teacher in an actual classroom and the consequentiality of edTPA. Moreover, she finds edTPA an intrusion into TCs' time and an amplification of their workload. She contends that it detracts from a TC's ability to maintain their cooperating teacher's standards and impedes the TC's ability to follow through on agreed-upon tasks. She stated that she has witnessed the friction between the TCs and their cooperating teachers concerning time commitments and classroom responsibilities that edTPA can cause.

Second, in addition to being a source of contention between TCs and their mentor teachers, she feels that edTPA is an inaccurate measurement tool because "a TC can be a great teacher in the classroom but a weak technical writer and fail the edTPA. Conversely, a TC can be a weak teacher in the classroom but a strong writer and pass the edTPA" (personal communication, February 7, 2016). Additionally, she mentioned that there is not an accommodation for first-hand observations and recommendations from the university supervisor. She noted that ideally, a university supervisor observes the TC several times throughout the semester, knows the strengths and areas needing improvement of the TC, and is familiar with the context of the school and classroom. Although edTPA requires TCs to complete the Context for Learning, she explains that there are important contextual details in classroom communities that are intangible, yet important. She reported that "a university supervisor is better suited to evaluate the contexts that affect a TC's ability to teach more than the edTPA dossier."

Turning to her third issue, technology problems, Ferrill noted that one technical glitch has the propensity to ruin a TC's edTPA score. She finds that most TCs try to be proactive to avoid problems. However, now that the world, in general, is relying on technology more and more, both TCs and external reviewers can experience technical problems. She mentioned that at Illinois State University there is support staff to resolve technical issues while TCs upload their materials into a computer interface to send to Pearson. Nevertheless, "every semester, the majority of TCs in [her] program have difficulty with the computer format component of edTPA."

Next, Ferrill finds that some of the Task 3 features reach beyond what a novice teacher can expect to know and be able to do. Every semester, she recounted, cooperating teachers spend substantial personal time explaining assessment processes and strategies for interpreting the data to TCs, sometimes at the expense of working on developing other classroom material. To implement a timeline that enables TCs to develop and complete an edTPA dossier, and yet have time to revise before the semester ends if necessary, she suggests vigilance with regard to TC time on (edTPA) task.

Fifth, she reported that she disagrees with the notion that a TC's justification of being an effective novice teacher hinges on one set of video clips. She adamantly stated that teaching to the test has been a failure. She feels that the short videos do not do justice in evaluating one's ability to become a teacher or not. For example, she pointed out that if an activity does not meet all requirements, even though it may be an effective activity or lesson, a TC's score could be lower than anticipated. While it is arguable that a *lowered* score on one rubric is not of major consequence, one or two less than desired rubric scores can result in an overall lower final edTPA score. She confesses that "in our state, the consequence of that lowered score can translate not only into a failure to obtain a teaching license but also a failure to graduate from the college—all because 15 minutes of selected video from one to two video clips may have been poorly chosen." While she acknowledged that it would take reviewers more time to evaluate several days of instruction or even one complete lesson, she restated that 15 minutes of video is insufficient.

Another one of Ferrill's concerns is the cost of edTPA because of the money going to Pearson and TCs paying for their portfolios to be reviewed. While the money is divided among reviewers and others, it speaks to the corporatization of education in the United States. She added that particularly because TCs may have to resubmit a portion of or an entirely new portfolio, the overall cost of the edTPA becomes burdensome, especially when combined with other tests that students must take and pass (see Hildebrandt & Swanson, 2014).

Her last concern, expressed in an email in which she approved our representation of her edTPA thoughts, entails her fear that edTPA, as it is now, does not provide for the full creativity of individual teachers to be adapted to their specific classrooms. She fears that teachers sacrifice their creative talents and strategies to conform to a model represented by edTPA's rubrics.

In conclusion, she noted that many of her edTPA concerns are becoming a negative reality. During the student teaching experience, she feels that edTPA's rigorous demands appear to work against TC success. She also feels that edTPA is changing the educational atmosphere in that many capable and enthusiastic young people are opting out of education—some citing edTPA as a significant reason for their career change. She feels that edTPA is a contributor to the shortage of language teachers in her area.

Next, Jennifer Eddy, a tenured assistant professor of world language education at Queens College of the City University of New York, added her opinion. She noted the need for highly effective language teachers who teach in the target language to serve as models for TCs. She pointed out that

> in 2010, ACTFL advanced a position statement on teaching in the target language where teachers use the target language at least 90% of the time. It continues to amaze us as we are in schools working with our TCs, that there are mentor teachers who, during instruction, talk about the target language in English instead of using the target language as the vehicle for instruction. (personal communication, January 24, 2016)

In addition to edTPA not demanding that TCs use the target language for instruction, she discussed that many times TCs are working with cooperating teachers who have little knowledge about performance assessments. And these in-service mentors can continue to advocate for practices that have been shown to be ineffective years ago. She stated that while they continue to strive for their TCs to be placed with highly effective language teachers, who teach and assess student learning using communicative approaches, they are not guaranteed one. She ended by stating that, along with colleagues around the nation, there are many language teachers working under renewable teaching certificates who have not embraced language teaching for communicative purposes. And those individuals may be assigned a student teacher and even serve as an external edTPA portfolio reviewer.

Eddy noted that, in fall 2013, her program participated in an edTPA pilot "and with that data, made significant logistical changes to the program" (personal communication, February 11, 2016). Although her program was well prepared for edTPA, in terms of pedagogical content knowledge and its application during the clinical phase, she reported that edTPA preparation necessitated increased contact hours and modified timing of content delivery. Dr. Eddy stated that subsequent data were collected over the following 2 years and those changes remain in practice today in her program. She summarizes her thoughts concerning the changes' effects and TC feedback in a forthcoming paper entitled *Reprise, Reciprocity, Re-Vision: Program Review Through an edTPA Lens*. The three current issues for her program include increased contact, timing of delivery, and cost, which are presented below.

Contact for Commentaries. Her world language education program always had 1 year of clinical student teaching: one semester at the middle school and one at the high school. Considering the longstanding, complete academic year of curriculum and assessment coursework, it was already a rigorous program. That rigor was especially salient because most of her program's TCs work additional jobs and have families. As periodical data collection showed, the program added 10 seminars to run concurrently with the initial clinical experience in the middle school to provide a reciprocal exchange of theory and practice.

Timing of Delivery. The initial clinical experience and the first curriculum course were always historically carried out in the fall, and high school student teaching and the second curriculum course were offered in the spring. As a result of edTPA, the program decided to front-load key pedagogical content, moving from 1 year to a year and a half total clinical experience. Now, the first curriculum course takes place in the spring, initial clinical experience is in the fall coupled with the new seminars, and the second curriculum course, along with high school student teaching and the ten seminars, occur during the TCs' final spring semester. The program collects video artifacts in both clinical experiences in order to give TCs the choice of which school site experience to use for their edTPA portfolios and to provide maximum video footage.

Cost. She noted that the $300 cost to submit edTPA is quite difficult for her TCs. The cost pushes the total cost for testing and certification requirements in New York State to about $2000. As a result, TCs complete the work but often do not submit it, creating a body of *nonsubmitters* across the division. She finds it discouraging because program faculty members can only recommend that TCs submit it and complete the certification process. She disclosed that "ultimately, TCs will need to submit it in order to continue for the master's degree, which is required to maintain certification in NYS."

In conclusion, Dr. Eddy stated that the demands of the edTPA commentaries required the reconfiguration of clinical coursework timing, with additional seminars necessary. The increased and earlier contact with TCs has proven to be a positive outcome for her program. The cost of submission and the consequences thereof remain large for her candidates and is the biggest edTPA challenge. She stated that,

> although pedagogical content and application of performance assessment are essential for our TCs to know and be able to do during their preservice preparation, one might consider the depth of some of the commentaries more suitable for in-service teachers after a year or 2 of experience. This move would ensure access to student learning plans and more consistent experience with diverse learners. In addition, as a salaried teacher, the burden of the exam cost is relieved. If implemented for professional, rather than initial, certification, edTPA assessment responses with identifiers removed could provide invaluable data to programs for Impact on Student Learning, as required to address CAEP Standard Four. One might consider the value of reconnecting the in-service teacher with the college to complete the loop, obtain feedback and witness genuine impact on K–12 student learning through a more discerning lens.

Then, we asked Dr. Victoria Russell, associate professor of Spanish and foreign language education at Valdosta State University, for her thoughts. She stated that as a university supervisor of Spanish and French TCs seeking certification, she is most concerned with the edTPA consequences for TCs who are English language learners (ELLs) and heritage speakers of a language other than English. Given that the edTPA portfolio requires extensive commentaries in English, this puts these ELLs and heritage speakers at a disadvantage compared to their native English-speaking counterparts. She noted that in her experience piloting the edTPA assessment in Georgia with seven teacher candidates in 2015, the candidates who were ELLs or heritage speakers of Spanish performed significantly worse on the edTPA assessment, as compared to the candidates who are native speakers of English. She went on to state that many of her TCs who were native English speakers but were weak in using the target language during instruction were able to perform very well on edTPA, even though they were unable to deliver 90% or more of their instruction in the target language, as recommended by ACTFL (2010) but not addressed by edTPA rubrics. Additionally, she mentioned that the edTPA portfolio only requires one or two video clips totaling no more than 15 minutes, in which candidates showcase their instruction. Much like Ferrill, she feels that these short segments are unable to demonstrate the TCs' competency as novice teachers, especially with respect to their proficiency level in the target language.

In her program, she noted that the ELLs and heritage speakers of Spanish had the lowest edTPA scores. These lower scores were particularly troubling, since one of the ELLs was named Student Teacher of the Year with strong evaluations from her mentor teacher and university supervisor throughout her final clinical practice semester. If it were not a pilot year, this individual would have been unable to obtain certification to teach Spanish in Georgia, in spite of her strong performance during her final clinical practice semester. Russell concluded that she and others are deeply concerned that edTPA may create a barrier to certification for ELLs and heritage speakers of languages other than English who seek Georgia certification to teach a world language.

Interestingly, Dr. Russell suggested we provide Ms. Sydney Earley's thoughts as a mentor teacher at Lowndes High School in Valdosta, Georgia in 2015. Ms. Earley stated,

> I do not think that the edTPA portfolio effectively demonstrates a teacher's ability to plan lessons because there is too much paperwork for these new teacher candidates to handle. In order for them to perform well throughout the actual teaching experience, which requires a ton of time both inside and outside of the classroom, the TCs do not have time to jump through yet another hoop in order to show the state what they want to see. If a student is

paired with a good mentor teacher, it is there that he or she really learns how to plan, figure out pacing, and deal with classroom management issues. By requiring the edTPA portfolio, TCs do not have time to learn from the real life experiences. Additionally, the workload is too much. Many of the TCs have bad experiences because they are so worried and consumed with edTPA that any additional work (e.g., lesson planning, grading, creating assessments and activities), which is actually the most important, seems like a whole lot. Because passing edTPA is a graduation requirement for the TCs with whom I work, it becomes the main focus, and in reality it says nothing about their actual teaching abilities. Teachers already have so much to do both inside and outside of the classroom. They need the time to properly and confidently prepare good lessons, which is impossible with the workload that is required from edTPA. (personal communication, February 10, 2016)

Another Georgia mentor teacher, Ms. Alicia T. Hiers of Colquitt County High School in Norman Park, worked with Dr. Russell's TCs during the pilot year and remarked,

As a mentor teacher, I find edTPA a most unwelcome distraction for student teachers and their mentors. It is my personal opinion that edTPA (as it is now) robs student teachers of precious observation and planning time. Additionally, student teachers are so busy formatting lessons into 10-page documents that they have no time to interact with students or develop teacher-student relationships that are an integral part of classroom success. edTPA should fit naturally and effectively into the clinical teaching experience. As it is, it demands that the natural flow of the classroom bend to meet its requirements. The student teachers that I have mentored since edTPA has been a requirement have not been able to experience fully the realities of classroom instruction because they have been kidnapped for 6 to 7 weeks and held ransom for a set of video clips and a collection of busy work. (personal communication, February 20, 2016)

These voices from the field raise many of the same concerns that we raised throughout this chapter, but in a more contextualized way. We encourage our language teachers and teacher education colleagues to continue discussing edTPA preparation and implementation challenges and to support each other so they can to help TCs succeed on edTPA within the parameters afforded in their given environment.

NEXT STEPS

With our colleagues, we raised the concerns above to provide constructive criticisms that inform edTPA developers and users, state and federal educational policy makers, and world language teacher educators and program directors about unintended consequences of edTPA implementation. Here we outline the next steps we anticipate taking as edTPA gains a foothold in our states and becomes consequential to our programs' evaluations.

Although our programs' TCs outperformed their national peers on all but one of the 13 rubrics, as noted in Chapters 4, 5, and 6, we find several areas of improvement possible. To begin, the one rubric on which our candidates did score lower was the final rubric, Analyzing Teaching Effectiveness, with a .20 difference on a 5-point scale (Hildebrandt & Swanson, 2014). Therefore, we will expand our efforts to provide TCs in our classes with real-life examples of instruction that meets students' learning needs and connects to lesson objectives. We anticipate exploring the phenomenon of learning objectives and their alignment with *Bloom's Revised Taxonomy* (Krathwohl, 2002) using the matrix introduced in Chapter 4.

Further, given the inadequate exposure to authentic student work samples and edTPA's focus on student feedback, we anticipate enlisting the help of former TCs who graduated from our programs to share samples of their assessments and the student work that was created to address those assessments. Those artifacts can include audio and video taped samples of performance assessments that demonstrate best language teaching and assessment practices. The resulting archive will prove invaluable as we will be able to provide more authentic student work and facilitate more meaningful feedback.

We also anticipate adding to our data set as more of our TCs complete their edTPA portfolios and submit them for review. With a larger data set, a more robust picture of TC edTPA performance can be developed. We hope that, with more data, we will be able to ascertain patterns that inform us of TC or student teaching placement characteristics that might influence scores on individual rubrics. These characteristics, we hope, may serve as an early warning system for future TCs who may struggle on edTPA and enable us to appropriately intervene. To complement our growing quantitative data set, we look forward to expanding our existing set of qualitative data from TCs who completed the portfolio.

We invite readers to contribute to the ongoing edTPA research agenda required to validate this assessment and align it with second language acquisition theory and research. We anticipate continuing to advocate for a world language edTPA that better aligns with language teacher education program expectations and we encourage other stakeholders to do the same. Our recent conversation with SCALE personnel causes us to be optimistic that necessary changes will be made to create an even better assessment of world language teacher effectiveness.

FINAL THOUGHTS

With edTPA now consequential in both of our states, we watch the process of its implementation unfold in real time. Our TCs have mentioned to us on many occasions that they feel left alone during the process of creating their externally reviewed portfolios. We adhere strictly to the guidelines for TC support and even take the time during the practicum to discuss these guidelines with TCs. At this point in our edTPA work, we are not convinced that the assessment is helping to create better novice language teachers, but time will tell. Nevertheless, edTPA is a central part of our programs and we will continue to do our best to help TCs become highly effective teachers.

As we conclude, we offer some final thoughts for each of our antici-pated audiences. First, we hope that legislators at the state and federal levels will recognize the need to listen to those *on the ground*—inservice and preservice teachers working in K–12 schools, along with those work-ing in colleges and university classrooms—from across the country who every day do the personal work of teaching. We hope that policymakers can take what they learn from those educators and apply that knowledge to enact smart educational policy at all levels. We advocate for policy that acknowledges that unequal access to resources influences student learn-ing, heeds local TC preparation and assessment expertise, respects finan-cial constraints to becoming a teacher, and encourages all facets of healthy child development, including caregiver and community support, healthy eating, early world language learning, the arts, and play. When legislators gain a greater understanding and respect of teachers and teacher educators, they can enact laws that support educators and their students instead of over testing them. We must all stay abreast of the national conversation surrounding the Every Student Succeeds Act, the recent reauthorization of the Bush administration's 2001 No Child Left Behind Act. While initial reactions appeared positive, there are several legislative issues that may adversely influence teacher preparation. For example, provisions in the act allow for the creation of teacher prepara-tion academies, which are nontraditional, nonuniversity programs like those funded by venture philanthropists (Strauss, 2015). It is disturbing to think that the critical work of teacher education could fall into the hands of individuals with little to no training as teachers themselves.

Next, we hope that SCALE will continue to listen to those in the field and make the necessary changes to the world language edTPA that we have presented above and those outlined by teachers and teacher educa-tors in other content areas. We also hope that SCALE will begin to investi-gate how dual language immersion should be assessed as it differs dramatically from traditional world language instruction. Further, the lack of world language exemplars and artifacts available to teacher education program faculty is a detriment to program and TC success. edTPA is a daunting task and a high-stakes assessment for all parties, especially for those who are in states with established cut scores. People need to be able to see and understand what constitutes an excellent portfolio and what does not. The stakes for so many teachers are high and every entity needs to support program faculty and TCs to their fullest extent.

We also hope that teacher preparation faculty members will get up-to-date on edTPA and find out what their respective states are doing regarding teacher education. It is imperative that teacher educators stay abreast of and get involved in formulating local, state, and national educational policy. We recommend networking with colleagues, presenting edTPA research, and sharing their experiences with others. For years many teachers have neglected to advocate publicly for teacher education and we need to voice our informed opinions. We feel that teacher educators must schedule ongoing discussions about edTPA in language departments, as well as in colleges of education, if TCs are to be fully prepared for the exigencies of edTPA. If programs are fortunate enough to have an edTPA coordinator on their campus, we prompt teacher educators to befriend this individual and get to know what is happening with edTPA across content areas. Additionally, we encourage others to become trained edTPA scorers. We also recommend staying abreast of the availability of support materials developed by AACTE and becoming aware of acceptable TC supports. If there is an opportunity to attend a conference on edTPA, the information gathered there could also be valuable to teacher education programs. Finally, it is imperative to create opportunities for TCs to practice with a mini edTPA before attempting this high-stakes assessment. We have found that TCs who developed a mini-edTPA dossier receive the highest scores on the assessment as compared to those who did not.

Finally, we hope that we have achieved our ultimate goal for this book—to help world language TCs to understand and perform successfully on the three edTPA tasks. edTPA is a relatively new assessment of beginning teacher readiness being implemented in 36 states and the District of Columbia (AACTE, 2016) to inform teacher education and licensure/certification decisions. Little empirical research on edTPA has made its way to public view, outside of findings reported by SCALE. The first mention of edTPA in the world language teacher education circles appeared in a brief introduction published in *The Language Educator* (Hildebrandt & Hlas, 2013). Until the publication of our 2014 article in *Foreign Language Annals*, no empirical studies of edTPA were present in the professional literature. This absence applies not just to world language teacher education, but to all content areas. We also believe this book to be the first that focuses so intently on edTPA. We bring the reader's attention to these facts not for self-promotion; rather, we hope that others will help us fill the gaps in the literature. As edTPA comes to influence teacher education policy and practices in over one half of this country's states, the need for validation studies and investigations of the assessment's consequential validity increases. We encourage others in world languages and other content areas to investigate edTPA in their own settings and raise their voices in the educational policy arena. We sincerely hope that our ideas, and those of our colleagues, have been useful.

REFERENCES

Adair-Hauck, B. (2007). *The PACE model: A dialogic and co-constructive approach to grammar explanation*. Paper presented at the New Jersey State Foreign Language Teachers Consortium, Princeton, NJ.

Adair-Hauck, B., Glisan, E. W., Koda, K., Swender, E. B., & Sandrock, P. (2006). The Integrated Performance Assessment (IPA): Connecting assessment to instruction and learning. *Foreign Language Annals*, *39*(3), 359–382.

Adair-Hauck, B., Glisan, E. W., & Troyan, F. J. (2013). *Implementing integrated performance assessment*. Alexandria, VA: American Council on the Teaching of Foreign Languages.

Airasian, P. W., & Miranda, H. (2002). The role of assessment in the revised taxonomy. *Theory into Practice*, *41*, 249–254. Retrieved from http://www.unco.edu/cetl/sir/stating_outcome/documents/Krathwohl.pdf

Alliance for Excellent Education. (2014). Summary Report Available on 2013 edTPA Field Test. Retrieved from http://all4ed.org/summary-report-available-on-2013-edtpa-field-test/

American Association for Colleges of Teacher Education. (2015). *edTPA handouts to share with* stakeholders. Retrieved from https://secure.aacte.org/apps/rl/resource.php?resid=268&ref=edtpa

American Association for Colleges of Teacher Education. (2016). *Participation map*. Retrieved from http://edtpa.aacte.org/state-policy

American Council on the Teaching of Foreign Languages. (n.d.-a). *ACTFL/CAEP program standards for the preparation of foreign language teachers*. Retrieved from http://www.actfl.org/assessment-professional-development/actflcaep

American Council on the Teaching of Foreign Languages. (n.d.-b). *The keys to planning for learning*. Retrieved from http://www.actfl.org/publications/books-and-brochures/the-keys-planning-learning

American Council on the Teaching of Foreign Languages. (2010). Use of the target language in the classroom. Retrieved from http://www.actfl.org/news/position-statements/use-the-target-language-the-classroom-0

American Council on the Teaching of Foreign Languages. (2012). *ACTFL proficiency guidelines 2012*. White Plains, NY: Author. Retrieved from http://www.actfl.org/sites/default/files/pdfs/public/ACTFLProficiencyGuidelines2012_FINAL.pdf

American Council on the Teaching of Foreign Languages. (2015). *ACTFL global engagement initiative*. Retrieved from http://www.actfl.org/advocacy/actfl-global-engagement-initiative

American Council on the Teaching of Foreign Languages. (2016). *About the American Council on the Teaching of Foreign Languages*. Retrieved from http://www.actfl.org/about-the-american-council-the-teaching-foreign-languages

Amrein-Beardsley, A., Collins, C., Polasky, S. A., & Sloat, E. F. (2013). Value-added model (VAM) Research for educational policy: Framing the issue. *Education Policy Analysis Archives*, *21*(4), 1–14. Retrieved from http://epaa.asu.edu/ojs/article/view/1311

Anderson, L. W., & Krathwohl, D. R. (Eds.). (2001). *A taxonomy for learning, teaching, and assessing: A revision of Bloom's taxonomy of educational objectives*. New York, NY: Longman.

Au, W. (2013). What's a nice test like you doing in a place like this? The edTPA and corporate education "reform." *Rethinking Schools*, *27*(4), 22–27.

Bachman, L. F., & Palmer, A. (2010). *Language assessment in practice: Developing language assessments and justifying their use in the real world*. Oxford, England, Oxford University Press.

Ball, D. L., & Forzani, F. M. (2009). The work of teaching and the challenge for teacher education. *Journal of Teacher Education, 60*, 497–511.

Bandura, A. (1997). *Self-efficacy: The exercise of control*. New York, NY: W.H. Freeman and Company.

Blackburn, B. R. (2015). Three tools to support ELL students. *Middle web*. Retrieved from http://www.middleweb.com/21607/3-tools-to-support-english-language-learners/

Blaz, D. (1999). *Foreign language teacher's guide to active learning*. London, England: Routledge.

Blaz, D. (2000). *Collections of performance tasks & rubrics: Foreign languages*. London, England: Routledge.

Blaz, D. (2006). *Differentiated instruction: A guide for foreign language teachers*. London, England: Routledge.

Bloom, B. S. (Ed.), Engelhart, M. D., Furst, E. J., Hill, W. H., & Krathwohl, D. R. (1956). *Taxonomy of educational objectives: The classification of educational goals. Handbook 1: Cognitive domain*. New York, NY: David McKay.

Bond, L. (1998). Culturally responsive pedagogy and the assessment of accomplished teaching. *Journal of Negro Education, 67*(4), 242–254.

Brown, H. D., & Abeywickrama, P. (2010). *Language assessment: Principles and classroom practices* (2nd ed.). White Plains, NY: Longman.

Burke, B. (2014). Forty years after Savignon, how far have(n't) we come? Students' perspectives about communicative language teaching in the 21st century. In S. Dhonau (Ed.), *Unlock the gateway to communication* (pp. 113–138). Eau Claire, WI: Central States Conference on the Teaching of Foreign Languages.

Buttaro, L. (2009). Language, learning, and the achievement gap: The influence of classroom practices and conversation on performance. *Language and Learning Journal, 4*. Retrieved from http://ojs.gc.cuny.edu/index.php/lljournal/article/view/458/547

Byram, M. (1997). *Teaching and assessing intercultural communicative competence*. Clevedon, England: Multilingual Matters.

California Commission on Teacher Credentialing. (2014). *Recommended passing score standard for the use of the edTPA in California*. Retrieved from www.ctc.ca.gov/commission/agendas/2014.../2014-10-3F.pdf

Camarota, S. A. (2011). A record-setting decade of immigration: 2000-2010. Retrieved from http://cis.org/sites/cis.org/files/articles/2011/record-setting-decade.pdf

Center for Advanced Research on Language Acquisition. (2013a). *Creating an assessment unit*. Retrieved from http://www.carla.umn.edu/assessment/vac/CreateUnit/step4.html

Center for Advanced Research on Language Acquisition. (2013b). *Creating an assessment unit: The interpretive mode*. Retrieved from http://www.carla.umn.edu/assessment/vac/CreateUnit/step4_interpretive.html

Center for Advanced Research on Language Acquisition. (2013c). *Step 4: Design performance assessments*. Retrieved from http://www.carla.umn.edu/assessment/vac/CreateUnit/step4_interpersonal.html

Center for Advanced Research on Language Acquisition. (2013d). *Step 7: Determine key learning activities/formative assessments*. Retrieved from http://www.carla.umn.edu/assessment/vac/CreateUnit/step7.html

Center on Education Policy. (2007, August). *Implementing the No Child Left Behind Teacher Requirements*. Washington, DC: Author.

Ceo-DiFrancesco, D. (2013). Instructor target language use in today's world language classrooms. In S. Dhonau (Ed.), *Multitasks, multiskills, multiconnections: Selected papers from the 2013 Central States Conference on the Teaching of Foreign Languages* (pp. 1–20). Milwaukee, WI: Central States Conference on the Teaching of Foreign Languages.

Clapham, C. (2000). Assessment and testing. *Annual Review of Applied Linguistics*, *20*, 147–161.

Clementi, D., & Terrill, L. (2013). *The keys to planning for learning: Effective curriculum, unit, and lesson design*. Alexandria, VA: ACTFL.

Cochran-Smith, M., Piazza, P., & Power, C. (2013). The politics of accountability: Assessing teacher education in the United States. *The Educational Forum*, *77*(1), 6–27.

Coladarci, T. (1992). Teachers' sense of efficacy and commitment to teaching. *Journal of Experimental Education, 60*, 323–337.

Coopersmith, J. (2009). *Characteristics of public, private, and bureau of Indian education elementary and secondary school teachers in the United States: Results from the 2007-08 schools and staffing survey* (NCES 2009-324). National Center for Education Statistics, Institute of Education Sciences, United States Department of Education. Washington, DC.

Cousins, J. B., & Walker, C. A. (2000). Predictors of educators' valuing of systemic inquiry in schools. *Canadian Journal of Program Evaluation* (Special Issue), 25–53.

Croft, S. J., Robbins, M. A., & Stenhouse, V. L. (2013). The perfect storm of education reform: High-stakes testing and teacher evaluation. *Justice Journal, 42*(1), 70–92.

Danielson, C. (2011). *Enhancing professional practice: A framework for teaching*. Alexandria, VA: ASCD.

Darling-Hammond, L. (2010). Evaluating teacher effectiveness: How teacher performance assessments can measure and improve teaching. Retrieved from http://files.eric.ed.gov/fulltext/ED535859.pdf

Darling-Hammond, L. (2012). Creating a strong foundation for the teaching career. *Phi Delta Kappan, 94*(3), 8–13.

Darling-Hammond, L., & Snyder, J. (2000). Authentic assessment of teaching in context. *Teaching and Teacher Education, 16*(5), 523–545.

Deci, E. L., & Ryan, R. M. (2002), Overview of self-determination theory: An organismic dialectical perspective. In E. L. Deci & R. M. Ryan (Eds,), *Handbook of self-determination research* (pp. 3–36). Rochester, NY: University of Rochester Press.

D'Agati, J. L. (2015). *edTPA use of materials and originality*. Retrieved from http://www.highered.nysed.gov/pdf/memo07232015.pdf

Donato, R. (1994). Collective scaffolding in second language learning. In J. P. Lantolf & G. Appel (Eds.), *Vygostskian approaches to second language research* (pp. 33–56). Norwood, NJ: Ablex.

Dörnyei, Z. (2001) *Motivational strategies in the language classroom*. Cambridge, England: Cambridge University Press.

Dörnyei, Z., & Ushioda, E. (2013). *Teaching and researching: Motivation* (2nd ed.). Cambridge, England: Routledge.

Dover, A. G., Schultz, B. D., Smith, K., & Duggan, T. J. (2015). Who's preparing our candidates? edTPA, localized knowledge and the outsourcing of teacher evaluation. *Teachers College Record*. Retrieved from http://www.tcrecord.org/content.asp?contentid=17914

Education Week. (2014, July 29). *10 tips for edTPA success*. Retrieved from http://www.edweek.org/tm/articles/2014/07/29/ctq_jette_edtpa.html

Elder, C. (2001). Assessing the language proficiency of teachers: Are there any border controls? *Language Testing, 18*(2), 149–170.

Elementary and Secondary Education Act of 1965, Pub. L. No. 89-10, 79 Stat. 27.

Ellis, R. (2001). Investigating form-focused instruction. *Language Learning, 51*(Supplement 1), 1–46.

Ellis, R. (2009). Corrective feedback and teacher development. *L2 Journal, 1*(1), 3–18.

Ellis, R. (2012). *Language teaching: Research & language pedagogy*. West Sussex, England: Wiley.

Ellis, R., Basturkmen, H., & Loewen, S. (2002). Doing focus on form. *System, 30*, 419–432.

Ellis, R., S., Loewen, S., & Erlam, R. (2006). Implicit and explicit corrective feedback and the acquisition of L2 grammar. *Studies in Second Language Acquisition, 25*(2), 243–272.

Even, R., & Markovitz, Z. (1995). Some aspects of teachers' and students' views on student reasoning and knowledge construction. *International Journal of Mathematics Education in Science Technology, 26*, 531–544.

Foreign Language Teacher Preparation Standards Writing Team. (2002). *Program standards for the preparation of foreign language teachers*. Retrieved from http://

www.actfl.org/sites/default/files/pdfs/public/
ACTFLNCATEStandardsRevised713.pdf

Foreign Language Teacher Preparation Standards Writing Team. (2013). *Program standards for the preparation of foreign language teachers.* Retrieved from http://www.actfl.org/professional-development/actfl-caep

Ford, D. Y., & Grantham, T. C. (2003). Providing access for culturally diverse gifted students: From deficit to dynamic thinking. *Theory Into Practice, 42*(3), 217–225.

Gass, S. M. (1988). Integrating research areas: A framework for second language studies. *Applied Linguistics, 9*, 198–217.

Gay, G. (2000). *Culturally responsive teaching: Theory, research, and practice.* New York, NY: Teachers College Press.

Gay, G. (2010). *Culturally responsive teaching: Theory, research, and practice.* New York, NY: Teachers College Press.

Georgia Professional Standards Commission. (2014). *Understanding the 2014 educator certification rule.* Retrieved from http://www.gapsc.com/Commission/policies_guidelines/Downloads/2014EducatorCertificationRuleChanges.pdf

Georgia Professional Standards Commission. (2015). edTPA standard setting decision. Retrieved from http://www.gapsc.com/Downloads/edTPA_Standard_Setting_Decision_071015.pdf

Georgia State University. (2015). *2015 status report: Georgia State University: Complete college Georgia.* Retrieved from http://enrollment.gsu.edu/files/2015/08/Georgia-State-University-CCG-Report-2015.pdf

Glisan, E. W., Adair-Hauck, B., Koda, K., Sandrock, P., & Swender, E. (2003). *ACTFL integrated performance assessment.* Yonkers, NY: American Council on the Teaching of Foreign Languages.

Glynn, C., Wesely, P., & Wassell, B. (2014). *Words and actions: Teaching languages through the lens of social justice.* Alexandria, VA: American Council on the Teaching of Foreign Languages.

Goe, L., Bell, C., & Little, O. (2008). *Approaches to evaluating teacher effectiveness: A research synthesis.* Washington, DC: National Comprehensive Center for Teacher Quality.

Goldhaber, D. (2007). Everyone's doing it, but what does teacher testing tell us about teacher effectiveness? *Journal of Human Resources, 42*, 765–794.

González, N., Moll, L., & Amanti, C. (2005). *Funds of knowledge: Theorizing practices in households, communities, and classrooms.* Mahwah, NJ: Erlbaum.

Gorski, P. C. (2010). *Unlearning deficit ideology and the scornful gaze: Thoughts on authenticating the class discourse in education.* Retrieved from www.edchange.org/publications/deficit-ideology-scornful-gaze.pdf

Gorman, K. A. (2013). *Breaking down the barriers: A guide to student services supervision.* New York, NY: Rowman & Littlefield.

Gregersen, T. (2005). To err is human: A reminder to teachers of language-anxious students. *Foreign Language Annals, 36*(1), 25–32.

Gregersen, T., & MacIntyre, P. D. (2014). *Capitalizing on language learners' individuality: From premise to practice.* Bristol, England: Multilingual Matters.

Griffiths, C. (2009). *Lessons from good language learners.* Cambridge, England: Cambridge University Press.

Guskey, T. R. (1988). Teacher efficacy, self-concept, and attitudes toward the implementation of instructional innovation. *Teaching and Teacher Education, 4*(1), 63–69.

Hai-Peng, H., & Deng, L. (2007). Vocabulary acquisition in multimedia environment. *US-China Foreign Language, 5*(8), 55–59.

Hall, J. K. (1999). A prosaics of interaction: The development of interactional competence in another language. In E. Hinkel (Ed.), *Culture in second language teaching and learning* (pp. 137-151). Cambridge, England: Cambridge University Press.

Harmer, J. (1983). *The practice of English language teaching.* London, England: Longman.

Hildebrandt, S. A. (2014). Mutually beneficial service learning: Language teacher candidates in a local community center. In K. Hoyt & P. Swanson (Eds.), *SCOLT Dimension Uniting the Corps: Uniting the Core* (pp. 111–123). Retrieved from http://www.scolt.org/index.php/publications/dimension/26-publications/39-scolt-publications

Hildebrandt, S., & Edwards, W. (n.d.). Foreign language autobiography. Retrieved from http://www.longwood.edu/assets/projectlinc/website--FL_autobiography_blank.pdf

Hildebrandt, S. A., & Eom, M. (2011). Teacher professionalization: Motivational factors and the influence of age. *Teaching and Teacher Education, 27*, 243–494.

Hildebrandt, S. A., & Hlas, A. C. (2013). Assessing the effectiveness of new teachers with edTPA™. *The Language Educator, 8*(3), 50–51.

Hildebrandt, S. A., Hlas, A. C., & Conroy, K. (2013). Comparing nine world language teacher preparation programs within and across three states. *NECTFL Review, 72*, 15–44. Retrieved from http://www.nectfl.org/sites/nectfl.drupalgardens.com/files/201308/NECTFL_September%202013.pdf

Hildebrandt, S. A., & Swanson, P. B. (2014). World language teacher candidate performance on edTPA: An exploratory study. *Foreign Language Annals, 47*, 576–591.

Hlas, A. C., & Hlas, C. S. (2012). A review of high-leverage teaching practices: Making connections between mathematics and foreign languages. *Foreign Language Annals, 45*(S1), S76–S97).

Hu, G. 2002. Potential cultural resistance to pedagogical imports: The case of communicative language teaching in China. *Language, Culture and Curriculum, 15*(2), 93–105.

Huang, S., & Eslami, Z. (2010). The relationship between teacher and peer support and English-language learners' anxiety. *English Language Teaching, 3*, 32–40.

Hymes, D. (1974). Ways of speaking. In R. Bauman & J. Sherzer (Eds.), *Explorations in the ethnography of speaking* (pp. 433–451). London, England: Cambridge University Press.

Hunter, M. (1982). *Master teaching.* El Segundo, CA: TIP Publications.

Illinois General Assembly. (2012). 105 ILCS 5/21B-30 http://www.ilga.gov/legislation/ilcs/fulltext.asp?DocName=010500050K21B-30

Illinois State Board of Education. (2012). Memo. Retrieved from http://www.isbe.state.il.us/licensure/pdf/higher-ed/edTPA/edTPA-summary1212.pdf

Illinois State Board of Education. (2013). edTPA support letter to districts. Retrieved from http://www.isbe.net/licensure/pdf/higher-ed/edTPA/district-letters/english.pdf

Illinois State Board of Education. (n.d.). Center for Educator Effectiveness. Services and information for higher education. Retrieved from http://www.isbe.net/licensure/html/higher-education.htm#tpa

Illinois State University. (n.d.). *ISU edTPA portfolio use non-disclosure agreement.* Normal, IL: Author.

Illinois State University. (2016). *IDS 274: Preparing for the edTPA.* Retrieved from https://education.illinoisstate.edu/downloads/teacher_education/IDS274Summer2016.pdf

Individuals with Disabilities Education Act, 20 U.S.C. § 1400 (2004).

Ithaca College. (n.d.). How do I prepare for my edTPA video recordings for my learning segment. Retrieved from www.ithaca.edu/actec/docs/edTPA_video.pdf

Kaye, C. B. (2004). *The complete guide to service learning: Proven, practical ways to engage students in civic responsibility, academic curriculum, and social action.* Minneapolis, MN: Free Spirit.

Kelleher, A. (2010). What is a heritage language program? Washington, DC: Center for Applied Linguistics. Retrieved from http://www.cal.org/heritage/pdfs/briefs/Who-is-a-Heritage-Language-Learner.pdf

Kramsch, C. 1993. *Context and culture in language teaching.* Oxford, England: Oxford University Press.

Krashen, S. (1981). *Second language acquisition and second language learning.* Oxford, England: Pergamon.

Krashen, S. (1985). *The input hypothesis: Issues and implications.* New York, NY: Longman.

Krashen, S. D., & Terrell, T. D. (1983). *The natural approach: Language acquisition in the classroom.* London, England: Prentice Hall Europe.

Krathwohl, D. R. (2002). A revision of Bloom's taxonomy: An overview. *Theory Into Practice, 41,* 212–218. Retrieved from http://www.unco.edu/cetl/sir/stating_outcome/documents/Krathwohl.pdf

Ladson-Billings, G. (1995). But that's just good teaching! The case for culturally relevant pedagogy. *Theory Into Practice, 34*(3), 159–165.

Lee, J., & VanPatten, B. (2003). *Making communicative language teaching happen* (2nd ed.). New York, NY: McGraw Hill.

Lewis, W. D., & Young, T. V. (2013). The politics of accountability: Teacher education policy. *Educational Policy, 27*(2), 190–216.

Lightbown, P., & Spada, N. (2013). *How languages are learned* (4th ed.). Oxford, England: Oxford University Press.

Long, M. (1996). The role of the linguistic environment in second language acquisition. In W. C. Ritchie & T. K. Bhatia (Eds.), *Handbook of language acquisition: Vol. 2. Second language acquisition* (pp. 413–468). New York, NY: Academic Press.

Loewen, S. (2005). Incidental focus on form and second language learning. *Studies in Second Language Acquisition, 27*(3), 361–386.

Lynn, M. (2014). Making culturally relevant pedagogy relevant to aspiring teachers. *Diverse: Issues in Higher Education*. Retrieved from https://secure.aacte.org/apps/rl/resource.php?resid=268&ref=edtpa

Lyster, R., & Ranta, L. (1997). Corrective feedback and learner uptake: Negotiation of form in communicative classrooms. *Studies in Second Language Acquisition, 19*, 37–66.

MacIntyre, P. D., & Gardner, R. C. (1994a). The effects of induced anxiety on three stages of cognitive processing in computerized vocabulary learning. *Studies in Second Language Acquisition, 16*, 1–17.

MacIntyre, P. D., & Gardner, R. C. (1994b). The subtle effects of language anxiety on cognitive processing in the second language. *Language Learning, 44*, 283–305.

Mackey, A. (1999). Input, interaction, and second language development. *Studies in Second Language Acquisition, 21*(4), 557–587.

Madeloni, B., & Gorlewski, J. (2013). Wrong answer to the wrong question: Why we need critical teacher education, not standardization. *Rethinking Schools, 27*, 4. Retrieved from http://www.rethinkingschools.org/archive/27_04/27_04_madeloni-gorlewski.shtml

Marzano, R. J. (2007). *The art and science of teaching: A comprehensive framework for effective instruction*. Alexandria, VA: Association for Supervision and Curriculum Development.

Massachusetts Department of Elementary and Secondary Education. (1999). *Foreign language curriculum frameworks*. Retrieved from http://www.doe.mass.edu/frameworks/foreign/1999/commode.html

Meuwissen, K. W., & Choppin, J. M. (2015). Preservice teachers' adaptations to tensions associated with the edTPA during its early implementation in New York and Washington. *Education Policy Analysis Archives, 23*(103). Retrieved from http://epaa.asu.edu/ojs/article/view/2078/1680

Moll, L., Amanti, C., Neff, D., & Gonzalez, N. (1992). Funds of knowledge for teaching: Using a qualitative approach to connect homes and classrooms. *Theory Into Practice, 31*(2), 132–141.

Muijs, D. (2006). Measuring teacher effectiveness: Some methodological reflections. *Educational Research and Evaluation: An International Journal on Theory and Practice, 12*, 53–74.

Muranoi, H. (2000). Focus on form through interaction enhancement: Integrating formal instruction into a communicative task in EFL classrooms. *Language Learning, 50*, 617–673.

Nassaji, H., & Fotos, S. (2011). *Teaching grammar in second language classrooms. Integrating form-focused instruction in communicative context*. London, England: Routledge.

National Association of Multicultural Education. (2014, January 21). *NAME position statement on edTPA*. Retrieved from http://www.nameorg.org/docs/Statement-rr-edTPA-1-21-14.pdf

National Center for Education Statistics. (2014). *The condition of education 2014*. Washington, DC: United States Department of Education, Office of Educational Research and Improvement.

National Commission on Excellence in Education. (1983). *A nation at risk: The imperative for educational reform: A report to the Nation and the Secretary of Education, United States Department of Education*. Washington, DC: Author.

National Council of Teachers of English. (2008). *English language learners*. Urbana, IL: Author.

National Standards Collaborative Board. (2015). *World-readiness standards for learning languages* (4th ed.). Alexandria, VA: Author.

National Standards in Foreign Language Education Project. (1999). *Standards for foreign language learning in the 2st century*. Lawrence, KS: Allen Press.

New York State Board of Regents. (2013). *Commissioner King announces scores needed to pass new edTPA exam*. Retrieved from http://www.highered.nysed.gov/edtpa.html

Nieto, S. (2010). *Language, culture, and teaching: Critical perspectives*. New York, NY: Routledge.

Nieto, S. (2013). *Finding joy in teaching students of diverse backgrounds: Culturally responsive and socially just practices in U.S. classrooms*. Portsmouth, NH: Heinemann.

Osborn, T. A. (2006). *Teaching world languages for social justice: A sourcebook of principles and practices*. Mahwah, NJ: Erlbaum.

Owen, S. J. (2015). Georgia's teacher dropout crisis: A look at why nearly half of Georgia public school teachers are leaving the profession. Georgia Department of Education. Available from https://www.gadoe.org/External-Affairs-and-Policy/communications/Documents/Teacher%20Survey%20Results.pdf

Palmer, E. (2015a). Commentary thinking organizers and helpful hints (World language version). Retrieved from https://secure.aacte.org/apps/rl/resource.php?resid=495&ref=edtpa

Palmer, E. (2015b). *Commentary review sheet*. Normal, IL: Illinois State University.

Palmer, E. (2015c). *Completion checklist*. Normal, IL: Illinois State University.

Paris, D. (2012). Culturally sustaining pedagogy a needed change in stance, terminology, and practice. *Educational Researcher, 41*(3), 93–97.

Pearson. (2014). edTPA scorer qualifications. Retrieved from http://scoreedtpa.pearson.com/become-an-edtpa-scorer/edtpa-scorer-qualifications.html

Pearson Education. (2016a). Recommended professional performance standard. Retrieved from http://www.edtpa.com/PageView.aspx?f=GEN_PerformanceStandard.html

Pearson Education. (2016b). edTPA for Illinois. Retrieved from http://www.edtpa.com/PageView.aspx?f=GEN_Illinois.html

Pearson Education. (2016c). edTPA for Washington. Retrieved from http://www.edtpa.com/PageView.aspx?f=GEN_Washington.html

Pearson Education. (2016d). Scores. Retrieved from http://www.edtpa.com/PageView.aspx?f=GEN_Scores.html

Peck, C. A., Singer-Gabella, M., Sloan, T., & Lin, S. (2014). Driving blind: Why we need standardized performance assessment in teacher education. *Journal of Curriculum and Instruction, 8*(1), 8–30.

Project LINC. (2015). Project LINC: Learning in inclusive classrooms. Retrieved from http://www.longwood.edu/projectlinc/index.html

Renaissance Partnership for Improving Teacher Quality. (2002). *Teacher work sample: Performance prompt, teaching process standards, scoring rubrics*. Bowling Green, KY: Author.

Richards, J. C., & Bohlke, D. (2011). Creating effective language lessons. Cambridge University Press. Retrieved from http://prodibing.fkip.unsri.ac.id/userfiles/lesson 20planning.pdf

Rosenbusch, M. H. (2005). The No Child Left Behind Act and teaching and learning languages in the U.S. Schools. *The Modern Language Journal, 89*, 250–261.

Rosenbusch, M. H., & Jensen, J. (2004). Status of foreign language programs in NECTFL states. *NECTFL Review, 56*, 26–37.

Rubin, J. (1975). What the "good language learner" can teach us. *TESOL Quarterly, 9*(1), 41–51.

Russell, J., & Spada, N. (2006). The effectiveness of corrective feedback for the acquisition of L2 grammar: A meta-analysis of the research. In J. Norris & L. Ortega (Eds.), *Synthesizing research on language learning and teaching* (pp. 133–164). Amsterdam, Netherlands: John Benjamins.

Ryan, J. E. (2004). The Tenth Amendment and other paper tigers: The legal boundaries of education governance. In N. Epstein (Ed.), *Who's in charge here? The tangled web of school governance and policy* (pp. 42–74). Washington, DC: Brookings Institution Press.

Sandrock, P. (2008). *Integrated performance assessment*. Retrieved from http://depts.washington.edu/mellwa/Events/20081105/sandrock_ipa_handout.pdf

Sandrock, P. (2010). *The keys to assessing language performance*. Washington, DC: ACTFL.

Sato, M. (2014). What is the underlying conception of teacher of the edTPA? *Journal of Teacher Education*, 1–14. Retrieved from http://jte.sagepub.com/content/early/2014/07/09/0022487114542518

Savignon, S. J. (1983). *Communicative competence: Theory and classroom practice*. Reading, MA: Addison-Wesley.

Sawchuk, S. (2013, December 2). Performance-based test for teachers rolls out. *Education Week*. Retrieved from http://www.edweek.org/ew/articles/2013/12/04/13assess_ep.h33.html

Sharma, R. C., & Mishra, S. (2007). *Cases on global e-learning practices: Successes and pitfalls*. Hershey, PA: IGI Global.

Schön, D. A. (1983). *The reflective practitioner: How professionals think in action*. London, United Kingdom: Temple Smith.

Schrier, L. L. (1993). Prospects for the professionalization of foreign language teaching. In C. G. Guntermann, (Ed.), *Developing language teachers for a changing world* (pp. 105–123). Chicago, IL: National Textbook Company.

Schrier, L. L., & Hammadou, J. A. (1994). Assessment in foreign language teacher education. In C. D. Hancock (Ed.), *Making the connections: Teaching, assessment, testing* (pp. 211–234). Lincolnwood, IL: National Textbook.

Schulte, A. (2012, December 14). Ann Schulte: Teacher performance assessment isn't the answer (Living in Dialogue). *Education Week Teacher*. Retrieved from http://blogs.ed-week.org/teachers/living-in-dialogue/2012/12/ann_schulte_teacher_performanc.html

Schulz, R. A. (2000). Foreign language teacher development: MLJ Perspectives—1916–1999. *The Modern Language Journal, 84*(4), 495–522.

Selinker, L. (1972). Interlanguage. *IRAL-International Review of Applied Linguistics in Language Teaching, 10*, 209–232.

Shinkfield, A. J., & Stufflebeam, D. L. (1995). *Teacher evaluation: Guide to effective practice.* Norwell, MA: Kluwer Academic.

Shrum, J. L., & Glisan, E. W. (2010). *Teacher's handbook: Contextualized language instruction* (4th ed.). Boston, MA: Heinle.

Shrum, J. L., & Glisan, E. W. (2015). *Teacher's handbook: Contextualized language instruction* (5th ed.). Boston, MA: Heinle.

Smith, M., & Scoll, B. (1995). The Clinton human capital agenda. *The Teachers College Record, 96*(3), 389–404.

Stanford Center for Assessment, Learning, and Equity. (n.d.-a). Using edTPA. Stanford, CA: Stanford University. Retrieved from https://secure.aacte.org/apps/rl/resource.php?resid=268&ref=edtpa

Stanford Center for Assessment, Learning, and Equity. (n.d.-b). edTPA fact sheet. Stanford, CA: Stanford University. Retrieved from https://secure.aacte.org/apps/rl/resource.php?resid=268&ref=edtpa

Stanford Center for Assessment, Learning, and Equity. (n.d.-c). edTPA myths and facts. Stanford, CA: Stanford University. Retrieved from https://secure.aacte.org/apps/rl/res_get.php?fid=1331&ref=edtpa

Stanford Center for Assessment, Learning, and Equity. (n.d.-d). Teachers who support teacher candidates. Stanford, CA: Stanford University. Retrieved from https://secure.aacte.org/apps/rl/res_get.php?fid=1622&ref=edtpa

Stanford Center for Assessment, Learning, and Equity. (n.d.-e). edTPA guidance for P-12 administrators and leaders. Stanford, CA: Stanford University. Retrieved from https://secure.aacte.org/apps/rl/res_get.php?fid=2425&ref=edtpa

Stanford Center for Assessment, Learning, and Equity. (2013a). 2013 edTPA field test: Summary report. Stanford, CA: Stanford University. Retrieved from https://secure.aacte.org/apps/rl/res_get.php?fid=827&ref=edtpa

Stanford Center for Assessment, Learning, and Equity. (2013b). edTPA support and assessment program. Stanford, CA: Stanford University. Retrieved from https://www.edtpa.com/PageView.aspx?f=GEN_PerformanceStandard.html

Stanford Center for Assessment, Learning, and Equity. (2013c). edTPA world language assessment handbook. Stanford, CA: Stanford University.

Stanford Center for Assessment, Learning, and Equity. (2014). edTPA guidelines for acceptable candidate support. Retrieved from https://www.edtpa.com/Content/Docs/GuidelinesForSupportingCandidates.pdf

Stanford Center for Assessment, Learning, and Equity. (2015a). edTPA world language assessment handbook. Stanford, CA: Stanford University.

Stanford Center for Assessment, Learning, and Equity. (2015b). Understanding rubric level progressions. Stanford, CA: Stanford University. Retrieved from https://secure.aacte.org/apps/rl/resource.php?resid=469&ref=edtpa

Stanford Center for Assessment, Learning, and Equity. (2015c). Making good choices: A support guide for edTPA candidates. Stanford, CA: Stanford University. Retrieved from https://secure.aacte.org/apps/rl/resource.php?resid =495&ref=edtpa

Stanford Center for Assessment, Learning, and Equity. (2015d). List of changes for edTPA handbooks for 2015-2016. Retrieved from https://secure.aacte.org/apps/rl/resource.php?resid=450&ref=edtpa

Stanford Center for Assessment, Learning, and Equity. (2015e). Educative assessment & meaningful support: 2014 edTPA administrative report. Retrieved from https://secure.aacte.org/apps/rl/res_get.php?fid=2183&ref=edtpa

Stanford Center for Assessment, Learning, and Equity. (2015f). Confidentiality and security of edTPA candidate materials and assessment data. Retrieved from https://www.edtpa.com/Content/Docs/ConfidentialityAndSecurity.pdf

Strauss, V. (2015, December 5). The disturbing provisions about teacher preparation in No Child Left Behind rewrite. *The Washington Post*. Retrieved from https://www.washingtonpost.com/news/answer-sheet/wp/2015/12/05/the-disturbing-provisions-about-teacher-preparation-in-no-child-left-behind-rewrite/

Stronge, J. H. (Ed.). (2005). *Evaluating teaching: A guide to current thinking and best practice* (2nd ed.). Newbury Park, CA: Corwin Press.

Swanson, P. (2008). Efficacy and interest profile of foreign language teachers during a time of critical shortage. *NECTFL Review, 62*, 55–74.

Swanson, P. (2012). Second/foreign language teacher efficacy: Multiple factors and their relation to professional attrition. *Canadian Modern Language Review, 68*(1), 78–101. doi:10.3138/cmlr.68.1.078

Swanson, P. (2013). Spanish teachers' sense of humor and student performance on the national Spanish exams. *Foreign Language Annals, 46*(2), 146–156.

Swanson, P., & Early, P. (2008). Digital recordings and assessment: An alternative for measuring oral proficiency. In A. Moeller, J. Theiler, & S. Betta (Eds.), *CSCTFL Report* (pp. 129–143). Eau Claire, WI: Central States Conference on the Teaching of Foreign Languages.

Swanson, P., Early, P. N., & Baumann, Q. (2011). What audacity! Decreasing student anxiety while increasing instructional time. In B. Özkan Czerkawski (Ed.), *Free and open source software for e-learning: Issues, successes and challenges* (pp. 168–186). Hershey, PA: IGI Global. doi:104018/978-1-61520-917-0.ch011

Swanson, P., & Huff, R. (2010). Georgia's rural foreign language teachers' sense of efficacy and how it relates to teacher attrition. *The Rural Educator, 31*(3), 16–29.

Tirosh, D. (2000). Enhancing prospective teachers' knowledge of children's conceptions: The case of division of fractions. *Journal for Research in Mathematics Education, 31*, 5–25.

Thanasoulas, D. (2001). The importance of teaching culture in the foreign language classroom. *Radical Pedagogy*. Available from http://www.radicalpedagogy.org/radicalpedagogy/The_Importance_of_Teaching_Culture_in_the_Foreign_Language_Classroom.html

Tuck, E., & Gorlewski, J. (2016). Racist ordering, settler colonialism, and edTPA: A participatory policy analysis. *Educational Policy, 30*(1), 197–217.

U.S. Department of Education. (2002). No Child Left Behind Act of 2001, Pub. L. No. 107-110, § 115, Stat. 1425. Retrieved from http://www2.ed.gov/policy/elsec/leg/esea02/107-110.pdf

U.S. Department of Education. (2004). New No Child Left Behind flexibility: Highly qualified teachers. Retrieved from http://www.ed.gov/nclb/methods/teachers/hqtflexibility.html

U.S. Department of Education. (2009). Race to the Top executive summary. Retrieved from http://www2.ed.gov/programs/racetothetop/executive-summary.pdf

U.S. Department of Education. (2011). *Our future, our teachers: The Obama Administration's plan for teacher education reform and improvement.* Retrieved from http://www.ed.gov/sites/default/files/our-future-our-teachers.pdf

U.S. Department of Education. (2014). *Improving teacher preparation.* Retrieved from www.ed.gov/teacherprep

U.S. Department of Education. (2015). Every Student Succeeds Act of 2015, Pub. L. No 114-95. Retrieved from https://www.congress.gov/bill/114th-congress/senate-bill/1177/text

Unity Community Center. (2015). Missions, values, and goals. Retrieved from http://web.extension.illinois.edu/lmw/unity/

Ur, P. (1996). *A course in language teaching.* Cambridge, England: Cambridge University Press.

Valdés, G. (1997). The teaching of Spanish to bilingual Spanish-speaking students: Outstanding issues and unanswered questions. In M. C. Colombi & F. X. Alarcon (Eds.), *La enseñanza del español a hispanohablantes: Praxis y teoría* (pp. 8–44). Boston, MA: Houghton Mifflin.

Valdés, G. (1999, October). *Heritage language students: Profiles and possibilities.* Paper presented at National Conference on Heritage Languages in America, Long Beach, CA.

Valdés, G. (2001). Heritage Language students: Profiles and possibilities. In J. K. Peyton & S. McGinnis (Eds.), *Heritage languages in America: Blueprint for the future* (pp. 37–77). Washington, DC: Center for Applied Linguistics.

VanPatten, B. (1996). *Input processing and grammar instruction in second language acquisition.* Norwood, NJ: Ablex.

Villa, R. A., Thousand, J. S., & Nevin, A. I. (2013). *A guide to co-teaching: New lessons and strategies to facilitate student learning* (3rd ed.). Thousand Oaks, CA: Corwin.

Vygotsky, L. S. (1978). *Mind and society: The development of higher mental processes.* Cambridge, MA: Harvard University Press.

Wang, S., & García, M. I. (2002). *Heritage language learners: A position paper.* National Council of State Supervisors of Foreign Languages. Retrieved from www.ncssfl.org/papers/NCSSFLHLLs0902.pdf

Wiggins, G., & McTighe, J. (2005). *Understanding by design.* Alexandria, VA: Association for Supervision and Curriculum Development.

Wilen, W., Bosse, M. I., Hutchinson, J., & Kindsvatter, R. (2004). Planning for teaching. In W. Wilen, J. Hutchison, & M. Ishler (Eds.), *Dynamics of effective secondary teaching* (5th ed., pp. 134–165). Boston, MA: Pearson.

Winerip, M. (2012, May 6). Move to outsource teacher licensing process draws protest. *The New York Times*. Retrieved from http://www.nytimes.com/2012/05/07/education/new-procedu-re-for-teaching-license-draws-protest.html?pagewanted=1&_r=3&

Woodrow, L. (2006). Anxiety and speaking English as a second language. *RELC Journal, 37*(3), 308–328.

Wong, H. K., & Wong, R. T. (2009). *The first days of school: How to be an effective teacher* (4th ed.). Mountain View, CA: Harry K. Wong Publications.

Yell, M., Katsiyannis, A., & Bradley, M. R. (2011). The individuals with disabilities education act: The evolution of special education law. In J. M. Kauffman & D. P. Hallahan (Eds.), Handbook of special education (pp.61–76). London, England: Routledge.

Zwiers, J. (2004/2005). The third language of academic English. *Educational Leadership, 62*(4), 60–63.

APPENDIXES

APPENDIX A

edTPA World Languages Lesson Plan Template

Teacher Candidate:		Estimated Lesson Duration:
Date:	Level(s):	School:
Mentor Teacher Signature for Approval:		

Formal Assessment of Prior Learning or Preassess-ment *(Beginning of Learning Segment)*	[The section for formal preassessment begins the lesson segment and does not need to be shown on subsequent lessons.]

Title of Lesson		
Standards	**ACTFL World Readiness Standards for Learning Languages (2014):** http://www.actfl.org/publications/all/world-readiness-standards-learning-languages All five ACTFL National Standards should be included in the Learning Segment.	

	State standards (GA and IL examples provided)
	Assessed Georgia Performance Standards: https://www.georgiastandards.org/standards/pages/BrowseStandards/ModernLanguageLatin.aspx
	GPS that are addressed but not assessed: https://www.georgiastandards.org/standards/pages/BrowseStandards/ModernLanguageLatin.aspx
	CCGPS Standards (links to other disciplines): https://www.georgiastandards.org/common-core/Pages/default.aspx
	Illinois Learning Standards for Foreign Languages: http://www.isbe.net/ils/foreign_languages/standards.htm
	Note: You may delete the links to the standards once you list the standards that you will address in your lesson plan. Please list the number and text of each standard that is being addressed. If only a portion of a standard is being addressed, then only list the part or parts that are relevant.
Central Focus (CF)	What is/are the important understanding(s) and core concept(s) that you want students to develop within the learning segment? In other words, what is the big idea?
Learning Outcomes	These should be measureable and aligned with the lesson standards, activities, and assessments. Students will be able to …
Language Forms	What grammar and vocabulary are covered in this lesson?
Interpersonal Language Functions	What speakers do and accomplish by using language (grammar and vocabulary) in meaningful contexts. Common interpersonal language functions include greeting, expressing likes/dislikes, making requests, giving and receiving information, et cetera. See p. 105 of Clementi and Terrill (2013) for their list of verbs under "interpersonal language functions." *Note: Language functions are associated with verbs found in your learning outcome statements.*
Academic Language Functions	Common academic language functions include defining, classifying, comparing/contrasting, explaining, arguing, interpreting, and evaluating ideas. See http://www.unco.edu/cetl/sir/stating_outcome/documents/Krathwohl.pdf for a description of Bloom's taxonomy and the various types and levels of knowledge.

Instructional Strategies and Language Tasks

In the section below (Lesson Activities), include what you and the students will be doing by sequentially describing the instructional strategies and learning tasks that will be included in the lesson. Emphasize how you will support the diverse needs of students in your class by describing how you will accommodate/modify for specific learner needs. Also, describe how assessments will be incorporated within and throughout your lesson.

Be sure to plan instruction for the following types of learners that may be in your class:

• Students with IEPs or 504 plans
• English language learners (ELLs)
• Readers who struggle in their first language
• Students at varying levels of language proficiency
• Students who are underperforming or those with gaps in academic knowledge
• Heritage Language Speakers
• Gifted students

You will need to plan supports that address the needs of specific individuals or groups with similar needs. Supports should include specific strategies to identify and respond to common errors and misunderstandings about the target language and/or cultural practices in the target language.

The learning segment (three lessons) should address all three modes of communication (interpretive, interpersonal, and presentational) within a meaningful cultural context.

Please include time estimates for each lesson activity.

Please include connections to students' everyday lives and at least one connection to another discipline in each lesson.

Note: You may delete the text above after you plan your lesson. However, you need to leave in the heading "Instructional Strategies and Language Tasks."

Lesson Activity 1 (Review, Recycle, or Warm-up)	**Teacher does:**	**Students do:**
Lesson Activity 2	**Teacher does:**	**Students do:**

Formative Assessment	Include *what* is being assessed and *if* you will be able to differentiate your assessment. Note: You may change the order of the formative assessments as needed.	
Lesson Activity 3	**Teacher does:**	**Students do:**
Formative Assessment	Include *what* is being assessed and *if* you will be able differentiate your assessment. *Note: You may change the order of the formative assessments as needed.*	
Closure	**Teacher does:**	**Students do:**
Instructional Materials	List pertinent resources and materials needed for this lesson, including technology.	
Instructional Resources	Cite all resources and materials using the current APA format.	

Formal Assessment or Post-assessment (*End of Learning Segment*)	[The section for formal post-assessment ends the lesson segment and does not need to be shown on preceding lessons.]	

The language used within this lesson plan template is attributed to: Stanford Center for Assessment, Learning, and Equity. (2015). *edTPA world language assessment handbook*. Stanford, CA: Author.

APPENDIX B

Foreign Language Autobiography

Name:

Please answer the following questions as thoughtfully as possible so that we can get to know each other. Print it out and bring to the next class as part of your homework.

1. Placement: Are you in the right class? Please describe your foreign language history. What courses have you taken before? How did you do in them, and how did you feel about them?

2. What are your fears (if any) about taking this class?

3. Think back on classes you have taken (not necessarily foreign language classes) that you really liked, and classes you have taken that you really despised. What was it that made you like them or despise them?

Good	Bad

4. Now, think about teachers you thought were good and bad. What traits make you classify them as good or bad?

Good	Bad

5. Complete the following statement – For me, foreign language is like ...

6. How is your anxiety level going into this class? If it is high, is there anything you can do to control it?

7. What are your goals for this class? This semester?

8. What are your passions?

Now, read the following:

Notes from your professor about this class and this semester.

Here is what I hope will happen this semester:

(a) You will gain confidence in your ability to learn and use foreign language.
(b) You will gain flexibility in career and educational choices.
(c) You will gain prerequisite skills to prepare you for additional experiences in foreign language.
(d) You will begin to read, write, listen to, and speak a foreign language, and work effectively in groups.
(e) You will learn about foreign language through real-world applications and see connections between foreign language and other disciplines. And you will learn about what the cultures of Spanish-speaking countries are like.
(f) You will find our classroom to be a nonthreatening environment, where you are ?encouraged to ask questions.

In the February 1995 issue of *The Teaching Professor*, Maryellen Weimer shares a letter that she gives to her students at the end of the semester. She says, "What I don't see in you, and wish I did, is intellectual risk-taking—a view of learning as a kind of ultimate bungee jump. I'd love for you to get past grades, to a place where you could see what happens to you in college has the power to change the way you think about yourself, and others in your life, about your work, and about your world."

"Race car drivers don't have speedometers. They're pointless. The drivers simply put the pedal to the metal and go as fast as the car will go. They back off only to prevent an accident. In contrast, most of you drive your intellectual machinery as if you were on caution laps. You are out there running, you weave from side to side to keep the tires warm, but you're clearly not up to speed. You're not racing. Why? Well, some of you don't like the track, and it is still early in your college season. You think that once you get into the real world, when it really counts, you'll run flat out. Bad move. You need to get the bugs out of your intellectual equipment now, while there is still time to make repairs and adjustments. You've got to run well consistently in every course.

"Start with one class, maybe just an assignment, and resolve that you are going to take personal responsibility for your education, and do better than you have ever done before."

It has been said that you do not have to be a natural talent to succeed in a foreign language. What is necessary is an open mind, risk-taking and hard work. I hope that you will keep this in mind this semester and in all of your other classes as well.

1. Any comments about what you just read?

2. Any final comments? Anything additional that you want me to know?

Adapted by Dr. Susan Hildebrandt and Dr. Wade Edwards from "One Creative Way To Begin Your First Day Of Classes: Foreign Language Autobiography" created by Richard Kalfus and available at http://www.actfl.org/files/public/TLE_Autobiography_082006.pdf

APPENDIX C

"Party Quirks" Classroom Management Activity

Explanation: You and your classmates are going to simulate a classroom of high school freshman during the first quarter of the school year. Each of you will have a role that you will act out as one of your classmates tries to "teach" the class. You will continue to play **your role** until the "teacher" engages in the **target teacher behavior**. You must stay in your role until the teacher does what will contain your behavior.

Your role: You whisper with your neighbor about the upcoming dance. You are not distracting to the whole class, but your attention is obviously NOT on the lesson.
Target teacher behavior: Proximity—teacher must be within 2 feet of you for at least 10 seconds.

Your role: You tap your pencil incessantly throughout the lesson.
Target teacher behavior: Eye contact—teacher must sustain eye contact with you for at least 5 seconds.

Your role: You are passing notes with the person in front of you.

Target teacher behavior: Intervention— teacher must take note from you or your partner. Until he/she does, you must continue to pass notes.

Your role: You put your head down on the desk, completely disinterested.

Target teacher behavior: Name usage—teacher must say your name (either in front of the whole class or just to you).

Your role: You whisper with your neighbor about last night's basketball game. You are not distracting to the whole class at first, but as the class goes on you and your neighbor become louder and louder.

Target teacher behavior: Proximity—teacher must be within 2 feet of you for at least 10 seconds on two different occasions.

Your role: You are writing a note to a friend, trying to hide it.

Target teacher behavior: Proximity—teacher must be within 2 feet of you for at least 5 seconds.

Your role: You are working on your math homework. You have your book open and are writing out algebra equations.

Target teacher behavior: Intervention—teacher must close your book or notebook.

Your role: You are having an awful day and are not interested in what the teacher is saying. You pout and cross your arms. You slouch in your chair and pout some more. Every minute or so, sigh heavily.

Target teacher behavior: Personal attention—teacher must kneel/bend down and have a miniconversation with you asking how you are doing or if you are okay.

Your role: Raise your hand every minute or so. When called on, ask questions that are off topic.

Target teacher behavior: Taking away attention—Teacher must ignore your hand being up for 2 minutes.

Your role: You drum your fingers on your desk for 10 seconds, stop for 10 seconds. Repeat.

Target teacher behavior: Eye contact—teacher must sustain eye contact with you for at least 5 seconds

Your role: You get up out of your chair to through away a piece of paper every minute or so.

Target teacher behavior: Name usage   teacher must use your name.

Your role: You have had too much Pepsi this morning and cannot stop shifting around in your chair.

Target teacher behavior: Eye contact—teacher must sustain eye contact with you for at least 5 seconds

Your role: You are a perfect angel and hang on the teacher's every word.

Target teacher behavior: N/A

Your role: TEACHER

ABOUT THE AUTHORS

Susan A. Hildebrandt, PhD, is an associate professor of applied linguistics and Spanish in the Department of Languages, Literatures and Cultures at Illinois State University, where she coordinates the world language teacher education program. Her research concerns world language teacher development, assessment, and professionalism, along with inclusive language teaching practices. She has taught Spanish in a variety of K–12 and postsecondary settings and has experience teaching world language teacher education courses in Iowa, Virginia, and Illinois universities ranging from a small liberal arts college, to a small former state normal school, to a large state university. A native of Wisconsin, she loves to travel, read, knit, sew, and hang out with her family, friends, and critters.

Pete Swanson, PhD, is an associate professor of foreign language teacher education and is the Foreign Language Teacher Education program coordinator at Georgia State University. He currently serves as president of the American Council on the Teaching of Foreign Languages. Before entering higher education, Dr. Swanson worked as a public school Spanish teacher in Colorado and Wyoming for more than a decade. Dr. Swanson has earned a international reputation as a leader in language teacher recruitment and his research has been published in highly esteemed journals and books. During his time at Georgia State University, the foreign language teacher education program has grown to become one of the largest language teacher programs in the nation with more than 100 students in the initial teacher education preparation program. Dr. Swanson resides in Atlanta with his family and enjoys traveling internationally and spending time with family and friends in the Rocky Mountains.

55954135R00128

Made in the USA
Middletown, DE
18 July 2019